MEXICO

WESTVIEW PROFILES • NATIONS OF CONTEMPORARY LATIN AMERICA
Ronald Schneider, Series Editor

† *Mexico: Paradoxes of Stability and Change,*
Daniel Levy and Gabriel Székely

† *Nicaragua: The Land of Sandino,* Thomas W. Walker

† *The Dominican Republic: A Caribbean Crucible,*
Howard J. Wiarda and Michael J. Kryzanek

Colombia: Portrait of Unity and Diversity, Harvey F. Kline

Also of Interest

† *The End and the Beginning: The Nicaraguan Revolution,*
John A. Booth

† *Revolution in El Salvador: Origins and Evolution,*
Tommie Sue Montgomery

† *Revolution in Central America,*
edited by the Stanford Central America Action Network

Development Strategies and Basic Needs in Latin America,
edited by Claes Brundenius and Mats Lundahl

Colossus Challenged: The Struggle for Caribbean Influence,
edited by H. Michael Erisman and John D. Martz

Oil, Money, and the Mexican Economy: A Macroeconomic Analysis,
Francisco Carrada-Bravo

† Available in hardcover and paperback.

MEXICO

Paradoxes of
Stability and Change

Daniel Levy
and
Gabriel Székely

Westview Press / Boulder, Colorado

TO OUR PARENTS

Westview Profiles/Nations of Contemporary Latin America

Jacket photo: Mexico City's famous Plaza de las Tres Culturas (Plaza of the Three Cultures) at Tlatelolco (Photo courtesy of the Mexican National Tourist Council)

Published in 1983 in the United States of America by
Westview Press, Inc.
5500 Central Avenue
Boulder, Colorado 80301
Frederick A. Praeger, President and Publisher

Library of Congress Cataloging in Publication Data
Levy, Daniel C.
  Mexico, paradoxes of stability and change.
  (Profiles. Nations of contemporary Latin America)
  Bibliography: p.
  Includes index.
  1. Mexico—Politics and government. I. Székely, Gabriel, 1953–   . II. Title. III. Series.
F1226.L59   1983   320.972   82-16028
ISBN 0-86531-020-3
ISBN 0-86531-394-6 (pbk.)

Printed and bound in the United States of America

Contents

Tables

Illustrations

Foreword

The election of Miguel de la Madrid in mid-1982 as Mexico's president underscored this country's remarkable political stability, institutionalized for half a century now after two decades of revolution and civil war. At the same time, Mexico once again has fallen into a severe economic crisis. Its foreign debt has reached an astronomical sum—nearly the highest in the world whether measured in per capita terms, as a proportion of GNP, or in relation to foreign exchange earnings. Then, too, there is the highly ambivalent relationship between Mexico and its northern neighbor, the United States, plagued by the former's memories of virtual rape in the mid-1800s and subsequent domination and by the latter's ingrained attitude of inherent superiority. Indeed, it can be said with considerable justification that Mexican immigrants ceased being "wetbacks" only when the post-1973 energy crisis forced the United States to turn toward Mexico as a source of gas and petroleum. Although most people in the United States believe that they know more about Mexico than about any other Latin American country, their perceptions of Mexican society and culture are far too often a mix of Tijuana and Acapulco plus the residue of any personal contact with Chicanos in this country. As a result, real understanding of this developing middle power remains sorely lacking, except, perhaps, in the bordering areas of the Southwest where contact between the two peoples is most intense and continuous.

The existing literature on Mexico is extensive and on many subjects highly informative. Yet the best is essentially monographic, going deeply into some rather narrow topic and rarely escaping the limitations of a single academic discipline. Once in a generation there have been books that successfully explained the essence of Mexico, at least from the perspective of the time. Into this category fall John Reed's coverage of the Revolution, Frank Tannenbaum's explanation of the Cárdenas era, and Howard Cline's portrayal of Mexico on the verge of industrialization. The Mexico of the 1980s is far more complex and marked by contradictions than even that of the 1950s; therefore a fresh and more systematic interpretation is badly needed. To this end Daniel Levy and Gabriel Székely have combined their talents and differing backgrounds to produce a superb synthesis that captures both the drama and tragedy of today's Mexico. Politics are at the center of their analysis, yet the Mexico that emerges from the pages of this book is a whole, not compartmentalized into society, economy, and culture with some assumed relationship to political life. Moreover, by examining the alternative policy prescriptions put forth by Mexico's major political-intellectual currents, they provide an added dimension for those interested not only in what Mexico is and how this came to be but also with where it is going and how it might get there.

Ronald Schneider

Preface

The common problems involved in coauthorship are especially challenging for those who try to bridge national boundaries. We are therefore happy, perhaps even surprised, to find ourselves far closer friends at the end of this book than when we began it. It has been a rewarding experience for both of us. Yet, it has not come easily. The continual struggle for mutually acceptable, compatible content and style has been as time-consuming as it has been trying.

It is only natural that the authors differ on many issues concerning Mexican politics. We have grown up in different nations, under different social and personal influences. Moreover, Levy has drawn predominantly on U.S. bibliographical sources and Székely predominantly on Mexican ones. All this does not mean that Levy represents "the U.S. view" and Székely "the Mexican view." It does mean that we have brought different sensitivities, different insensitivities, and different educational and research experiences and resources to the task. We believe that it is important for those U.S. citizens interested in Mexican politics to hear not just from U.S. but also from Mexican authors.

We have resolved our political differences in a few ways. First, we have divided responsibility. We have each written four chapters, shaping them to our own tastes: Levy wrote chapters 1, 2, 4, and 6; Székely wrote chapters 3, 5, 7, and 8. Nonetheless, we have both criticized and strongly influenced each other's chapters. Second, we have compromised. Where disagreement could be reduced, the chapter author adjusted his work. In those few cases where disagreement proved intractable, we chose to delete specific thoughts rather than to risk a schizoid product. Third, we have restricted the scope of our work. We have not attempted to develop and elaborate our own normative preferences. Instead, we have tried to analyze the principal realities of

Mexican politics. In doing so, we have focused on how Mexico has managed to achieve a degree of political stability unmatched in Latin America and on what Mexico has and has not reaped, politically, economically, and socially, from this stability. However obvious and compelling the degree of political stability, it has manifested itself amid complex, sometimes subtle, paradoxes of development. We happen to agree a bit more substantially in our analysis of Mexican reality—the stability and the paradoxes—than in our normative preferences. We each strove to be as objective as possible, but we recognize that our political views inevitably influenced the content and structure of every chapter.

In the process of writing this book, we have interacted with many scholars, from both sides of the border. Their insights have contributed significantly, although we naturally assume responsibility for the final product. We wish to thank Juan M. del Aguila and Rose Spalding for their chapter-by-chapter comments on the entire manuscript. Several other colleagues also offered valuable comments, usually sharing their special expertise on one or two individual chapters. We thank Silvia Arrom, Bruce Bagley, Roderic Camp, Arturo Cruz Sequeira, Cynthia Hewitt de Alcántara, Lorenzo Meyer, Cynthia McClintock, Kevin Middlebrook, Dale Story, and Gustavo Vega. April Levy deserves our gratitude for her editing and for originating the idea of binational coauthorship. Ron Schneider and Lynne Rienner, academic and editorial engineers of Westview's Nations of Contemporary Latin America series, have been generous in their support, advice, and encouragement; we particularly thank Lynne Rienner for her vote of confidence in approving a significant increase in the length of this study. Finally, we thank photographers Rodolfo Romo de Vivar and James P. Brochin for taking and providing most of the photographs we use and Rosa María Casas and her staff for facilitating access to the library of the Mexican Embassy in Washington, D.C.

For varied sorts of support we thank the following institutions with which we have been associated during the writing of the book: Yale University, the State University of New York at Albany, the National Autonomous University of Mexico, the George Washington University, and the Overseas Development Council.

Daniel Levy
New Haven, Connecticut

Gabriel Székely
Mexico City

MEXICO

THE UNITED STATES

ARIZONA

NEW MEXICO

TEXAS

Mexicali

BAJA CALIFORNIA-NORTE

La Paz

BAJA CALIFORNIA-SUR

GULF OF CALIFORNIA

PACIFIC OCEAN

SONORA

Hermosillo

CHIHUAHUA

SINALOA

Culiacán

DURANGO

COAHUILA

Saltillo

Monterrey

NUEVO LEÓN

TAMAULIPAS

Ciudad Victoria

ZACATECAS

S.L.P.

NAYARIT

Tepic

AGUASCALIENTES

GUANAJUATO

Guadalajara

JALISCO

COLIMA

MICHOACAN

Morelia

QUERÉTARO

HIDALGO

Pachuca

MEXICO

Toluca

D.F.

TLAXCALA

Jalapa

PUEBLA

MORELOS

Cuernavaca

GUERRERO

Chilpancingo

VERACRUZ

OAXACA

TABASCO

Villahermosa

CAMPECHE

Tuxtla Gutiérrez

CHIAPAS

GUATEMALA

GULF OF MEXICO

YUCATAN

Mérida

QUINTANA ROO

Chetumal

B.H.

Abbreviations
B.H. = British Honduras
D.F. = Federal District
S.L.P. = San Luis Potosi

Note: All unlabeled capital cities have the same name as the state in which they appear. For example,
         the capital of Durango is Durango.

1

Introduction

POLITICAL STABILITY AND DEVELOPMENT

A Model of Political Stability?

Perhaps the most striking feature of Mexican politics has been its extraordinary stability—indeed, the Mexican regime has been uniquely stable within Latin America. Since 1973 alone, Argentina has swung from military to civilian to harsher military rule, Chile from liberal reformist to Marxist to rightist authoritarian rule, Peru from leftist military to rightist military to civilian rule, and Uruguay from civilian to military rule. Similarly, we need go back only to 1964 and 1958 respectively to record notable regime transformations in Brazil and Venezuela; to go back a half century would be to include multiple transformations in most major Latin American nations, as well as the notoriously unstable smaller ones such as Bolivia. Not only the countries of Latin America but also much of the Third World beyond has found political stability an elusive goal.

Mexico has been different: Mexico has maintained the same political regime for more than fifty years. It is the only major Latin American nation not to have had a military coup in the post–World War II period. Every president selected since 1934 has survived his six-year term and then peacefully relinquished the office to his successor. Since at least the 1940s, despite these leadership changes, the regime has almost always held close to a basic mode of national development emphasizing political stability with economic growth. Although economic crises in 1976 and 1982 qualify the generalization, Mexico has been unusually successful in achieving these two goals. Consequently, those interested in such development, from political scientists to politicians to foreign governments to bankers, have frequently pointed to Mexico as a model, a model to be assessed and even emulated.[1]

1

What, then, does Mexico look like after its extended period of political stability? To agree that Mexico has been uniquely stable is not necessarily to agree on whether stability has been a blessing or a problem. Those who disapprove of the present situation and favor fundamental changes may well regard political stability as either a neutral fact or an obstacle to desired change. Much depends on the relationships one sees between political stability and other components of development. Some see political development in terms of a combination including regime stability, institution building, and widespread inclusion of the citizenry. Others find this definition morally bankrupt and conceive of development in terms of meaningfully independent participation or of democracy. Still others emphasize economic development, either in terms of production, industrialization, and per capita income, or very differently, in terms of resource distribution. An emphasis on resource distribution overlaps various concepts of social development, focusing on such issues as the distribution and quality of education, health care, and other services.[2] Many works have attempted to explore the relationships among some of these criteria of development. Here we focus on the relationship between political stability and other development criteria. Specifically, we need to ask how various factors have contributed to political stability and, even more important, what political, economic, and social realities have characterized stable Mexico.

Political Stability Amid
Deep and Pressing Problems

Political stability should not imply the absence of political (or economic and social) change and flexibility, examples of which are found throughout the book. Political stability, as used here, refers to the maintenance of the regime and its basic development model. Nor does the stability of the regime guarantee the passivity (let alone the well-being) of its citizens. There have been many protests in Mexico, including violent ones, and the regime has continually faced numerous and serious threats. That the Mexican regime is now in crisis is debatable; that Mexico itself is in crisis, in the broader sense of facing huge and recently aggravated economic and social problems, is less debatable. Mexico's crisis demands our attention, partly because of the threat it may pose to the regime's stability, especially if long-standing economic growth falters badly, but principally because the crisis itself stems from underlying problems that begin to tell us what a stable Mexico has and has not accomplished.

Chapter 2 briefly highlights the dimensions of the deep economic crisis that surfaced in 1981, while Chapter 5 analyzes in much greater depth the sources as well as the dimensions of Mexico's ongoing economic

Modernity and wealth emerge side by side with extreme poverty in one of the central paradoxes of Mexican development. (The sign reads "expropriated lands" and gives a file number.) (Photo courtesy of Rodolfo Romo de Vivar)

and social problems; our purpose in this introduction is to give a feel for the immediacy of some of these problems in everyday Mexican life. Decades of political stability and economic growth have surely alleviated some of the terrible social and economic problems that have historically plagued Mexico. But they have just as surely not alleviated others. And this very contrast may sharpen the threat to the system's survival. For whether the result is called a revolution of rising expectations, frustrated aspirations, or relative deprivation, it is less a people's abject circumstances that tempt them to rebel than their perception that these circumstances are unnecessary and unjustified; and the subjective view of what is unjustified is often made in comparison to the promise of development and the visible privileges enjoyed by others.[3] We will look briefly at both long-standing problems, made keener by their juxtaposition to increasing privilege, and at new problems caused perhaps by the forward motion of development itself.

Poverty, malnutrition, disease, unemployment, underemployment, illiteracy, and inadequate education are examples of old problems that still endure, now alongside increasing wealth and opportunity. Income distribution is one of the most unequal in the world and it is becoming even more unequal (see Chapter 5). In medicine, modern facilities have expanded while many still rely on folk cures and herbs. Rural Mexico still manages only second grade as its average educational achievement, a figure typical of the Third World's poorer nations, even though nearly 15 percent of the population (compared to roughly 2 percent in 1960) now has access to higher education, a figure close to that for much of Europe.[4] Transportation offers another case of increasing contrasts. In urban settings, developed Mexico uses automobiles, taxis, or modern buses that take only as many passengers as there are seats; less developed Mexico must rely more on older buses, often packed tightly. Between cities, developed Mexico travels by plane, car, or first-class bus equipped with air-conditioning, stereo music, toilets, assigned seats, and sometimes even complimentary soft drinks. The second-class buses are rarely equipped with any of these features and pack in as many passengers, often carrying fruit, fowl, and other market wares, as can be made to fit.

We have looked briefly at cases in which development has produced results for almost all to see but for only some to share. We now turn to cases in which the quality of life has actually diminished for most Mexicans, though again mostly for the less privileged. Population growth, both a product of development and a contributor to many chronic problems, illustrates the point. Mexico's population may not have been substantially larger in 1872 than it had been during the Spanish conquest three and a half centuries earlier; but, in the twentieth century, as political stability replaced revolutionary violence, the population began to soar. Furthermore, development has furthered population growth by extending life expectancy. The population grew at about 1 percent per year early in this century, 1.7 percent per year in the 1930s, and 3.4 percent per year in the 1960s. Indeed, Mexico came to have one of the fastest population growth rates in the world. The population reached 68.5 million by 1980, and roughly one in two Mexicans is under fifteen (meaning largely, although not fully, unproductive).[5] As population soars, more food has to be produced, more health care and education provided, more land distributed, just to stay even. And much more employment must be created.

Perceiving the dangers of unbridled population growth, the government began to act. As "candidate" for president in 1970, Luis Echeverría boasted of his opposition to population control, eagerly presenting himself as the proud father of eight children; as president, Echeverría helped initiate a governmental family planning program. The birthrate has slackened impressively, from a peak of roughly 3.7 percent per year to slightly less than 3 percent per year, but this rate remains high even for the Third World. Most projections would put Mexico's population over the 100 million mark by the end of the century.

Mexico's urbanization is another phenomenon that can be identified simultaneously with lack of development and development itself. Mexico's cities still do not have industrial bases that provide sufficient employment, income, and opportunity for their citizens, yet cities grow as population grows and as frustrated but aspiring villagers leave their more traditional settings. The uprooting social effects of migration may bring special problems for the migrants themselves and for increasingly overcrowded cities.[6] The valley of Mexico, including Mexico City, has roughly one-fifth or more of the nation's population. It also has perhaps the worst air pollution in the world. Atmospheric contamination rose by up to 50 percent in 1979 alone; the automobile—a product of development—was a major contributor.[7]

The automobile makes Mexican urban life difficult in other ways as well. Mexico City's traffic jams have become unbearable; they worsened drastically during the 1970s. Mexico City residents who drive to work may spend up to four hours daily in transit. Estimates of work hours lost are staggering. The city's traffic, crowded into a few main streets, is worse than in any U.S. city, and its rush hours are far longer. Yet, despite the automobile's problems, public transportation is not a satisfactory alternative. Mexico City's *metro* (subway) does carry about 2 million passengers daily, and it is clean, quiet, and efficient and is expanding its routes. But the system offers less adequate service than it did a few years ago simply because it cannot accommodate the increased passenger load. For a few hours each morning and again each evening the metro is a battleground, again much worse than the subway system in any U.S. city. For their own protection in the crunch hours, women and children are literally separated from men and funneled toward different sections of the train platforms.

And now, amid Mexico's troubles, oil blazes onto the scene. Chapter 7 will analyze how different observers foresee different impacts of oil on Mexican problems. For now we might note that some see oil as a blessing allowing Mexico—finally—to cope with many of its chronic problems or to stay even where it would otherwise be losing ground, while others see oil perpetuating or even aggravating these problems, as the benefits oil produces go to a few and the inflation it produces affects all. Some evidence for both perspectives on oil's impact can be found in oil's initial impact on the profound economic crisis that received so much attention in the mid-1970s. It is true that oil drove economic growth from its nadir in the mid-1970s back to and even above its characteristic post–World War II rates. But it also has helped to drive inflation to a new postwar high of 30 percent in 1980, a rate that had become much higher by 1982, by which time even the renewed growth halted.

Moreover, oil-based growth has symbolized how Mexican development has favored big industry over agriculture, especially subsistence agriculture. In fact, Mexico at present is threatened by the loss of its traditional self-sufficiency in many basic foods. Examples include corn (basic to the ubiquitous *tortilla*, or flat corncake), sugar, rice, beans, and other vegetables and fruits, as well as coffee and cotton. "Crude for food" is an exchange many Mexicans fear as they see themselves forced to rely on the oil-thirsty United States to feed themselves. Thus, in 1980, Mexico declared self-sufficiency in basic grains to be a major national *goal*. This declaration was really an implicit admission of the failure of the "rural modernization" policies (e.g., new techniques to overcome production problems) pursued since 1940 as part of the growth-stability development model. Rural modernization never led to concomitant "rural development" (defined as progress in the way people live). In fact, rural modernization was really aimed not so much at rural but at urban development, accepting rural misery in the hope of inexpensively feeding the growing urban population.[8] Despite its own suffering, rural Mexico had succeeded in feeding Mexico. Now, the regime acknowledged, new policies would be required in order to prevent even that achievement from slipping away (see Chapter 5 on the SAM program).

However serious and worsening many of Mexico's social and economic problems have been, they have not, at least not yet, transformed Mexican politics. Political stability has persisted. And it has persisted despite continual assertions that a house divided against itself cannot stand, that the development/nondevelopment contradictions are too deep, that the status quo is untenable, that fundamental change is inevitable. Most works written in the 1950s and 1960s argued optimistically that political, economic, and social development criteria usually—perhaps naturally—complement and even promote one another. This had supposedly been the experience of U.S. and West European development. Because Mexico had already achieved both political stability and economic growth, many observers assumed that meaningful political participation, as well as more equitable distribution of the wealth and improved social-welfare indicators, were likely to follow. Others believed that the negative side of the development ledger would pull down the positive side, tearing political stability asunder. Many commentaries emphasized either-or propositions: Frustrated aspirations would have to be *either* satisfied, probably through the democratic, reformist, or socialist option, *or* more directly repressed, probably through a right-wing, authoritarian, or fascist option. Unless something was done—soon—the system would be undone.[9]

Increased guerrilla activity in the late 1960s and early 1970s seemed to support the either-or interpretations. In those years, guerrillas polarized politics, or made latent polarization overt, and the regime bolstered its repressive apparatus. Guerrilla activity has had a rich history in Mexico, and its intensity increased in both urban and rural areas. Even the government and the press came to refer to a crisis of political terrorism, no longer dismissing guerrilla activity as common banditry. A rash of political kidnappings shook Mexico in the early 1970s. Senator Rubén Figueroa, leading Monterrey industrialist Eugenio Garza Sada, and the president's own father-in-law were among the victims. Some, like Garza Sada, were assassinated. Others, like Figueroa, were released, probably after the government secretly acquiesced in guerrilla demands. A perception of government weakness enhanced the guerrillas' image. Combined with the economic crisis (flight of capital out of Mexico, inflation, devaluation of the *peso*) and with controversial land seizures, this perception of government weakness contributed to somewhat rash speculation about possible military intervention in Mexico's proudly civilian system. But the guerrilla threat peaked and declined, and the regime was still intact. One of the best-known guerrilla defeats was the 1974 killing of Lucío Cabañas, a former primary school teacher, who had for seven years led guerrilla operations in the mountains and who was probably involved in the Figueroa kidnapping. Still, if the guerrilla threat has subsided, it has by no means vanished; it is especially active in such poor and mountainous states as Guerrero.

The single most dramatic recent political crisis peaked in 1968. Students opposing the regime's authoritarian and conservative policies went beyond the usual bounds permitted for dissent in Mexico and were violently repressed. By its harsh action, the regime "solved" the problem of open and organized political dissent, but it left a deep problem of political legitimacy.[10]

The legitimacy problem is less dramatic than the guerrilla or student protests, but it is a deep and difficult one. The official party has shown some weaknesses in most recent elections, raising serious doubts about the regime's popular support. Abstention rates have become much higher than the regime would like. Some observers have even remarked that the "party of abstention" could be viewed as the regime's toughest electoral opponent. Chapter 3 considers this challenge to legitimacy and the new party challenges that have consequently been engendered. But it also considers the regime's responses to the challenges, including its strong victory, with high turnout, in the 1982 elections.

Despite varied challenges, whether manifestly political or rooted in deep and perceptibly aggravated socioeconomic problems, Mexico (at least up until now) has remained politically stable. Stability has been shaken but not undone. The predictions that have proven most accurate are those that emphasized the viability of Mexico's political regime and the flexibility of that regime to meet otherwise destabilizing problems (see Chapter 4). Indeed, at the pinnacle of the perceived threat to its stability, just a few years after crises had toppled many other Latin

American regimes, the Mexican regime peacefully transferred power from one administration to the next. This key shift from President Luis Echeverría (1970–1976) to President José López Portillo (1976–1982) will therefore be analyzed from various political, economic, and foreign policy perspectives in subsequent chapters. The new administration proudly proclaimed the regime's viability. Its minister of programming and budget and the subsequent president of Mexico, Miguel de la Madrid, expressed the regime's optimism this way: "We have history, we have ideology, we have the system, and we have the leaders." Nor is all this propaganda or the wishful thinking of biased sources. Foreign investors, for example, generally see in Mexico a favorable environment, stable into the future. Compared to the 1976 Echeverría–López Portillo transition, the 1982 López Portillo–de la Madrid transition, despite Mexico's seriously mounting economic problems, was not surrounded by speculation about imminent regime collapse. Instead, many domestic and foreign news commentaries initially stressed the regime's remarkable and revitalized stability, although such commentaries were naturally tempered as Mexico slumped into a terrible economic crisis during 1982. One could point out that severe economic crises inevitably pose threats to political stability; in fact, this book repeatedly stresses that Mexico's political stability has been fundamentally tied to economic growth. Or one could emphasize how remarkable Mexico's political stability must be to have survived economic problems that would have toppled many Third World regimes.

Yet the future of Mexico's political stability is by no means certain. A key factor is economic growth, because although the regime has survived sporadic growth crises, it has not faced sustained growth problems comparable to the ongoing social problems. One's forecasts, hopes, and proposals depend largely on which of many contrasting factors are emphasized, as Chapter 8 shows. Just as the crises of the recent past have not resulted in instability, so the persistence of stability to the present does not guarantee its continuation. Mexico's vaunted stability could conceivably be undone even in the near future.

By now it should be obvious that this text (either too timid or too sober) avoids predictions. Instead, it will seek to understand the logic of Mexican politics. But such logic does not imply inevitability. For example, although we cannot hope to explain fully Mexico's extraordinary political stability, we can try to come as close as possible to that goal. Should stability lose its hold tomorrow, all the best explanations of how it once functioned might suddenly seem to have been at least partially inadequate.[11] What is clear is that the much-discussed "contradictions" of Mexican development have not (yet?) resolved themselves, that either-or propositions have not (yet?) materialized. This does not mean that we avoid considering alternatives to contemporary political patterns. It does mean that we look hardest at what continues to be Mexico's reality.

LAND AND POPULATION

This book is about Mexico's politics in the broadest sense, including its economics, sociology, and history. It is not truly an introduction to Mexico in general because it does not deal with those areas that fall primarily outside the political sphere. Still, we need some background on the land and population to understand the context in which Mexican politics operate. One need not believe that geography, natural resources, regionalism, culture, ethnicity, and demography determine politics to believe that they affect politics, presenting different opportunities and challenges. And surely it is mostly the people whom we ultimately care about when we study politics, just as it is the people whom politics affect.

The Land

Geographically, Mexico is both large and varied. Its 760,000 square miles (1,968,000 square kilometers) make it the third largest nation in Latin America, after only Brazil and Argentina, and one of the ten largest in the world. A profound geopolitical aspect is the 2,000-mile (3,200-kilometer) northern border with the United States. Also important, although less so, is the 600-mile (960-kilometer) border with Guatemala and the 160-mile (260-kilometer) border with newly independent (1981) Belize. Beyond these southern borders lies the rest of Central America.

Apart from the issues of Mexico's sheer size and borders, two geographical factors that deserve mention in the political context are natural resources and regional diversity. Mexico is neither unusually unfortunate nor—except as oil may change this—unusually fortunate in its natural resources. There is, however, a myth of special richness. Historian Daniel Cosío Villegas has traced the roots of that myth to the early colonists.[12] Spanish conquerors succumbed to a combination of calculated exaggeration (aimed at securing greater support from Spain) and enthusiastic miscalculation. Subsequently, both Mexicans and foreigners have sometimes perpetuated the myth, sometimes in order to blame those in power for Mexico's failures, sometimes to stereotype Mexicans as lazy, undisciplined, or ignorant, thereby perhaps seeking to justify foreign involvement.

On the positive side, Mexico is rich in minerals. Justly famous for its gold and silver since colonial times, Mexico has remained a leading producer of silver. Other important mineral resources have included lead, zinc, copper, and sulfur. Mexico also has some good ranching and timber lands, as well as fishing waters. Oil, of course, has now become the foremost natural resource.

Realists must also appreciate the harsher economic side of Mexican geography. Mexico lost much of its best agricultural land in nineteenth-century warfare with the United States. Today most of Mexico's land is mediocre agriculturally, and much of the rest is on the coasts; unfortunately, Mexico's climate is very varied, not just by latitude and longitude but by height above sea level, and the coastal climate is not generally favorable. Indeed, the climate tends to be hot from sea level to 2,000 feet (600 meters), before becoming more temperate to 8,000 feet (2,400 meters) and cooler above that height. Rainfall is also a problem, insufficient in some regions, excessive in others. More than half of Mexico is dry; about one-fourth, mostly mountainous area, is rainy and temperate; and the rest is tropically rainy.

Mexico also suffers from rugged topography. Its mountains hinder not only large-scale agriculture but also transportation and communication. And they impede national homogeneity by dividing Mexico into regions. It is not difficult to appreciate the divisions. Mexico City is 7,000 feet (2,100 meters) above sea level and still lies in a valley. If the air pollution level permitted, a person in Mexico City could see himself surrounded by mountains. If he then journeyed overland to the east or west, the descent would come only when nearing the coast, a dramatic descent demonstrating at once Mexico's physical beauty and its challenging topography.

Different commentators have suggested different but related regional divisions. The government itself has divided Mexico into five regions.[13] The North Pacific, with the states of Baja California, Sonora, and Sinaloa, is the second largest in land. But because much of the land is desert, the region has a relatively small population. The North stretches from the Sierra Madre Occidental (mountains connected with the Sierra Nevada in the United States) to the Gulf. Comprising San Luis Potosí, Zacatecas, Chihuahua, and Coahuila, it has roughly 40 percent of the land, including plains and the Sierra Madre Oriental (connected to the Rocky Mountains). It has about 20 percent of Mexico's population. So the main geographical features of the northern half of Mexico are the two Sierra Madre ranges, with the plateaus in between. Central Mexico, surrounding the Federal District, is the third largest region in area but includes roughly half the population. This region is itself a valley ensconced in high volcanic terrain. The Gulf Coast, including Veracruz, Tabasco, and the Yucatán, is a flat lowland region, relatively small in size and population. Finally, the South Pacific is the most rural region, resembling parts of Central America more than it does much of Mexico.

Mexico's topography and regionalism make the nation effectively larger in terms of achieving political or cultural homogeneity than sheer size would indicate. They have a good deal to do with Mexico's ethnic, cultural, social, and occupational divisions.

The Population

As Mexico is large and diverse in geography, so it is large and diverse in population.[14] Its 1980 population of 68.5 million puts it among the world's ten most populous nations. Mexico is the largest nation in the Spanish-speaking world, trailed far behind by Argentina and Colombia, the next largest in Latin America, as well as by Spain itself, the region's mother country.

Most Mexicans are the product of two very different ethnic groups, native Indians and colonizing Spaniards. Few Spanish women came to the New World, making miscegenation between Spanish males and Indian females inevitable. Some of the political ramifications of the Indian-European mixing are explored in Chapter 2. *Mestizos* (mixed Indian and Spanish) vary from mostly Indian to mostly Spanish, but in general the balance inclines more toward the Indian side than it does in most other major Latin American countries. Within Mexico, the balance is different in different regions, as what may be typical skin color or height in one region would not be typical in another.

Estimates vary on how many relatively pure Indians live in Mexico. Definitions themselves vary. Some anthropologists rely more on physiognomy, others more on cultural habits, others on whether people are bound to their land rather than mobile or on whether they have greater ties to their villages than to the nation. Some rely on people's self-perceptions. Most definitions lead to an estimate that there are a few million Indians. For example, probably around 5 percent but possibly up to 10 percent of all Mexicans speak only or primarily an Indian language, although there has been a trend away from such monolinguism since 1930, just as other distinctive traits have been diminishing.[15] Diversity is reflected in the many Indian languages, of which Maya and Nahuatl are merely the two most common. Different Indian groups concentrate in different regions, mostly in southern and central Mexico. The people, as well as the land, in certain areas of southern Mexico have more in common with Central America than with the rest of Mexico. Thus, culturally and economically, as well as geographically, many Mexicans are a long way from Mexico City. Descendents of the Mayas are concentrated in the south and the Yucatán, Zapotecs and Mixtecs in Oaxaca, Tarascans in Michoacán, fiercely independent Yaquis in Sonora, and Aztec descendents in various parts of Mexico. Different groups have their own languages, customs, dances, music, and clothing; they may also have their own economic systems, often based on maize and home industries, such as pottery and textiles, or on collective labor, concentrating on one key product to trade with other villages. In short, Mexico is fragmented not just by divisions between Indians and others, but even by differences among the Indians themselves.

We cannot describe Indian worlds without soon describing mestizo worlds. It is less important to fix the exact number of Indians than to appreciate how much the Indian presence has affected social norms, cultural relations, and political habits in the larger society. *Compadrazgo* (a godparent relationship), for example, is an Indian custom but also a Mexican custom.[16] Most Mexicans, not just Indians, eat corn and beans and tortillas, even though more and more Mexicans rely increasingly on packaged, canned, and processed products. Indian culture fuses with Spanish Catholicism to produce special hybrids. Mexico is therefore not as religiously homogeneous as one might infer from the fact that well over 90 percent of the people are Catholics (most of the rest are Protestants, and roughly 50,000 are Jewish). The Virgin Mary is a central symbol for many, but the dark-skinned Virgin of Guadalupe is a central symbol for more. Many Mexicans, especially in rural areas, observe the Day of the Dead, while Catholics in much of the world observe All Soul's Day. Although the Day of the Dead borrows some customs from All Soul's Day practices, it also adds particularly Indian aspects. This is not to say that the Catholic Church has been unimportant in Mexico's political history (see Chapter 2) but that Indian influences are part of the religious experiences of many Mexicans. Additionally, many Indian words have made their way into the "Mexican" language. Even the very name "Mexico" may come from an Indian root such as Mexica, one of the Aztec tribes, or Mexitl, an Aztec epithet for God.[17] And it is not by chance that Mexico's most famous museum is the Anthropological Museum. The plaque dedicating the museum (in 1964) acknowledges Mexico's debt to its Indian heritage: "Mexico today pays homage to indigenous Mexico, in whose example it recognizes essential characteristics of its national origins."

Ethnic diversity goes beyond all the degrees of the Indian-Spanish mix. Blacks were brought to Mexico as slaves in colonial times. Just as Indians tend to be clustered in certain regions, so blacks, or more commonly, Mexicans of mixed black-mestizo origin, are clustered along the coasts. Veracruz, for example, resembles a Caribbean as much as an inland Mexican city in many ways. Additionally, ethnic regionalism is naturally accompanied by cultural regionalism. In music alone, what is typical changes from mariachi bands to *zapateados* (rapid step dancing characteristic of Veracruz and the north) to Caribbean *salsa*.

For all its diversity, however, Mexico is one nation. Indeed, the degree of homogeneity is increasing. Indian enclaves are receding, although slowly. Spanish is increasingly the pervasive language. Modern trans-portation and communication have played a unifying role, and expanding educational facilities have played a socializing role. Urbanization also diminishes the intensity of some regional differences; by 1980, perhaps nearly three-fourths of the population lived in urban areas (the figure varies depending on the definition of "urban area"). Most Mexicans living outside the major cities live in villages, not in rural isolation, and migration from villages to cities continues at a rapid pace. Mexico City and its environs have roughly 15 million inhabitants. In fact, Mexico City may soon become the largest city in the world. Confronted by urban over-population, Mexico has recently attempted to decentralize but has not yet reversed the overwhelming centralization of political, economic, and intellectual life, as well as population, in Mexico City.

Most important to our study is the centralization of political life in Mexico City. Political centralization itself has been a great source of national integration. Despite regional, topographical, ethnic, and cultural cleavages, unified political power is indeed concentrated in Mexico City, in the government, in the executive branch, in the presidency. All Mexico, although in different degrees, falls under this authority. Most political roads lead to the capital. This political centralization seems especially remarkable when one considers the centrifugal forces, geographical and cultural, with which Mexican politics must cope. In the ensuing chapters (especially 3 and 4), we explore the regime's relative success in establishing its political authority.

MEXICO'S IMPORTANCE FOR THE UNITED STATES

Mexico's sheer size and its extraordinary political stability notwith-standing, the most obvious reasons for U.S. readers to be interested in Mexican politics stem from geographical proximity and economic and cultural interactions. Analysis of U.S. relations with its third largest trading partner and of specific bilateral issues appear in Chapter 6 in the broader context of Mexican foreign policy. Here we focus only on the United States's increased interest in and need for knowledge about Mexican politics.

Brazil is the only Latin American nation that can be considered more important than Mexico in terms of population and economic production, but for the United States there is little question about Mexico's preeminence. Yet U.S. interest in Mexican politics generally has been minimal.[18] Ever since the 1973 announcement of Mexico's great oil resources was taken seriously, however, there has been an upsurge of U.S. news coverage. President Carter established a major presidential commission on Mexico, a rare indicator of special U.S. interest in one nation, and the United States and Mexico established a consultative commission that went well beyond any of its bilateral predecessors reaching back to 1960. The commission was reorganized in 1979 into eight policy-oriented groups (e.g., trade). In 1981, López Portillo, one of the few heads of state to have met with president-elect Reagan, became one of the first to meet with the newly inaugurated U.S. president.

Unfortunately, this encouraging growth of interest comes up against long-standing barriers to understanding. Mexico's renowned poet-essayist Octavio Paz posed the problem this way:

> When I was in India, witnessing the never-ending quarrels between Hindus and Muslims, I asked myself more than once this question: What accident or misfortune of history caused two religions so obviously irreconcilable as Hinduism and Muhammadanism to coexist in the same society? . . . How could I forget that I myself, as a Mexican, was (and am) part of a no less singular paradox—that of Mexico and the United States? . . . In general, Americans have not looked for Mexico in Mexico; they have looked for their obsessions, enthusiasms, phobias, hopes, interests—and these are what they have found. In short, the history of our relationship is the history of mutual and stubborn deceit, usually involuntary though not always so.[19]

At their worst, U.S. views of Mexicans, and therefore, indirectly, of Mexican politics, are still colored by the stereotypes of indolence and immaturity nurtured in Hollywood and in the advertising media. Even today, a prominent weekly like *Time* (October 8, 1979) will imprint such stereotypes onto its analysis of Mexican policymaking, entitling a cover story on Mexico-United States relations "Mexico's Macho Mood." U.S. views are frequently colored by biases induced by its own preoccupations, especially with anticommunism.

Observers may differ on the degree to which geographical proximity naturally breeds understanding or resentment between Mexicans and their northern neighbors. They may also differ on the degree to which greater knowledge would reduce bilateral tensions. But few doubt that this knowledge would make for more intelligent handling of Mexico–United States affairs.

Another reason that U.S. readers should learn more about Mexico is that the United States *domestically* is greatly influenced by its southern neighbor. One reason that Mexico's influence on U.S. life sometimes fails to attract greater attention is that U.S. influence on Mexican life is even more obvious and pervasive. In fact, we cannot begin to know contemporary Mexico without appreciating the enormous extent of U.S. cultural as well as economic penetration. Thousands of U.S. citizens have retired in Mexico, and thousands of others have bought vacation homes there.

More important, many Mexicans come to live by behavioral norms exported by the United States. The Castro family in Oscar Lewis' anthropological classic *Five Families* illustrates the point: Pancake mix breakfasts substitute for tortillas, fried beans, and chili; U.S. cosmetics and toys become "necessities."[20] Processed food reshapes the diet, and "burgers," Shakey's Pizza, and Kentucky Fried Chicken are found in Mexican cities. English words creep into Mexican speech, especially as the majority of films and much of the television and music in Mexico come from the United States. Mexico's most widely read magazines are adaptations of *Reader's Digest* and *T.V. Guide*. Early in 1982, Mexico opened a huge U.S.-style amusement park ("Adventure Kingdom"). And, although soccer remains the number one sport, U.S.-style football is more popular than in any other Latin American country, baseball more popular than in all but a few.

But cultural penetration is very much—and increasingly so—a two-way phenomenon. Hispanics may soon surpass blacks as the biggest minority in the United States, and Mexican-Americans, or Chicanos, are the largest Hispanic subgroup. The Chicano presence is especially large if we consider the term broadly, including all those of Mexican descent, whether U.S. citizens or not. In fact, the United States is now perhaps the fifth-largest Spanish-speaking nation in the world! Continuing migration is one major root of the Chicano population in the United States, but another is simply the population inhabiting the land taken from Mexico by the United States in the nineteenth century; thus there are now wry jokes about a Mexican reconquest via population growth. Catering to the Mexican-American population, dozens of Spanish news periodicals and hundreds of Spanish radio and television stations have arisen in the United States. Television from Mexico comes via cable to major U.S. cities such as Los Angeles, New York, and Washington. Food, music, and language provide further manifestations of Mexican culture in the United States. Even the U.S. "national pastime" has felt a Mexican influence, most notably with Fernando Valenzuela's award-winning 1981 season as baseball's top box-office attraction. Education provides a good example of an important Mexican influence on the United States, even though the U.S. influence on Mexico is greater. True, U.S. money and academic models have helped shape some of Mexico's universities, especially private ones, and many of Mexico's ablest students attend U.S. graduate schools. But the Autonomous University of Guadalajara has more U.S. medical students than does any school in the United States, and there are more and more Chicanos in U.S. schools, from primary school through university. Half the kindergarten pupils in Los Angeles have Spanish surnames. Bilingual education and Chicano-relevant curriculum are prominent in some locales. Finally, there are many institutional interchanges between Mexican and U.S. universities.

Political muscle has been building less rapidly than cultural influence, but "Chicano consciousness" has grown in recent years. The political impact is naturally strongest in the Southwest, where most Chicanos live, but it is also significant in major urban centers, such as Chicago. Recognition of this power was evident in the 1980 presidential election, when Reagan and Carter both focused their campaigns on the Mexican-American vote more than any major party candidates had ever done. Candidate Reagan unabashedly tried to enhance his image in the Mexican-American community by traveling to Mexico, just as Senator Edward Kennedy had done during his losing quest for the Democratic nomination. As important, Mexico has made clear its growing concern for persons of Mexican descent living in the United States.[21] President López Portillo, on a September 1979 visit to the United States, boldly addressed Hispanics on the need to give a political voice to the cultural consciousness they share with Mexico. "We would like to deal with an organized community," the president declared, adding that "we are proud that you proudly maintain an identity with us."

Nowhere are the fates of Mexico and the United States more obviously intertwined and two-directional than at the border.[22] Millions live within a short distance of the extensive border, and the politics, economies, and cultures on each side are shaped by those on the other side. One can think of influences ranging from party affiliation, to labor-capital interchanges, to language and family ties. The degree of interchange is reflected by the fact that this is the world's busiest border. Already by 1972 the number of yearly crossings at the San Isidro–Tijuana point alone reached the 25 million figure.[23] In 1982, the effects of sharp peso devaluation were perhaps most vividly illustrated on the border, as increasing numbers of Mexicans crossed northward to seek work, or at least to convert pesos to dollars, while U.S. citizens crossed southward to take advantage of suddenly lower prices.

And yet, despite the volume of border interaction, and even some important homogenizing effects, nowhere is it more obvious how utterly different the two nations are. Where else does a border juxtapose two societies so ethnically, culturally, socially, economically, and politically different? One might think of Israel and its Arab neighbors. Or one could point to political divisions in Germany and Korea, or to religious divisions in Ireland and in India-Pakistan, but not to such accumulated differences. Moreover, this accumulation of Mexico–United States differences, far from being random, describes a critical division between the less developed and the more developed world. Focusing just on the division between wealth and poverty, per-capita income in the United States is roughly six times that in Mexico.[24] Entrance and exit lines at the border also symbolize the Mexico–United States development gap. Entrance into

Mexico is usually immediate, no lines, virtually no inspections, no wait. Exit from Mexico into the United States frequently is an ordeal, involving long lines, careful and tedious inspections (including indignities for Chicanos reentering the United States, who may be suspected of seeking illegal entry), and delays sometimes lasting for hours.

Despite bilateral influences and interdependency, any study of Mexican politics must appreciate the enormous underlying differences between the two nations. It will not then be surprising that Mexican politics generally are very different from U.S. politics, or that Mexican political stability has a different legacy and contemporary meaning from U.S. political stability. The challenge for us is to begin to understand Mexican politics on its own terms.

CHAPTER SUMMARIES

The following brief outline indicates the major concerns of each chapter. Chapter 2 provides a historical overview of how the bases of contemporary stability have developed. A central question is how stability could be forged against a historical background often characterized by instability. By analyzing the degree to which certain political, economic, and social goals were achieved in previous periods, the chapter helps provide a historical context within which to evaluate contemporary Mexico. Chapter 3 analyzes the major actors in Mexican politics and the principal structures through which they participate in the political system. A central challenge here is to understand how a developed network for citizen participation coexists with the regime's strong control over participatory structures. Political parties receive special attention. Chapter 4 provides a broad view of the political system. It analyzes how well political stability is reconciled with other political goals: political freedom, political equality, political change. The chapter tries to show how extraordinary stability has been consistent with mixed achievements in these other political areas.

Chapter 5 turns to the economic model that has at once benefited from and buttressed Mexico's political stability. Here we discuss how some enviable economic achievements have coexisted with a terribly unequal distribution of wealth and its consequent social problems. This chapter also analyzes the economic crisis of the mid-1970s and how its apparent resolution has failed to remove its fundamental causes, thus not averting the renewed economic crisis faced in 1982. The relationship between Mexico's domestic and foreign policies is discussed in Chapter 6. We try to show how Mexico's own conservative development model has been compatible with a seemingly leftist foreign policy and how Mexico's traditional dependence on the United States has squared with

Mexico's increased assertiveness in foreign policy. Specific attention is given to Mexican relations with Central America and, particularly, to critical Mexico–United States policy problems (migration, trade, drugs, tourism). Chapter 7 focuses on what is possibly the single biggest contemporary policy issue in Mexico and in Mexico–United States relations: oil. The chapter serves as a case study exemplifying key trends developed in preceding chapters, including some different ways in which oil may affect the major characteristics of Mexican development. The debate surrounding the best ways to spend oil revenues raises issues concerning alternative futures in Mexico. The relationship between these futures and contemporary reality is pursued in Chapter 8.

NOTES

1. Probably the best-known contemporary work on development that focuses on political stability is Samuel P. Huntington's *Political Order in Changing Societies* (New Haven, Conn.: Yale University Press, 1968). Huntington regards Mexico as "highly successful in political development," attributes the nation's economic growth to its political stability, and accords Mexico special attention as a model of stability. Quote is from p. 324; also see pp. 315–324 and passim.

2. From 1954 to 1970, Mexico followed a pattern known as *desarrollo estabilizador* (stabilizing development), which involved such policies as stable domestic prices and a stable foreign exchange rate. Dissatisfied with the results of desarrollo estabilizador, President Luis Echeverría (1970–1976) tried to introduce *desarrollo compartido* (shared development). The different efforts by Echeverría and López Portillo to modify and revitalize the basic development model are analyzed in subsequent chapters.

3. One such classic analysis of the causes of revolt is found in Alexis de Tocqueville's *The Old Regime and the French Revolution*, trans. Stuart Gilbert (New York: Doubleday, 1955). One more modern, empirical affirmation is Ted Robert Gurr's *Why Men Rebel* (Princeton, N.J.: Princeton University Press, 1970).

4. On rural education, see "Postración educativa," *Excélsior*, editorial, December 1, 1979. Perhaps 40 percent of the population of rural Mexico is still illiterate. On higher education, United Nations Educational, Scientific and Cultural Organization, *Statistical Yearbook 1977* (Paris: UNESCO, 1978), p. 151, indicated 6 percent for 1970 and 10 percent for 1975; expansion has continued at a fast pace.

5. The datum on historical stagnation comes from Frank Tannenbaum, *The Struggle for Peace and Bread* (New York: Columbia University Press, 1950), p. 10. On recent growth, see Thomas E. Weil et al., *Area Handbook for Mexico* (Washington, D.C.: Government Printing Office, 1975), pp. 36–38, 44.

6. For relevant discussions see Clifford Kaufman, "Urbanization, Material Satisfaction and Mass Political Involvement: The Poor in Mexico City," *Comparative Political Studies* 4, no. 3 (1971):295–320; Wayne A. Cornelius, "Urbanization as

an Agent of Latin American Political Stability: The Case of Mexico," *American Political Science Review* 63, no. 3 (1969):833–957.

7. "El valle de México," *Uno Más Uno*, December 6, 1979, referring to research at the National Polytechnic Institute; and David Siller and Miguel Angel Velázquez, "Los índices de contaminación," *Uno Más Uno*, December 21, 1979.

8. The "modernization-development" contrast is elaborated in Cynthia Hewitt de Alcántara, *La modernización de la agricultura mexicana 1940–1970* (Mexico City: Siglo XXI, 1978), p. 283 and passim.

9. See, for example, Octavio Paz, *The Other Mexico: Critique of the Pyramid*, trans. Lysander Kemp (New York: Grove Press, 1972), p. 45: "Here is the dilemma: either the developed Mexico will absorb and integrate the other, or the under-developed Mexico . . . will end up by strangling the developed Mexico." One of the widest-read "either-or" formulations can be found in Pablo González Casanova, *Democracy in Mexico*, trans. Danielle Salti (London: Oxford University Press, 1970), pp. 158–197.

10. On the causes and consequences of the 1968 confrontation, see Daniel Levy, *University and Government in Mexico: Autonomy in an Authoritarian System* (New York: Praeger Publishers, 1980), pp. 28–37.

11. The issue need not be seen as continued stability versus regime dissolution. Intermediate solutions are possible. Historians who look back on Mexico in the 1970s and 1980s may disagree as to whether the regime persisted, with deft accommodation to heightened challenge, or fundamentally changed.

12. Daniel Cosío Villegas, *American Extremes*, trans. Américo Paredes (Austin: University of Texas Press, 1964) pp. 7, 162–171.

13. Weil et al., *Area Handbook for Mexico*, p. 14.

14. For an up-to-date analysis of Mexico's population see Francisco Alba's *The Population of Mexico: Trends, Issues and Policies*, trans. Marjory Mattingly Urquidi (New Brunswick, N.J.: Transaction Press, 1982).

15. Peter Coy, "The Indians of Mexico," in *Latin America and the Caribbean: A Handbook*, ed. Claudio Véliz (New York: Praeger Publishers, 1968), pp. 705–706.

16. Compadrazgo relationships may bind a community together and make it more self-sufficient by imposing reciprocal obligations. Where compadrazgo ties rich and poor, for example, the poor may receive material help and security in return for which the rich may receive labor, a sense of community identity amid their wider "modern" interactions, and firmer support for political stability.

17. Weil et al., *Area Handbook for Mexico*, p. 8.

18. For an analysis of this coverage, still surprisingly small, at least until 1978, see Thomas Michael Laichas, "Mexico in the U.S. Press: A Quantitative Study, 1972–1978," in *Statistical Abstract of Latin America*, Vol. 20, ed. James W. Wilkie (Los Angeles: UCLA Latin American Center Publications, 1980), pp. 582–594.

19. Paz forcefully added that Mexican views of the United States are equally ill informed. "The idea that Mexican people have of the United States is contradictory, emotional, and impervious to criticism; it is a mythical image." "Reflections: Mexico and the United States," trans. Rachel Phillips, *The New Yorker*, September 17, 1979, p. 136. Cosío Villegas, *American Extremes* (p. 29),

20   INTRODUCTION

made similar two-way points. In fact, because the United States must divide its attention among so many nations and regions, while Mexico is so tied to the United States, the imperative to "know thy neighbor" should be especially clear for Mexicans.

20. Oscar Lewis, *Five Families* (New York: Basic Books, 1959).

21. See, for example, Rodolfo O. de la Garza's account of the recent growth of Chicano-Mexican ties: "Demythologizing Chicano-Mexican Relations," in *Mexico-United States Relations*, ed. Susan Kaufman Purcell (New York: Academy of Political Science, 1981), pp. 88–96.

22. For an overview and orientation to the recent books on the border, see María Patricia Fernández Kelly, "The U.S.-Mexico Border: Recent Publications and the State of Current Research," *Latin American Research Review* 16, no. 3 (1981):250–267.

23. Weil et al., *Area Handbook for Mexico*, p. 11.

24. World Bank, *World Development Indicators* (annex) (Washington, D.C., 1980), p. 135.

2

A Brief Political History

I repeat that we are nothing except a relationship: something that can be defined only as a part of a history.

Mexico has a plurality of pasts, all present and at war within every Mexican's soul.

—Octavio Paz[1]

To understand contemporary Mexico, one must understand its past or, more accurately, its pasts, for Mexican history is rich in conflicts and cataclysmic changes. Many of these changes seemingly brought victories for certain principles, but the victories often proved ephemeral. Probably few countries celebrate so many holidays, partly because victories were so frequently followed by defeats, necessitating future victories. We focus here on five continually glorified principles or goals: *political stability, political liberty, economic growth, increased economic equality,* and *national independence.* Special attention is given to the epic twentieth-century struggle for stability, seen against a historical backdrop in which extraordinary instability was the norm. Obviously, not all the ostensible goals have in fact been pursued by all those who have shaped Mexican history. Mexicans have disagreed sharply—and still do disagree—citing different victories and defeats, heroes and villains. Nonetheless, these goals represent recurrent themes in Mexican history. Indeed, they still command wide support among Mexicans, despite a lack of consensus on their exact meaning or priority. The exploration of these goals in different eras should therefore help provide a conceptual coherence to our chronological overview. (A summary of the U.S. role in Mexican history is left for Chapter 6.)

21

PRECOLONIAL AND COLONIAL ERAS

The Indians who inhabited Mexico in the precolonial period form an integral part of contemporary Mexico. They were not driven into historical oblivion by their European conquerors; instead, they mixed with them. As Octavio Paz wrote: "The historical memory of [U.S.] America is European, not American. . . . Exactly the opposite is true of Mexico, land of superimposed pasts."[2]

Mystery surrounds much of the early history of Mexico's Indians, but it seems likely that they were attracted to the region by such favorable factors as the warm climate and available water. With the shift from hunting to agriculture and more permanent settlement came higher civilizations of Olmecs, Mayas, Toltecs, and Teotihuacanos. In the twelfth century, the Aztecs abandoned the arid north for the fertile central valley, built Tenochtitlan (later Mexico City), conquered their enemies, and established an empire complete with governors of the provinces, tax collectors, courts, and ruling military-religious castes. Aztec rule has been compared to contemporary Mexican rule—both forged a centralized stable system of a markedly authoritarian and hierarchical nature. But Aztec rule is also remembered as a symbol of *Mexican* independence, violated but never fully vanquished by the foreign conquerors who would establish "New Spain."

Only a few hundred Spaniards under Hernán Cortés conquered Mexico in 1519. They were aided by superior weaponry and by fortuitous native religious beliefs that white gods would one day appear. Most of all, they were aided by the lack of unity among Mexico's Indians. The Aztecs ruled over other tribes, and some of these saw in the commotion surrounding the Spanish arrival an attractive opportunity to rebel. Images of a simple, harmonious, peaceful society succumbing to the warlike invaders are misleading. Precolumbian Mexican society was quite politically complex and conflictual. Some Indians defied Cortés; others were unsure, submissive, or even supportive. Leading the defiant ones—current allusions by gastronomically stricken tourists to "Moctezuma's revenge" notwithstanding—was not the Aztec emperor Moctezuma, but his defiant nephew, Cuauhtémoc. It is Cuauhtémoc who is today memorialized in Mexican books, monuments, and street names as the early symbol of independence.

Some contemporary Mexicans, particularly conservatives, emphasize positive features of Spain's three-century colonial rule. Most important was the introduction of Christianity. For those who believe that Christianity offers the route to godliness and salvation, this event can hardly be overemphasized. Care was taken to protect the Indian, while hoping to convert and assimilate him. How different this was from the English settlers' efforts to push aside the natives. A degree of political integration and stability was achieved, and Mexico City became one of the two central poles of development (Lima was the other) for all of Spanish America. Even some limited degree of self-government could be found. Finally, there is something to be said for the sheer courage and perseverance of the early conquerors.

Most Mexicans, however, have a more mixed or even negative image of the colonial era. To the extent that the Spaniards sought assimilation, they did so on the basis of paternalistic imposition of their own religion, values, and privileges. Even the Spanish who settled in Mexico were themselves exploited by Spain's mercantile economic system. The system robbed Mexico of its mineral riches while prohibiting free trade with any but the mother country. Certainly most Mexicans were not favorably affected by the colonization; a rigidly unequal social hierarchy insured that. At the top were the Spaniards, or *peninsulares*, followed by *criollos*, who were of Spanish descent but born in Mexico, followed much further down by mestizos, and still further down by the Indian masses. The Indians' plight probably worsened, in fact, as settlers carved out large estates at the expense of traditional communal landholdings. Overall, Spanish rule was paternalistic, elitist, and authoritarian. Crown and church together saw to that. Stability was probably the goal that fared best in the colonial era.

A contrast of Mexican and U.S. colonial experiences provides fascinating insights into contemporary differences. One major contrast involved the mother countries themselves. Spain had an absolute monarchy, strong church-state ties, and a still largely feudal economic system. At least by comparison, England appeared to have a more limited monarchy, a more vibrant parliament, more self-government, greater church-state separation, and leadership in the capitalist industrial revolution. Spain's organic, holistic, corporatist, conservative tendencies contrasted with England's more individualist, pluralist, liberal ones.

Another key contrast involved the native populations themselves. Whereas the English confronted nomadic tribes, the Spanish confronted relatively highly developed civilizations. The first would be swept aside, the second could not be. Thus the English transplanted their relatively liberal politics and culture largely intact, while Spain mixed its more conservative culture with those of a hierarchical native society. Within Spanish America itself, an interesting contrast emerged. Those countries (e.g., Mexico and Peru) with the most highly developed Indian civilizations naturally attracted the colonizers' greatest interest; whether one emphasizes the colonizers' oppression of the native civilizations or the blend of two hierarchical civilizations, these countries became very inegalitarian in their political, economic, and social affairs. Those countries (e.g., Argentina and Uruguay) with less developed Indian civilizations attracted less colonial interest; then, in the nineteenth century, European immigrants, with their liberalism, found fresher terrain on which to establish themselves. In a sense, therefore, countries with the most formidable Indian and colonial heritages were handicapped in pursuing many of the goals often subsequently associated with "development."

THE FIRST CENTURY OF INDEPENDENCE

Mexico's eventual political independence in 1821 resulted from a combination of weakened rule in the wake of Napoleon's conquest of Spain and accumulated Mexican grievances—especially when socioeconomic gains achieved through reforms were followed by setbacks and frustrated rising expectations. Criollos and privileged mestizos battled the peninsulares and their Spanish establishment. But the revolt was no struggle for the deprived masses. In this configuration, Mexico resembled most of Spain's rebellious colonies.

The most interesting Mexican twist was the involvement, albeit aborted, of many Indians. Their leader was Miguel Hidalgo, priest (for Indians had become Christians), champion of the oppressed, nationalist (whose leadership role in the independence struggle is still recalled in annual ritual by Mexico's president on the night of September 15), "Captain-General of America,"—and failure. It was not Hidalgo's brutal methods that sealed his fate; it was his utter lack of military skill and criollo desertion. His successor, although more successful, was also to be betrayed by wealthy criollos. The relatively privileged had never forgotten that they had more to fear from the aspiring masses than from unyielding elites. Like the revolution of a century later, the War for Independence (1810–1821) was complicated, meandering, protracted, decentralized, and ultimately unfulfilling for the masses. In fact, independence came only when the Mexican upper class finally turned against Spain, partly because Spain itself had now adopted a liberal constitution!

Not surprisingly, then, the War for Independence did not produce an egalitarian revolution. Nor did it bring political stability. And the lack of stability went hand in hand with economic problems. In turn, these political and economic failures made Mexico's new national independence very fragile. The early independence period is especially interesting for its illuminating political-economic contrasts to contemporary Mexico. Indeed, it has been called the "era of anarchy."

Independent Mexico inherited an economy in dreadful shape.[3] Mexico was in debt, its treasury was bankrupt, and the nation lacked strong commercial ties to European markets. In short, a crippled economy desperately needed a great deal of capital. This view was shared by those who would become "liberals" and those who would become "conservatives." Differences emerged when, for example, liberals wanted to promote private enterprise at the expense of a strong church and state, two institutions that conservatives wanted to uphold. Yet many conservatives were not simply harking back toward a bygone or feudal age; they favored powerful banking institutions and foreign investment.

Unfortunately, the Mexican state could not attract the needed capital without first establishing political stability—and this it could not do. Only two presidents completed their four-year terms during the thirty-five year span from 1821 to 1856. Part of the problem was regional. Centralists wanted to build power in Mexico City, federalists in the provinces. More directly, most of the problem was economic. Governments did not have the resources to meet basic legitimizing needs, to make it worthwhole *not* to revolt. This economic problem was clearly tied to the regional problem. Central governments could not extract more resources from society without engendering provincial challenges. Without those resources they could not even pay the army, thus provoking military coups. So just as Mexico could not get needed economic capital without stability, it could not establish stability without needed capital. Understanding the relationship between political instability and economic stagnation during much of the nineteenth century will help us to appreciate, by contrast, the stability-growth relationship in much of the twentieth century.

Only against this backdrop of deeply rooted political and economic problems can one begin to imagine the spectacular personal successes that notoriously irresponsible or incompetent leaders often achieved over responsible ones. Soon after Mexico freed itself from Spain, Augustín de Iturbide appointed himself emperor; thus far the main result of independence was criollo royalty. As governments rose and fell quickly in the ensuing decades, a perverse continuity was the incredible tenacity of Antonio López de Santa Anna, Mexico's most despised, traitorous, duplicitous native son, who in 1848 presided over the loss of roughly half Mexico's territory in war with the United States. Santa Anna's most consistent preoccupation was self-interest. Among his favorite self-designations were Most Serene Highness, Father of the Country, Savior, and Perpetual Victor. It is a sad commentary on Mexico's political instability from the 1820s to the 1850s that the last title had some validity. Almost no one could establish a viable government with a viable economic base.

Mexico's problems were greatly aggravated by foreign intervention. France, Great Britain, and Spain all demanded reparations for losses suffered during Mexico's turmoil. In 1864, France named Austrian Archduke Maximilian to rule Mexico. As in the war with the United States two decades earlier, Mexican independence suffered as domestic strife and instability weakened the nation's ability to defend itself. This time, however, Mexico eventually defeated the foreigners, and liberals regained power.

Although they did not achieve sustained political stability, liberals held the upper hand for much of the third quarter of the century, era of the reform (La Reforma). Their accomplishments were numerous. They permitted many political liberties, including elections, although with limited suffrage. They attacked the church's enormous privileges, reducing its large tracts of (untaxable) lands, its immunity before the law, and its control over social affairs such as education and marriage. They expanded public educational facilities. Mestizos and a growing bourgeoisie captured some privileges previously reserved for a small elite. And the reform's great leader, Benito Juárez, was himself an Indian from the poor state of Oaxaca. Historian Daniel Cosío Villegas called the liberals a "group of men without equal in our history, men with the virile optimism of those who feel a nation being born from their own hands, and for whom liberalism was a new religious faith."[4] Yet there is a perhaps less flattering evaluation. Classic nineteenth-century advocates of individualism, the liberals opposed traditionalism and communitarianism, whether oriented toward the church or the Indian. The liberals worshipped liberty, not equality.

In fact, however one evaluates the liberals' ideology, their reform's reach exceeded its grasp. It had greater success in limiting church privileges than in establishing a new liberal order. Regional oligarchs took advantage of formal democratic structures to thwart progressive change, so that both Juárez and his liberal successor had to rule largely through specially invoked executive authority. Ultimately, the liberals fell in 1876 to a military coup headed by Porfirio Díaz, who had been a general in Mexico's successful effort to end the French intervention.

Even when the liberals lost power, the traditional conservatives could not regain control. Instead, with Díaz as Mexico's supreme leader from 1876 to 1910, a new political philosophy reigned. This was the era of positivism, which stressed that progress derives from science and order. Like liberalism, positivism was imported from Europe by most Latin American nations, but few felt its impact as strongly as Mexico. Like liberalism, positivism based itself mostly on "progressive" Europe and was generally indifferent or hostile to both tradition and egalitarianism. Unlike liberalism, positivism did not characteristically embrace individual liberty.

The achievements of the *porfiriato* (1876–1910) were substantial. Foremost were political stability and economic growth. Stability must be appreciated against the new nation's background of instability. Governments had come and gone so often that the military had become a very desirable career for upwardly mobile mestizos, one offering good chances to reach positions of power and corruption. Instability frustrated Mexican efforts to attract waves of European emigrants, who instead took their skills to Argentina, Uruguay, or the United States. Most important, political instability had doomed the more significant efforts to attract foreign capital and technology. Now, finally, Mexico had an extended period of political stability. This stability, in turn, contributed to dramatic economic growth. Thus the porfiriato reversed the vicious cycle of economic weakness and political instability that had characterized the early independence period. Foreigners gave Mexico high credit ratings and made secure, profitable investments. Railroads, oil, electricity, steel, and sugar mills led the way. "Rails and Progress" boasted one prominent slogan. The strong porfiriato regime also succeeded in extracting increased tax revenues from the domestic population. National income soared, along with exports and imports.

Order and growth were achieved, however, with disdain for liberty and equality. Divisions of power between the national and state governments and separation of powers within the national government were bypassed as Díaz centralized political might into his own dictatorial hands. The reform's free elections, speech, and press were lost. The government co-opted peasants, gunmen, and bandits by offering good salaries, uniforms, and power and turned these *rurales* loose to repress any dissent in the countryside. And considerable repression was necessary in order to implement policies that were not just dictatorial but economically harsh for the masses. Mexico's development model required cheap peasant and urban labor and no strikes.

Positivism provided the handy rationale that the intellectually fittest must forge a necessary, natural path to progress. Neither ignorance nor short-sighted humanitarianism should impede that progress. Thus, the government did not need to worry that it was providing, for example, terrible education in rural areas. Economic growth was expected to help the rich, the small middle class, and—through trickle-down economics— even the poor. In fact, only the first two expectations were fulfilled. Large landholders increasingly pushed peasants off their land into laborer status, which often culminated in debtor status. Conditions worsened at the turn of the century, when world depression hit hardest at the masses. After decades of "order and progress," wages and living standards were deteriorating for many, and probably more than four in five Mexicans remained illiterate.[5]

While most Mexicans suffered, foreigners prospered. The porfiriato encouraged foreign penetration of major sectors of Mexico's economy. Independence took a giant step backward.

Parallels to contemporary Mexican politics (since 1940) are striking.

Leadership for both regimes emerged from the ruins of movements (the reform, the revolution) to change society. Underprivileged masses do not benefit, at least not nearly in proportion to economic growth, and dissent is repressed. Yet the stick is combined with a carrot of co-optation, as expanding bureaucracies offer jobs, and money from corruption is available. Both regimes are also enlightened enough to couple repression with intelligence, promoting scientific and professional pursuits, whether for the sake of "positivism" under the porfiriato or "modernization" in the contemporary system. Both use the trappings of democratic liberalism to obscure authoritarian behavior. (Díaz showed rare candor when he referred to Congress as "my herd of tame horses.") Both have molded strongly positive relationships between political stability and economic growth. And both could reasonably claim that, whatever their shortcomings, the real alternative in Mexican history has not been democratic and widely shared prosperity, but destructive political instability, a crippled economy, and consequent vulnerability to foreign intervention.

In fairness, however, there are also important differences between the past and present regimes. Today's uses a smaller stick and a larger carrot than the porfiriato did. Repression and exclusion have become less extensive. Peasants, and especially organized workers, fare better than before. The middle class has grown significantly, partaking of a measure of liberty and an expanded measure of economic opportunity. Finally, both social and political mobility are greater.

REVOLUTION

The marked lack of social and political mobility under the porfiriato contributed to its fall. Aging regimes that do not let in rising groups or circulate elites risk overthrow by those excluded. Economic growth had spawned new interests that felt thwarted by the porfiriato dictatorship. Intellectual foundations for rebellion were established by a reborn liberal movement that demanded, at a minimum, free elections, a free press, and a return to the reform's 1857 constitution. The regime reacted with repression. The economic situation made matters worse. In response to a depression, the government adopted harsh policies (e.g., calling in loans) and thereby alienated even some of the elites. Politically, Díaz fumbled his one major show of flexibility, an announcement of his personal retirement, by retreating into typically rigged reelection. This about-face was the match that ignited a flammable accumulation of grievances. So, almost a hundred years after the start of the war of independence, an equally protracted and far bloodier revolution began.

Like many revolutions, Mexico's started with a moderate stage. So brittle had Díaz's dictatorship become that it collapsed without any revolutionary push. Mexico's new president, Francisco Madero, was a young foreign-educated idealist from a wealthy landowning family. His slogan, "effective suffrage, no reelection," tells us as much about what he did not champion (fundamental socioeconomic change) as what he did (political reform). Madero was no fiery revolutionary. He restored the reform's basic tenets, including a free press and individual property rights. He also restored free elections, but, as earlier, suffrage was really limited to only part of the population. A form of political liberty, not political equality, and certainly not economic equality, was Madero's abiding principle. Courageous as he was, Madero ultimately failed because he neither smashed the old regime (its politicians, civil service, army, church, and entrenched economic interests) nor controlled the revolutionaries bent on so doing. The first—and, according to some, the last— really competitively elected president of Mexico in the twentieth century was murdered in a 1913 coup, covertly aided by the United States. The coup installed dictator Victoriano Huerta, destroyed political freedom, and inaugurated the revolution's most violent epoch. Like the democrat Madero, the dictator Huerta did not thoroughly overhaul the porfiriato's governing elite.[6] Had either Madero or Huerta consolidated his power, the events of 1910 to 1913 might, in retrospect, hardly be seen as revolutionary.

At least three major armies were pitted against the new dictatorship. They were by no means united among themselves, however. Emiliano Zapata led peasant forces from the south. Their chief demand was clear: land. When Madero urged moderation, Zapata withdrew his support, effected land reform in his home state of Morelos, and pressed to spread the revolution. Zapata's forces had a coherent revolutionary program but were perhaps essentially conservative socially. Even their cry for land was an attempt to preserve their communal, insulated traditions. The second army, Pancho Villa's forces, lacked a similarly coherent program but displayed the violent revolutionary zeal popularly attributed to them.[7]

The third army, the constitutionalists, was led by Venustiano Carranza. This group was the least revolutionary of the three. It was composed largely of ranchers and self-made men. If it did not represent society's established elite, neither did it represent primarily the masses. Perhaps the key factor was that the group included many of those excluded from the Díaz regime's ruling elite. The porfiriato had proved itself incapable of sufficient personnel turnover, incapable of sufficient incorporation of young elites, and therefore vulnerable to rebellion from frustrated aspirants. By 1915 the constitutionalists were rising to political supremacy. Allied with the powerful "Northwest Group," Carranza defeated the zapatistas and villistas after these groups had abandoned Mexico City and returned to their regional strongholds.

"Before the Revolution." Porfirio Díaz and "los científicos" (wise men). The cabinet (1909) represents the old guard. (Photo courtesy of Juan M. Cassola)

More revolutionary turmoil than revolutionary change came in the next few years. Carranza himself had been a landlord, a senator during the Díaz regime, a governor during the Madero regime, and a *cacique* (regional strongman with his own army) before leading the constitutionalists to power. Reform was thus limited in part by Carranza's rather nonrevolutionary values; but it was promoted by his keen political sense. Carranza understood that a degree of reform was necessary to consolidate the new regime. Thus he would have to support the 1917 Constitutional Convention. The convention probably went well beyond Carranza's own wishes and certainly promulgated a truly revolutionary doctrine. The Constitution is a strongly nationalistic proclamation, asserting Mexico's control over its natural resources. It pledges land reform. It pledges labor rights, such as a minimum wage, an eight-hour day, improved working conditions, workmen's compensation, maternity leave laws, freedom to shop at other than company stores, and even some employer responsibility for health, housing, and educational opportunities. It has been called the first modern socialist constitution, preceding the Soviet Union's. At the same time, however, like Mexico's earlier reform, it replicates many U.S. concepts meant to guarantee political freedom: federalism, separation of powers, a bicameral congress, an elaborate Bill of Rights. The framers

"The Revolution Peaks." Pancho Villa in the presidential chair, with Emiliano Zapata on his right (1914). Their revolutionary forces did not long occupy the capital, the focus of political power. (Photo courtesy of Juan M. Cassola)

of Mexico's constitution attempted to include what they perceived as the best of both worlds.

Carranza's effort in 1920 to circumvent free elections by installing a puppet successor led to his own murder and a coup by the Northwest Group. The group installed its leader, Alvaro Obregón, as president. From 1920 to 1924, Obregón pushed beyond Carranza's restrained reform, particularly in labor and educational policies. Mexico built schools and launched a literacy campaign. Whereas Carranza, the politician, did what he thought the circumstances dictated, Obregón, the statesman, more actively pressed for reform in keeping with his own vision of a new society. If Díaz had represented repression of demands for socioeconomic change and Madero a gentlemanly ignorance or indifference, Carranza represented political acquiescence and Obregón active partnership.

Plutarco Elías Calles, another leader of the Northwest Group, peacefully took over the presidency in 1924, but his plot to circumvent the no-reelection rule by reinstalling Obregón in 1928 was abruptly foiled by Obregón's murder. Calles nonetheless remained the supreme power

"The Revolution Fails." By 1920, after Zapata's death, some of his generals allied themselves with Obregón. This alliance may symbolize the defeat of a true peasant revolution and the peasants' subsequent incorporation into the regime's highly inegalitarian system. (Photo courtesy of Juan M. Cassola)

behind the throne until 1934. He was revolutionary in his attack on the church but failed to push many promised social reforms. His major accomplishment, without doubt, was to forge Mexico's uniquely successful one-party system. Although his successor pursued a more revolutionary course, Calles pointed Mexican politics in its present direction: political stability (with substantial limits on liberty) and economic modernization (centralized banking, improved tax collection, financial stability, agricultural credits, infrastructural development, and increased U.S. economic penetration of the Mexican economy), without effective redistribution of the newly generated wealth.

If Calles thought he had appointed yet another subservient successor in Lázaro Cárdenas (1934–1940), he soon learned otherwise. Cárdenas's strength derived from the strong bond he established with Mexico's masses. Never before or since has the revolution produced such a revered figure. Contemporary reverence for Cárdenas is reverence for the major absent but not forgotten goal of the revolution: greater equality. If the porfiriato provides the great historical parallel to the contemporary regime, Cárdenas' administration provides the great symbolic alternative.

As governor of Michoacán in the 1920s, Cárdenas had established his commitment to agrarian reform. He dramatically demonstrated this commitment, while deepening his mass support, by campaigning for president throughout the country for one and a half years. As president, he distributed more land than had all his revolutionary predecessors combined, even though there had been significant distribution since 1920. Ironically, this distribution may not have reduced income inequality or improved real wages for the masses. Peasants got land, but in the form of small plots, without the adequate capital, irrigation, or skills to develop them. Yet Cárdenas cut through the usual cynicism of Mexican politics. Undoubtedly, much of his reform represented a pragmatic response to the worldwide depression, but Cárdenas also acted out of his own reformist convictions. He established mutually warm, trustful feeling with the masses. He also placed reins on official luxury. That Mexico underwent only a small shift from rural to urban areas in the 1930s is an indication of the hope that Cárdenas gave the peasants on the land.[8] Finally, Cárdenas was revered for nationalizing the oil industry in 1938. Mexico's masses had reason to feel that Cárdenas was *their* president.

Cárdenas's conception of an activist state at the service of the people had little in common with democratic notions about political liberty. Reforms would be initiated more from the top down, "for the people," than from the bottom up, "by the people." Peasant and worker demands were carefully handled through the official party. Labor should restrain itself, Cárdenas could argue, because it was properly integrated into a progressive state, which was, after all, one of its major employers. Educational policy tried to elevate socialist solidarity above the free interchange of conflicting ideas. Like his predecessors, from whom he differed notably in socioeconomic approaches, Cárdenas directly pursued political stability much more than political liberty or bourgeois freedoms. Cárdenas's first major step to guarantee the strength of the presidency was, ironically, to expel Calles, the man who had originally appointed him but who then persisted in trying to undermine him. Cárdenas proceeded to assert his central authority over regional as well as labor caciques whenever he felt them to be threatening that authority. At the end of his term, by bypassing leftist leaders within the party to appoint instead a moderate as his successor, Cárdenas in effect chose to institutionalize rather than to intensify the revolution.

AFTER THE REVOLUTION

Some observers have questioned the degree to which a revolution really occurred. They point out that Mexico merely switched one elite for another, that the plight of the masses was not substantially improved.

A recent cartoon shows one peasant asking another, "Who finally won the revolution, the zapatistas or the villistas?" Answer: "Neither one; the Revolutionary Family governs us."[9] Leaders like Cárdenas emerge less often, those like novelist Carlos Fuentes's Artemio Cruz more often.[10] For Cruz, revolutionary goals are quickly subordinated to material goals. He becomes preoccupied more with Paris or New York than with Mexico. He uses the power of the state to repress rather than to help the less privileged.

Revolutions need not change everything to be revolutions, however. And in fact, many important changes were achieved. A fossilized oligarchy was replaced by a much broader ruling elite. Peasant participation guaranteed that certain policy consequences, such as land distribution, would flow from the regime change. Labor became a major institutionalized political factor. A new political order, based on a strong civilian party structure, was born. And if violence is any criterion of revolution, Mexico's upheaval more than qualifies.

Mexico's transformation also included a cultural revolution. Nationalism was a key factor, although foreign influences remained strong in education and some related cultural fields.[11] The revolution weakened the explicitly European orientation of the Díaz regime and focused on Mexico's indigenous roots. The Indian was increasingly depicted not as an exotic savage, but as a mature person—even the source of all that was good in Mexico—in literary works such as Gregorio López y Fuentes's El Indio [The Indian]. Pedro Lamicq's Piedad para el Indio [Mercy for the Indian] called for the integration of the Indian into Mexican life. José Vasconcelos wrote of the mission of the cosmic, Ibero-American race as a fortuitous blend of Indian, European, and African roots. Composers such as Carlos Chávez and Silvestre Revueltas would work repeatedly with folk themes. Writers such as Samuel Ramos, Jesús Silva Herzog, Octavio Paz, and Leopold Zea would explore the essence of Mexicanism. Archeologists would pursue their unique exploration of Mexico's roots. Architects associated ornament with bourgeois decadence and strove instead to transmit revolutionary values. But it was the painters who made the greatest impact, particularly with their grand murals depicting indigenous and revolutionary themes. Among the most famous were Diego Rivera, David Alfaro Siqueiros, José Clemente Orozco, and Rufino Tamayo. One could speak of a distinctly Mexican style. Cultural independence had taken great strides, even if one could argue that U.S. media have significantly changed the situation in recent decades. And to all this one would have to add a consideration of popular nationalistic culture, epitomized by the revolutionary ballads, such as La Cucaracha, which, with considerable folkloric embellishment, hark back to distinctly

Diego Rivera's mural at the National Palace captures both Mexico's revolutionary turmoil and its official pride in its indigenous roots. "Huelga" means "strike," an important part of the revolutionary heritage. (Photo courtesy of Rodolfo Romo de Vivar)

Mexican themes. Importantly, folk music and dance are prominently and proudly featured at official government gatherings.

Political-economic consequences of the revolution for the post-1940 system will of course be analyzed throughout the rest of this book. Suffice it here to offer a very brief chronological overview. President Manuel Avila Camacho (1940–1946) concentrated on taming revolutionary fervor, whether directed against the church or against the United States. A positive accomplishment was the creation of Mexico's social security system. His successor, Miguel Alemán (1946–1952) became at least the symbolic antithesis to Cárdenas, the antihero of leftist historical interpretations. Alemán strongly favored industrialization, business interests, and the trickle-down approach to distributing wealth, explicitly pursuing economic growth while hoping that all might eventually benefit from the bigger pie. Agriculture, notably communal agriculture, plunged into a low-priority status, which the regime would maintain for decades. Nevertheless—and this is crucial to the institutionalization and stability of the Mexican regime—Alemán did not specifically undo all of Cárdenas's reforms or declare them illegitimate. Alemán's successor, Adolfo Ruiz Cortines (1952–1958), then proclaimed a "balanced revolution," that is, one balanced between the *alemanista* and *cardenista* approaches. His moderation, integrity, popularity, and relative inactivity made him something of a Mexican Eisenhower.

Next, López Mateos (1958–1964) declared himself a leftist "within the revolution." But nearly all administrations since 1940 have really inclined more to the alemanista pole. By the mid-1950s the state role in the economy had diminished, leaving more leeway to the private sector, and still greater emphasis was given to industry over agriculture. López Mateos readily repressed labor, particularly the rebellious railroad workers, in order to protect the sanctity of the growth-stability model. Gustavo Díaz Ordaz (1964–1970) went still farther, repressing even middle-class university students when he perceived a possible challenge to the regime. His administration's strong inclination toward the alemanista pole was unquestioned.

Luis Echeverría (1970–1976) showed once again that "leftist" presidents are not above authoritarian repression. Although he granted a greater degree of freedom than his predecessor, he also clamped down on governors, the press, and peasants. In socioeconomic affairs, Echeverría made the major post-1940 attempt to deviate from the alemanista model, but he achieved only mixed results. He managed some success in subsidizing food and housing and increased the government's control over certain economic sectors, including communications, commerce, industry, and foreign investment. But he failed dismally in other attempts, such as tax reform. His overall effort to alter the development model, to fortify the public and domestic sectors, and to redistribute wealth a bit earned him the enmity of foreign economic interests and of Mexico's middle and upper classes. Mexico's economy plunged deeper into disaster, culminating in the 1976 peso devaluation. It is important to understand that Echeverría deviated from the alemanista model fundamentally not because he was an irresponsible radical adventurer, as many of his detractors would have it, or because he was a dedicated revolutionary, as many of his ardent supporters would have it; he acted mostly because he saw serious crises within the development model.

José López Portillo (1976–1982) successfully restored the confidence of those who are sympathetic to Mexico's basic development model, at least until 1981. Political stability seemed surer, the economy once again grew at enviable rates, and the middle and upper classes and foreign and domestic investors were pleased. Political reform was extended. Mexico maintained its progressive hue in foreign policy, notwithstanding the moderation of strident rhetoric. During most of López Portillo's administration, political liberty probably flourished more than it had for at least several administrations. On the other hand, government policies appeared to retreat from Echeverría's banner of fundamental reform. Austerity measures were imposed, and wage increases were held far below the rate of inflation. The regime acknowledged that no new grants of land to peasants would be undertaken. Overall, there was an effort to move away from heady populist politics in favor of more rationalized, technocratic policies. We will explore signs that some important modifications in the basic development model did in fact continue under López Portillo, but the overriding point is that economic growth, not increased economic equality, was once again viewed as political stability's most critical partner. The widespread belief, necessarily very tentative, that Miguel de la Madrid would continue the stability-growth emphasis is based partly on his personal background, mostly on the fact that this emphasis has been the overwhelming choice of almost all governments since 1940.

But uncertainty became dominant as the worst economic crisis in decades enveloped Mexico in the year prior to de la Madrid's inauguration. The peso, which had held steady for more than two decades at 12.5 to the U.S. dollar before weakening to roughly 25 in 1976, plummeted to 45 in early 1982 and to 70 by later that year, with even more alarming unofficial exchange rates. Inflation, which had held at less than 5 percent annually from the late 1950s through the 1960s before increasing markedly in the 1970s, shot up to over 60 percent by 1982, even by the government's own accounts. And against an enviable background of decades of strong growth rates, stymied for only a few years in the 1970s, the government was forced to predict zero growth for one to two years. Additionally, capital flight accelerated, the government seriously cut its spending, its subsidization of basic goods to consumers, and its public works projects (while helping to bail Mexico's largest private concern out of its own deep crisis), and government, business, and labor clashed over wage and price policies. In September 1982, the government announced a dramatic move: It was taking over all domestic private banks. Amid such deep crisis, Mexico was forced to count on foreign interests for a multi-billion-dollar rescue package. More than US$4 billion would come from International Monetary Fund credits, an almost equal amount from combined U.S. sources, and additional aid from European central banks. Naturally, such aid flows largely on donor terms, as with increased U.S. oil purchases at preferential prices. Although the international impact of oil prices and interest rates had contributed to Mexico's economic crisis, López Portillo's return to the basic tenets of Mexico's vaunted stability-growth model seemed either less complete or less desirable than many had previously thought.

INSTITUTIONALIZATION

The question is continually asked and never adequately answered: How can a revolution be institutionalized? Most observers agree that the revolution has indeed died, probably around 1940, although the date has been debated.[12] Contemporary Mexico has followed a model of stable development, not revolutionary change. By institutionalizing its revolution, Mexico has simultaneously cemented certain changes already achieved by the revolution and shielded the system from further revolutionary change. The story is revealed through the political histories of certain key societal institutions.

The Party

Development of Mexico's official political party was the linchpin of institutionalization. Calles was the party's principal architect. Having failed to help restore Obregón to the presidency in 1928, Calles sought a mechanism by which to perpetuate the regime after he himself left office. He ably persuaded most regional and labor caciques that a centralization of political power was in their interests. This centralization was especially important because the early revolutionary period had been characterized by strong centrifugal forces. Calles proposed that caciques band together through a central party to perpetuate certain privileges, as all would be lost if the existing disorder continued. Recent events spoke loudly for Calles: Madero, Zapata, Carranza, Villa, and Obregón had all met unnatural deaths. Violence continued to surround most local as well as national elections. Three contenders were killed in the 1928 presidential campaign. Religious warfare continued with violent intensity (see below). Moreover, Mexico was now headed into the worldwide Great Depression, which was bound to exacerbate worker discontent. Mexico's power-holders needed political order.

Calles was remarkably successful. Enough power-holders bought the message (some allowing themselves to be bought out of politics with lucrative business opportunities) for the new party to take on considerable power. From the nineteenth century on, parties had lacked cohesiveness, often rising and falling with their leaders. Furthermore, the party "system" had been highly fragmented, with many weak parties. But from fifty-one registered parties in 1929, Mexico was down to four by 1933.[13] And the more ex-president Calles ruled and dispensed favors through the party, the stronger that party became. Thus the regime overcame the regional dispersion of political power that had often contributed to instability. The party was a mechanism to centralize political power in Mexico City.

Yet the party might have faded early. Institutionalization of the regime was one reason that Calles built the party; perpetuation of his own political power was another. But any possibility that the party would be merely a personal vehicle for Calles ended when Cárdenas, as president, cut Calles loose from the party.[14] More important, Cárdenas did not try to extend his control over the party after his own term. Given his enormous popularity, this was a considerable victory indeed for the cause of institutionalization. Instead, Cárdenas used his popularity to strengthen the party. He reorganized it from a regional basis, so important initially to bring in the local caciques, to a functional basis, so important now to incorporate the masses. The hero of land distribution organized local peasant leagues into an official agrarian sector. He similarly backed the organization of a giant central labor union. Those who failed to join up soon found themselves powerless. Influence and benefits, after all, now came through the party. So Mexico had successfully created a party that brought into the system the peasant and working masses whose rising expectations may otherwise have created further revolutionary pressures. Cárdenas was neither the first nor the only leader to favor such incorporation, but he was the most successful. Calles had brought the elites together into a common forum, and Cárdenas completed the picture by bringing in the masses.

Given the plight of peasants and workers in recent decades, Cárdenas's incorporation of them into the official party may be seen as ultimately producing greater gains for political stability than for equality or liberty. By not excluding peasants and workers from the formal political structure, the regime would not allow them to develop *independently*. Serious attempts to pressure the regime for fundamental socioeconomic reform in contemporary Mexico often receive neither support nor even indifference but damaging opposition from official peasant and worker representatives. Additionally, the party's nonrevolutionary nature was probably reinforced by the 1942 inclusion of a "popular sector" composed of diverse groups (small industrialists, professionals, youth, women's groups), mostly of middle-class background, with little revolutionary heritage or outlook. In 1946 the party, originally the National Revolutionary Party, then the Party of the Mexican Revolution, assumed its present name: Institutional Revolutionary Party (PRI). As we will discuss in the next chapter, it has dominated Mexico's party system ever since.

The Military

The rise of a strong party contributed greatly to taming Mexico's military. Cárdenas actually brought the military into the party structure. He reasoned that the military was involved de facto in politics already—better to integrate it into an institution controlled by others.

The significance of taming the military can be grasped by looking at historical experience. Nineteenth-century Mexico had one of the "worst" records of military intervention in politics of any Latin American nation.[15] Local armies loyal to given caciques were decisive political forces. Military might most often determined who ruled Mexico. The armed forces served as prime vehicles of social mobility: Soldiers might rise through the ranks, but power-seekers could also realize their dreams by toppling existing governments. Although Juárez, and especially Díaz, made some progress in curbing the military, the military remained active even after the revolution. Obregón and his successors took matters more in hand with a carrot-and-stick approach. They put all generals on the federal payroll, eventually provided social security for soldiers, and allowed ample opportunities for corruption; they also purged disloyal generals, shifted others away from their power bases, and slashed military expenditures.

The results have been startling. Mexico boasts steady civilian rule. This loss of power by the military was not sudden, however. Even after the military's dominant and direct role in politics ended and even after the military as an institution was excluded from the formal party structure, army generals headed the party until 1964.[16] No civilian was elected president until Alemán's election in 1946. Nonetheless, the military's decline was sure. Generals within the PRI increasingly made room for civilian domination. In reality, several of Alemán's immediate predecessors had been warriors only by loose, image-inflated definition anyway, but every president since Alemán has clearly been a civilian. Eight military officers held cabinet positions unrelated to defense between 1929 and 1946; only one has done so since 1946. Officers held fifteen governorships in 1940; there has been, at most, only one serving as governor at any time since 1964. There have been military challenges, such as a rebellion in 1938 and a general's electoral campaign in 1940, but the ease with which the civilian regime turned back these challenges really showed the regime's strength rather than its vulnerability. Besides, even such limited challenges have been less frequent since 1940 than previously.

The taming of the military has been startling by comparison not only with Mexican history, but also with almost all of contemporary Latin America. It has been common for the military to topple governments and, increasingly, to rule directly for extended periods. Even in countries where civilians ostensibly rule, they often must share considerable power with the military. Not in Mexico. The Mexican government has been in the hands of a professional civilian elite, not just soldiers in mufti or soldiers newly turned civilian.[17] Compared to its regional counterparts, Mexico's military has much less power to veto or influence civilian policy, or to demand big payoffs for nonintervention. As one indicator, Mexico spends much less of its budget on the military than do most Latin American countries.

This does not mean that Mexico's military lacks functions. It means that these functions *serve rather than threaten* the civilian system. The military watches for potential threats to stability. It is an arm of repression against those—rural guerrillas, peasants, workers, and occasionally students—who mount significant challenges to the regime. The military also engages in certain infrastructural development projects. Its allegiance to the civilian rulership is a source of legitimacy for both groups.

Mexico's military may appear unique, but it is really the civilian political system that is unique. The civilian system determines the military role. Unlike the situation in most of Latin America, conservative interests can count on Mexico's civilian structure to maintain political order and economic privilege. Were this structure to fail in the future, the military role could well change. In fact, interesting signs of change have very recently appeared and will be examined in the next chapter. For decades, however, Mexico's military has been uniquely institutionalized within the civilian-dominated political structure.

The Church

As with peaceful military-regime relations, the importance of peaceful church-regime relations must be seen against a turbulent historical background. In precolumbian and even colonial Mexico, dominant religions and political institutions were generally tightly bound, but church influence often constituted a powerful counterweight to the newly independent government. Church ownership of perhaps one-third of Mexico's land gave it extraordinary resources.[18] Together with other large landholders, the church significantly shaped conservative Mexican politics. Political liberals and many capitalists seeking a more open economic system therefore challenged the church. The reform's 1857 constitution seriously eroded church power. Although liberal ideology was clearly an important force, the reform's attack on the church must also be seen in the context of the governmental instability, rooted in inability to raise adequate revenues, that had characterized newly independent Mexico. The church's land was nontaxable, depriving the state of badly needed revenue.

Despite positivism's antireligious bias, church influence recovered somewhat during the porfiriato. So the revolutionaries felt it necessary to attack church privileges again. The Constitution of 1917 denied rights of property ownership to religious institutions or personnel, forbids church participation in politics, limits participation in education, denies voting rights to the clergy, and gives government the authority to designate places of worship and to fix a maximum number of ministers for each state. Church-state tensions peaked under Calles. Until 1926 there had been only limited enforcement of anticlerical constitutional provisions, although there were certain stiff measures, such as the drafting of priests. Calles then launched a virulent antichurch crusade, provoking armed rebellion from many Catholics (the *cristero* rebellion). Calles's crusade must be understood in terms of his unyielding attempts to centralize political power and the potential threat to Mexico's revolution still posed by the church. The regime would accept the church only after the regime itself became more secure and the church in turn retreated from political affairs. Cárdenas relaxed the crusade, although his neo-Marxism guaranteed anticlerical politics. His successor displayed no such negative posture toward the church: "I am a believer," he declared. The period in which revolution had preempted Catholicism as Mexico's only sanctioned religion was over.

Today, the church's presence mocks harsh constitutional restrictions. There are seminaries, church-run schools, religiously inspired universities, priests walking about in clerical garb. Government employees receive "spring vacations," which could just as accurately be called vacations for Holy Week (the week between Palm Sunday and Easter). All this is possible because the church no longer threatens the regime. It is, in fact, functional to it. Church activities offer living proof of a degree of political liberty. More important, in Karl Marx's terms, religion is a flower on the chains of repression, a flower that deflects the masses' attention from their material plight (although it is not held fundamentally responsible for constructing those chains). And the church may be a useful coun terweight to forces pushing the regime in more leftist directions.[19]

This is not to say that the church's principal aims are political rather than spiritual. Nor is it to say there are no church-state tensions. Many Catholics resent the government's antichurch posturing. The government, for its part, wants to keep church influence minimal. Strong mass allegiance to the church, contrasted to increasingly manifest apathy about the government, is embarrassing, to say the least. The outpouring of enthusiasm by perhaps 20 million Mexicans for Pope John Paul's 1979 visit was uncomfortably similar to the preference shown by the Poles for their pope over their premier. The regime is also wary of the now important role of reform-minded priests in much of Latin America, particularly in authoritarian nations such as Brazil and Chile and in Central America. The era of inevitable church allegiance to Latin America's conservative states is over. Mexico's church now has an active minority, spearheaded by the likes of the "red bishop" of Cuernavaca and the progressive bishop of San Cristóbal de las Casas, who argue that the masses deserve a better material fate in *this* life. For the most part, however, the church lacks the independent political power it previously had or even the independent power it still has in certain other Latin American countries.

The University

Few, if any, major institutions seem to lend themselves as readily to dissent and disorder as the university. Although rarely capable of unilaterally destroying regimes, universities often initiate and then help lead potentially destabilizing coalitions. And Mexico's university had a history of turmoil to rival that of the military or the church.

Porfirio Díaz's positivists had no sooner opened their National University (1910) dedicated to progress and order than the revolution ripped it apart. Sheer revolutionary turmoil was one factor. Beyond this, the university became a special target of revolutionary assault. It was indicted for challenging the revolutionary regime's authority, with serving the elite and esoteric ends, rather than the masses and practical problem-solving. Many in Congress wanted to cut all ties to the university, and indeed, subsidies ceased in 1934. Calles was especially harsh, as he was against the church. "The state should control education at all levels, from elementary to university. . . . Unfortunately, university youth is 80 percent or more reactionary and tries to . . . dislodge the revolutionaries from power and thus keep them from combating . . . capital and the clergy."[20] Nor did Cárdenas's victory suggest much relief. He strongly supported a socialist constitutional reform. Although it was implemented only sporadically, it was used by the likes of labor boss Vicente Lombardo Toledano to battle defenders of pluralist academic freedom. Cárdenas made it clear that there would be no government subsidies until the university joined actively in the "social program of the revolution." Many professors resigned in protest.

The university, divided but mostly antagonistic to the government, remained the scene of considerable disorder. Between 1933 and 1944 not one of its rectors (presidents) lasted more than two years. Nor was the revolutionary fight restricted to higher education; many teachers were assassinated in the countryside. Yet while both Calles and Cárdenas wanted revolutionary control, they also wanted order, as their party-building efforts suggest. So in 1929 the government granted partial autonomy to the university and in 1933, full autonomy. One idea behind these grants was to placate university opposition. Another was that the autonomous university, without government funds, would soon perish, opening the way for creation of a truly revolutionary or "proletarian" institution. Meanwhile, Cárdenas proceeded to establish a government-run National Polytechnic Institute, geared to serve the revolution as the university would not.

As expected, the university simply could not survive without government funds and therefore increasingly pledged its loyalty to the revolution. A new statute passed in 1944 limited student and faculty power, establishing instead a strong rectorship and what many considered to be a U.S.-style governing board. Such a board, and its appointed rector, were far less likely than students and professors to engage in disorder or to challenge the regime. The university itself became much more stable. Whereas the rectorship had changed hands twenty-three times in the thirty-five years between the revolution's inception and the new statute, it changed hands only nine times in the next thirty-five years. Rarely since 1944 has disorder at the National University seriously threatened the regime. When it does, as in 1968, the government is likely to resort to repression.

On balance, however, the government went even further than the university to reach a modus vivendi. It resumed its subsidies to and greatly reduced its ideological assaults on the university. It invited faculty, alumni, and administrators into government positions. Most of all, it ceased to insist that the university be revolutionary, instead allowing it considerable autonomy. Indeed, this autonomy has not characteristically been used to promote revolutionary ends, such as fundamentally changing Mexico's social structure. The regime no longer pressed for a revolutionary university *once the regime itself was no longer revolutionary.* Early in 1946 it changed the socialist amendment on education, replacing the doctrine of class struggle with the doctrine of national unity.

Like the army and church, the university performs certain functions that reinforce the government's position. One good example is the training and recruitment of political elites. Mostly, the government merely tries to guarantee that the university not be a significant destabilizing force. The government still has great trouble with the university—more than with the church—but for decades neither institution has seriously threatened the regime, nor been forced into revolutionary lockstep with it.

REPRISE

With its unusually inclusive official party, civilian control over the military, and modus vivendi with the church and university, Mexico's contemporary regime has protected itself from many of the traditional threats faced by other Latin American regimes. As Samuel Huntington has written, a weak political system in which different social forces competed with each other amid feeble political institutions transformed itself into a system in which these social forces have been largely subordinated to strong political institutions.[21] Probably the most important autonomous center of power limiting the Mexican regime's authority today is business, domestic and foreign. But business has generally reinforced, not diluted, the institutionalization just described. It has supported the regime's basic development model, based on political stability and economic growth. In sum, the regime has tamed those forces it has had to tame in order to guarantee its stability, leaving a degree of autonomy only where such autonomy could be afforded. (The contemporary relationship between regime stability and group freedom and power is pursued in Chapter 4.)

It would be more charitable to compare the results of such institutionalization to the realities of Mexican history than to any standard elaboration of revolutionary goals. Where the postrevolutionary regime has failed to fulfill historical aspirations, it has hardly been unique in Mexican history. Where the regime has had more success, there is more, but hardly uniform, historical precedent. Greater individual political liberty has rarely been achieved in Mexico; the principal precedent might be the reform period. Rarer still has been any sustained effort to decrease economic inequality. The key symbolic precedent here would be the Cárdenas years. In the struggle for national independence, the war against Spanish colonial rule and the revolution emerge as the two most notable victories, although neither prevented significant economic and cultural dependency on foreign powers. Finally, the contemporary regime's clearest success lies in its achievement of political stability and economic growth along with it. Although the porfiriato provides one strong historical precedent, the frequent turbulence in Mexican history makes the contemporary regime's achievements in this regard seem considerable indeed.

We close this chapter with a brief schematic summary of how Mexico has historically approached the interrelationships among political stability, political liberty, economic growth, decreased economic inequality, and national independence.

The Spanish crown stressed, quite successfully, colonial political stability combined with economic gain for the mother country. It obviously did not consider offering much more than the modicum of democratic liberties it granted to its own citizens in Spain, and it even more obviously opposed independence for the colonies. It delegated the inequality issue to the church, insuring that it would be approached far more as a spiritual than an economic issue.

Clearly, the criollos of the early nineteenth century pursued national independence as their prime goal, hoping that independence would subsequently underpin their own political and economic control. As those Indians who joined in the independence struggle soon discovered, the criollos were staunchly opposed to spreading economic resources. Nor did the criollo movement, like that of the privileged classes in the United States, begin to establish a democratic system. Such a system did, however, emerge as a chief preoccupation of many of Mexico's nineteenth-century liberals, whose crowning success came with the reform and 1857 constitution. Democracy was deemed compatible with both political stability and economic growth. The new order would naturally benefit the masses, it was argued, but opinions were more mixed as to the degree of *direct* effort that should be made on their behalf. The liberals proved their commitment to independence by opposing perpetuation of colonial customs and by fighting to oust the French occupation forces. Conservatives were generally more sympathetic to Mexico's inherited colonial culture and less sympathetic to liberal democracy. Nonetheless, they generally shared the liberals' frustrated concern for political stability and economic growth, and neither group raised the banner of economic equality. As the reform gave way to the porfiriato, the latter ushered in a ruling creed that displayed unusually clear priorities. Political stability and economic growth were the twin idols. As strong national independence would be incompatible with economic growth, foreign investment was encouraged. And as, allegedly, neither stability nor growth could be intelligently guided if the system betrayed itself by pandering to principles of political democracy or economic equality, progress was entrusted to "survival of the fittest," not to the popular will.

The porfiriato's vaunted political stability exploded early in the twentieth century. Francisco Madero, Mexico's first leader of the revolutionary period, broke sharply with the positivists' political beliefs, although not so sharply from their economic beliefs. Among the grassroots movements, both the zapatistas and villistas struggled to decrease inequality and to promote independence, while remaining relatively indifferent to Madero's brand of liberal democracy; the zapatistas were especially concerned to achieve a political order that would allow them to return to peaceful agricultural pursuits. Carranza's constitutionalists began to point Mexico away from both the maderista emphasis on political democracy and the zapatista and villista emphasis on economic redistribution, moving instead toward contemporary priorities of stability and growth. Calles intensified these tendencies.

Under Cárdenas the Mexican Revolution was recalled to its goals of national independence and egalitarianism, although the revolution's emphasis on political stability rather than liberal or bourgeois democracy was maintained. In Cárdenas's view, greater national independence and more equal distribution of wealth were not just compatible with but were necessary to political stability; without them, Mexico would be an unstable pawn of powers from without and a time bomb to be detonated by its own deprived masses from within. Alemán's followers, on the other hand, would see direct efforts to redistribute wealth as obstacles to economic growth; the two economic goals could be compatible only when growth expanded opportunities and the overall size of the economic pie. Alemanistas basically felt that foreign investment, credit, and trade lead to growth and therefore stability. Interestingly, there has been no major, consistent split between cardenistas and alemanistas regarding political liberty; such liberty may be accepted, even encouraged, but only insofar as it does not endanger political stability or economic growth. As the contemporary regime (since 1940) has inclined decidedly toward the alemanista position, the pursuit of political stability has been consciously tied to the pursuit of economic growth.[22]

We can find reflections of indigenous, colonial, liberal, conservative, positivist, and revolutionary pasts all present today. But neither all these pasts nor the various principles they have promoted are *equally* represented in contemporary Mexican politics. In general, contemporary Mexico has been most successful in attaining the historical goals of political stability and economic growth, less successful in attaining the goals of national independence and political liberty, and least successful in attaining the goal of increased economic equality.

NOTES

1. The quotes are from, respectively, Octavio Paz, *The Other Mexico: Critique of the Pyramid*, trans. Lysander Kemp (New York: Grove Press, 1972) p. x; and idem, "Reflections: Mexico and the United States," trans. Rachel Phillips, *New Yorker*, September 17, 1979, p. 148.

2. Paz, "Reflections," p. 140.

3. Political liberty increased, mostly for the criollos, but not for most Mexicans. The following two paragraphs in the text derive largely from Frank Safford, "Bases of Political Alignment in Early Republican Spanish America," in *New Approaches to Latin American History*, ed. Richard Graham and Peter H. Smith (Austin: University of Texas Press, 1974), especially pp. 72, 91–92; and Barbara H. Tenenbaum, "Straightening Out Some of the Lumpen in the Development," *Latin American Perspectives* 2, no. 2 (1975):7–9.

4. Daniel Cosío Villegas, *American Extremes*, trans. Américo Paredes (Austin: University of Texas Press, 1964), p. 10.

5. Frank Tannenbaum, *Mexico: The Struggle for Peace and Bread* (New York: Columbia University Press, 1950), p. 154.

6. Peter Smith, *The Labyrinths of Power: Political Recruitment in Twentieth Century Mexico* (Princeton, N.J.: Princeton University Press, 1979), p. 163.

7. Hollywood has produced a number of colorful movies about the Mexican revolution and its leading personalities. Unfortunately, most tell us more about Hollywood than Mexico. One of the finest and most intimate scholarly books, unusually well written, is John Womack's *Zapata and the Mexican Revolution* (New York: Knopf, 1969).

8. James Wilkie, *The Mexican Revolution: Federal Expenditures and Social Change Since 1910* (Berkeley: University of California Press, 1967), p. 256.

9. *Los Supermachos*, January 23, 1975.

10. Carlos Fuentes, *The Death of Artemio Cruz*, trans. Sam Hileman (New York: Farrar, Straus, 1964).

11. See Frederick C. Turner's account of revolutionary nationalism and even xenophobia, *The Dynamic of Mexican Nationalism* (Chapel Hill: University of North Carolina Press, 1968). Also see Mary Kay Vaughan's account of persistent dependence on foreign thought, *The State, Education, and Social Class in Mexico, 1880–1928* (DeKalb, Illinois: Northern University Press, 1982).

12. Standard reading on this issue is Stanley Ross, ed., *Is the Mexican Revolution Dead?* (New York: Knopf, 1966). Even more skeptical in tone is Peter Calvert, "The Mexican Revolution: Theory or Fact," *Journal of Latin American Studies* 1, no. 1 (1969):51–68.

13. Pablo González Casanova, *Democracy in Mexico*, trans. Danielle Salti (London: Oxford University Press, 1970), p. 34.

14. For a detailed account of Cárdenas's efforts at party institutionalization, see Wayne A. Cornelius, "Nation-Building, Participation and Distribution: The Politics of Social Reform Under Cárdenas," in *Crisis, Choice and Change: Historical Studies of Political Development*, ed. Gabriel A. Almond, Scott C. Flanagan, and Robert J. Mundt (Boston: Little, Brown and Co., 1973), pp. 392–498. Naturally, we do not mean to imply that the revolution's preoccupation with institution-alization and stability began only in 1929. It is embodied, for example, in the ideology and efforts of Alberto J. Pani, who served in high policy positions under seven consecutive constitutionally elected presidents from 1910 to 1933. See Keith Allen Haynes, "Orden y Progreso: The Revolutionary Ideology of Alberto J. Pani," paper presented at the Sixth Conference of Mexican and U.S. Historians, Chicago, September 1981.

15. Samuel P. Huntington has called Mexico "the worst." *Political Order in Changing Societies* (New Haven, Conn.: Yale University Press, 1968), p. 256.

16. Robert K. Furtak, *El partido de la revolución y la estabilidad política en México* (Mexico City: UNAM, 1978), pp. 217–218. For further accounts of the institutionalization of the military see Edwin Lieuwen, *Mexican Militarism: The Political Rise and Fall of the Revolutionary Army, 1910–1940* (Albuquerque: University of New Mexico Press, 1968); and Jorge Alberto Loyoza, *El ejército mexicano (1911–1965)* (Mexico City: El Colegio de México, 1970).

17. John Conklin has given supporting data for 1940–1965 and starkly contrasted Mexico to other Latin American nations. "Elite Studies: The Case of the Mexican Presidency," *Journal of Latin American Studies* 5, no. 2 (1973):247–269.

18. Frank Brandenburg, *The Making of Modern Mexico* (Englewood Cliffs, N.J.: Prentice-Hall, 1964), p. 188. For a detailed account of the struggle to institutionalize the church, see Nicolás Larin, *La rebelión de los cristeros (1926–1929)* trans. Angel C. Tomás (Mexico City: Ediciones Era, 1968). For an English-language source on the state-church issue see David C. Bailey, *¡Viva Cristo Rey!* (Austin: University of Texas Press, 1973).

19. Thus, for example, the church has deplored the violent means of Mexican guerrillas and Castroites. President Echeverría, in inimitable style, turned the tables a bit by using progressive religious ideals to attack conservatives! Monterrey industrialists, he declared, were bad Christians because of their selfish pursuit of wealth rather than social justice.

20. Quoted in Sebastian Mayo, *La educación en México* (Rosario, Argentina: Editorial BEAR, 1964) pp. 261–262. Our account of the struggle to institutionalize the university is drawn from Daniel Levy, "University Autonomy Versus Government Control: The Case of Mexico," Ph.D. dissertation, University of North Carolina, 1977, pp. 66–151.

21. Huntington, *Political Order in Changing Societies,* p. 318.

22. For a lengthy and readable single-volume overview of Mexican history the reader is referred to Michael C. Meyer and William L. Sherman, *The Course of Mexican History* (New York: Oxford University Press, 1979). A good source on the twentieth century is Wilkie, *The Mexican Revolution.* The most comprehensive source on Mexican history is the series of volumes entitled Historia General de Mexico and published by El Colegio de México.

3

Political Institutions and Actors

Political participation is the process in which individuals, groups, or classes in a society articulate their material interests, their ideological preferences, or their particular conception of the public interest. The first section of this chapter identifies the formal state and societal institutions through which Mexican political participation takes place. Special consideration is given to the roles of the president, the heads of key ministries, and those in other federal positions as well as to the participatory roles of the ruling party (PRI), labor, the peasants, and the business community. Nonelectoral forms of political participation by actors such as the media, intellectuals, and what sociologists have referred to as *marginados* (including slum inhabitants and many Indians and unorganized workers) are left for Chapter 4.

In the second section, our discussion of the political parties and the 1977 political reform focuses on elections, one potentially important form of political participation, considering such questions as: What are the ideologies and constituencies of the opposition parties, as compared to the PRI? Is a more truly multiparty system evolving in Mexico? What is the significance of the recent political and electoral reforms?

STATE INSTITUTIONS

A critical characteristic of the Mexican state is the unusually strong position of the president relative to that of any other formal authority. Power is highly centralized and checks and balances are minimal, even though Mexico is nominally a federal republic modeled after the U.S. system of government. Congress has been practically a rubber stamp, passing nearly all laws proposed by the president without effecting major

51

Mexico's National Palace, built in the sixteenth century (although remodeled and enlarged several times since), remains a powerful architectural reminder of Spanish colonial influence. But it also represents the seat of centralized political power in Mexico and in the presidency. (Photo courtesy of Rodolfo Romo de Vivar)

modifications; the judicial branch of government has exhibited only a slightly greater degree of autonomy.[1]

Because most important legislation is initiated and carried through to approval by the president, there is hardly any opportunity for effective interaction between citizens and their representatives during the lawmaking process. However, groups and individuals may occasionally influence the way in which laws and policies are actually implemented. A common element of day-to-day politics in Mexico is the presentation of demands to local and state governments, to departments of the federal bureaucracy, and even directly to the president. As the ultimate authority, the president can overrule an interpretation of the law made by any other government authority; this practice of reinterpreting written law also occurs at lower levels of government. This mechanism for managing demands provides some welcome flexibility in a system generally characterized by rigidity and a lack of efficiency, but it also contributes to widespread corruption. The group or individual with better contacts and resources is more likely to attain a favorable interpretation of a law or policy. (Of course, this is only one feature of the Mexican system that invites corruption.)

The president has broad powers to choose his team of close associates.

He chooses the ministers of defense and navy after close consideration of the merit system prevailing in their respective bureaucratic structures. The new president usually appoints other ministers from his group of long-time friends and collaborators. In addition, although every new president has to negotiate with some powerful groups about certain positions in his initial cabinet, as time goes on he progressively replaces those ministers who pose some problems and eventually attains full control of his cabinet. In the end, all ministers try to be as loyal as possible to him, partly because the outgoing president chooses his successor from among the members of his cabinet (see Chapter 4). The president, who is elected every six years for only one term, has very broad dismissal as well as appointive powers, and his actions in this respect need not be sanctioned by any other authority.

Juxtaposed to the weakness of the Congress and the courts, the strong presidency confers very broad powers upon the members of the cabinet. The sixteen ministers and the holders of cabinet-level positions, such as the directorships of the state oil monopoly (Petróleos Mexicanos—PEMEX) and the Central Bank and the mayoralty of Mexico City, specialize in a number of tasks in which they enjoy formal autonomy from other officials. Generally, the major intragovernmental constraints on ministerial activities are imposed by the president himself, who personally approves most of his ministers' important proposals.

One can identify a certain hierarchy of influence among ministries according to the command over resources each enjoys. A few examples illustrate this point. In the area of domestic politics, the minister of the interior (Gobernación)—with functions overlapping those of the U.S. F.B.I. and Interior and Justice departments combined—is chiefly responsible for the state's internal security. In fact, this broad responsibility gives the minister far-reaching powers. He should be aware of every major political event in the country, in particular of all legal and extralegal actions with political implications. He is also the chairman of the Federal Electoral Commission. His position allows him to know better than any other cabinet member the critical details about how the Mexican political system works and to extend his contacts and exercise his authority throughout the nation. Naturally, every president chooses a man he trusts to be his minister of the interior. For such reasons, this minister has often become president in the subsequent administration.

The heads of the Ministry of Finance and of the Central Bank make most major decisions in the fields of fiscal and monetary policies. These institutions have usually favored policies geared to attaining the maximum possible rates of economic growth, even at the expense of lower-income groups. The Ministry of Commerce elaborates more specific policies affecting the interests of the business community, and the Ministry of

National Resources and Industrial Development heads the public sector of the economy, which is very large by U.S. standards.

Other important roles are played by the Ministry of Agrarian Reform, which deals with demands from the peasantry; the Ministry of Agriculture and Water Resources, which is in closer contact with large farmers; the Ministry of Labor, which deals with labor disputes and with working conditions in general; and the Ministry of Programming and Budget (previously Presidencia), which was reorganized by López Portillo to coordinate the actions of all other governmental agencies wherever possible, supervise the budget, and draw up a national development plan. Although it is not intended to become a super-ministry, Programming and Budget has assumed great influence. In 1980, López Portillo appointed his son as undersecretary. Programming and Budget has also been a source of well-organized and, in some cases, previously undisclosed information and statistics. This constitutes a welcome improvement over the long-standing lack of information on many subjects. With the appointment in September 1981 of the minister of programming and budget, Miguel de la Madrid Hurtado, as the next president of Mexico, the role of this agency took on additional significance.[2]

There is much to be learned about the actual influence of the minister of defense in the political process. In fact, this question is intimately linked to the broader question of military participation in politics. In Chapter 2 we argued that such participation changed from near-dominance of the outcome of the revolution to much more limited functions in support of the emerging civilian regime years later. However, two qualifications to our earlier statement are in order. First, there are no empirical studies concerning the many middle- and lower-level positions that are apparently occupied by members of the armed forces in practically all agencies of the federal government. Such information is necessary in order to have a more complete picture of the military's role. Second, an emerging change in perceptions about how national security interests are best served may provide the rationale for a more visible role by the military. Minister of Defense Félix Galván, who has been the most outspoken minister of defense in many years, has defined the term "national security" very broadly as "maintaining a socio-economic and political equilibrium which is guaranteed by the armed forces."[3] This is a perspective on national security that is shared by most Latin American military leaders—including many who have assumed the reins of government by force. However, it also reflects the fact that, as a neighbor of the United States, Mexico has not worried much for a long time about the external aspects of its national security. Moreover, the Central American republics have been far too weak to pose a threat from the south.

This does not mean that the military is totally unconcerned about the defense of the country from external threats. For example, the ongoing political turmoil and generalized instability in Central America and the Caribbean, as well as events related to the achievement of independence of Belize in November 1981, have been a growing source of concern in Mexico City. During two weeks in December of 1980, the Mexican Army conducted maneuvers before López Portillo and a number of guests of the Guatemalan high military command. More than 40,000 soldiers (including parachutists) participated (in the southern states of Chiapas and Tabasco), along with several air force T-33 jets, tanks for delivery of medium-range rockets, and helicopters.[4] These maneuvers were justified on the grounds that Mexico must be ready to protect its oil fields. One could picture a worst-case scenario in which governmental or other forces in Central America, unhappy with Mexico's policies toward the region, might attempt to sabotage the oil fields in southeast Mexico.

Defense Minister Galván has been shopping around for some time for supersonic jets to add to Mexico's combat capabilities. In 1977, a request was made to the United States, following a similar request by Guatemala, to buy twenty-six Northrop F5-E fighters for more than US$150 million. Later, U.S. Tiger planes and Israeli Kfir jets (following Galván's visit to Israel in early 1981) were considered for purchase. Following approval by the Reagan administration, Mexico finally decided to buy more than a dozen F5-E fighters, and it has bought thirty-eight modern Swiss Pilatus planes.[5] These decisions were made at a time when Mexico had stepped up its domestic output of weapons already in its arsenal. And in 1981 Mexico planned to export G3 automatic rifles, medium-range rockets, and tanks to Pakistan and other as yet undisclosed nations. Apparently, Mexico is seeking markets for its arms outside Latin America; its sponsorship in international fora, such as the UN Special Session on Disarmament in 1978, of limitations and prohibitions on the transfer and use of certain conventional weapons within the region prevents it from exporting to other Latin American countries.

All these developments have combined to change traditional perceptions about the meaning and the needs of national security. It seems that its external dimension is now a matter of concern to policymakers. This change is being promoted by a Defense Ministry that is seeking, just as many other governmental agencies are, to legitimize its competition for the financial resources available from oil exports. In this sense at least, the military's public visibility is likely to increase during the coming years. Given the fact that Mexico's extraordinary stability for several decades has been based in large part on the limited role of the military, any change could be critical indeed.

Supersonic F5-E fighters bought from the United States in 1981 symbolize the growing modernization and visibility of Mexico's military. (Photo courtesy of the Northrop Corporation)

SOCIETAL INSTITUTIONS AND ACTORS

The second set of institutions to be discussed includes all those that are not formally part of the state but that make demands on state institutions. These include the ruling political party, labor, the peasantry, and the business community.

The Ruling Political Party

In Mexico, a key role in the political process has been played by the official political party, the PRI. There is a very strong and direct link between the PRI and the state, but they are different. The party is in charge of mobilizing support to legitimize the state. That is, the party's single most important task is to legitimize and to provide an ideological base of support for the state rather than to press the demands of its formal constituency on the state. On the other hand, this does not prevent the individual mass organizations of the party from pressing such demands.

Furthermore, it is the group of politicians in control of state institutions at any given time—as opposed to the politicians in control of the party—that is in charge of substantive policymaking, and the party has little voice in the formulation of policy. And the personnel of party and state are not the same, although government ministers may come from the party ranks, and government officials are not bashful about using their positions to promote PRI candidates, as illustrated in the 1982 campaign.

The party formally incorporates three major groups: the peasantry, the workers, and the "popular sector," or middle-class groups. Those observers who see this incorporation as a mechanism for the subordination of independent action by these groups point to the "corporatist" nature of Mexican politics. Corporatism refers to "a system of interest representation linking . . . associations of civil society with decisional structures of the state," and "state corporatism" refers to the dominance of the state over these associations.[6] In this respect, the successful corporative control of even a limited number of working-class organizations has been enough to maintain political stability. (Only unionized labor is incorporated in the workers' sector of the party.) For example, it has been estimated that of 8 million wage earners in urban areas in 1970, only 26 percent were unionized. A majority of labor unions are located in key industries in the production process and in the most urban-industrial states of México, Nuevo León, and Jalisco and in the Federal District. These four geographical areas account for more than 50 percent of all unionized workers.[7] Thus, political stability has been maintained by exercising corporative control over only one-quarter of the working people in urban areas. Moreover, these workers, compared to nonunionized workers, receive disproportionate amounts of the benefits of social programs sponsored by the state. Such programs include education, health insurance, and credits for housing.

A similar situation exists in the countryside. Although the benefits of the agrarian reform program have not been extended to all, the government has provided some organized peasants with land and other resources for the production process. The fact that much less has been done for unorganized peasants has not visibly and critically undermined political stability. A central question, therefore, is just what explains why the majority of *unorganized* workers and peasants—who have benefited little from the revolution—have not stood up again (as they did in the revolution) for their rights. Frankly, this question has been inadequately explored by students of Mexican politics. Some common explanations are that background and political culture may lead to a lack of effective effort in influencing policy; that provision of material benefits to some groups creates for others the illusion that they might eventually become recipients; and mostly, that fear of repression prevents the unorganized poor from actively seeking to improve their lot. More substantive research is necessary before reaching definitive conclusions. What follows, therefore, will focus on relations between the state and *organized* labor and peasants, relations that have been studied more systematically and may thus provide us with a better understanding of some of the key features of political participation in Mexico.

The Role of Organized Labor

The foundation in 1912 of the Casa del Obrero Mundial, the headquarters of Mexico's emerging labor movement, represented one of labor's first organizational efforts. At the outset, it was met with an unfriendly attitude and even repression by Francisco Madero's government and later by Victoriano Huerta's government. In 1914, a year after Huerta's coup, Huerta himself was overthrown and the Casa was able to resume its activities in a new building provided by Venustiano Carranza's closest ally, General Alvaro Obregón. This was the beginning of what turned out to be a pattern of a very strong association between the labor movement and the emerging political regime. In 1915, after months of internal divisions and debate, the Casa decided to stand on the side of Carranza and Obregón in their struggle against the revolutionary peasant leaders! A formal pact was signed in Orizaba, near Veracruz, where Carranza's government was then located. The pact included a commitment on the part of the Casa's leaders to send a number of brigades to the military front. These brigades participated in battles at El Ebano and Celaya against Pancho Villa's forces, and in Veracruz they helped to crush some of Zapata's battalions. So labor provided brigades to defeat what many would consider the most truly revolutionary armies of the people.

In spite of its contribution to his victory, however, labor's relations with Carranza were always precarious. In fact, had it not been for the efforts and vision of General Obregón, labor might have been much more severely repressed and left out of the political process. The peak point of confrontation with Carranza came on July 31, 1916, when the leader of the Electrical Workers Union called for a general strike. The main demand was that wages be paid in gold instead of paper money, which had a constantly changing value and was not always honored. Following Carranza's repression of the strike, Obregón approached some of the more moderate leaders to suggest that they close the Casa for good and instead form a study group to propose legislation favorable to labor during the upcoming Constitutional Convention in early 1917. He committed himself to futhering labor's cause. The outcome was perhaps the most progressive social and labor legislation in the world at the time, contained in Article 123 of the new Constitution of February 5, 1917.

Another outcome, crucial to the stability of the emerging regime, was the formulation of an alliance between labor leaders and the victorious military leaders. By 1918, the alliance was formalized by the establishment of a national labor confederation—the Mexican Regional Labor Confederation (CROM)—with assistance provided by the state.

The following year CROM's leader, Luis Morones, participated in the formation of a labor party to support Obregón's candidacy for the presidency. CROM played a similar role in 1924, in support of General Elías Calles. By 1928, however, CROM's relations with the state started to deteriorate as Morones himself sought to become president. The confederation suffered a split in the early 1930s. In 1936, President Lázaro Cárdenas threw his support behind Vicente Lombardo Toledano, who became the first leader of the newly created Confederation of Mexican Workers (CTM). Its membership reached about 700,000 by 1938, when it was incorporated by Cárdenas into the official party (at the time called the Party of the Mexican Revolution)—a step consistent with the regime's objective of developing close ties with organized labor.

Some of labor's leaders were drawn into the Chamber of Deputies over the years, while others participated in the policymaking process, together with representatives of the government and business. In addition to these co-optation mechanisms, some unions were granted special privileges to secure their loyalty to the regime. However, this strategy did not always work as expected because of the complex nature of labor's organizational structure. Although the CTM progressively became the dominant labor organization (estimates of its current membership range from 1.5 to 3.5 million), several very important unions fall outside CTM's control—even though they may belong to the PRI. One such union, the Federation of Unions of State Workers (FSTSE), which is part of the PRI's popular sector, includes the powerful governmental bureaucracy and those employed in the low-cost, state-sponsored national educational system (with a total of about 1 million members). Other very important unions include the railroad, electrical, and telephone workers' unions, among others. Totaling more than 400,000 members, these unions are noteworthy not only for their relative strength, stemming from their critical position in the economy, but also because some of them have at times posed the most serious challenges to corruption and state control over the labor movement. For example, the Electrical Workers Union has remained an independent-minded organization in spite of repression against it on several occasions. The Railroad Workers Union conducted a series of strikes leading to the nationalization of railroads in the mid-1930s; in 1958 and 1959, the union demanded an increase in salaries, participation in management, and labor's autonomy from the state. Before 1968, no other massive independent political action had been met with

60 POLITICAL INSTITUTIONS AND ACTORS

such repression as that faced by the railroad workers in the late 1950s. The regime forcefully reminded organized labor of the importance attached to close and smooth relations between them. In much less dramatic fashion, the point was made again when the Telephone Workers Union's efforts at democratization in the late 1970s receded only after the army's outright repression of its strike.

Such examples illustrate that state-labor relations in Mexico are not without serious conflict. In fact, the potential for conflict is always present, given the fact that labor's leaders do not simply stand by and do nothing for their constituencies. On the contrary, if the official political party itself does little to foster labor demands, affiliated mass organizations may indeed do something on their own. Of course, this does not mean that labor is best characterized as a strong and independent participant in the Mexican political process; corporatism is still the modal pattern in state-labor relations in Mexico. What it does mean is that sectors of the labor movement have demonstrated some capacity, albeit limited, to act independently from the state and the official party in order to pursue their own interests. Continued high levels of inflation and unemployment could make control over suffering unions increasingly difficult—as the upsurge in strikes and mobilization favoring autonomy from the state during the 1970s already indicates. However, as long as organized labor remains a political actor that is strongly allied with the state, political participation probably will be kept within certain limits. Moreover, the unorganized majority will be kept marginal. Finally, those unions that have recently declared their independence from state control are still too small to represent a dramatic change in state-labor relations.

Peasant Participation and Land Reform

Analysis of peasant participation in politics often focuses on the central issue of the struggle over land ownership. There has generally been a substantial gap between peasants' demands for land and the effective actions of the various governments. Bureaucratic red tape, the pace of population growth, and the inability of industry to absorb all of the labor freed by the agricultural sector are among the factors explaining this continuing gap between demand for and supply of land. Another important consideration is the limited availability of land for cultivation, given Mexico's geographical profile. In this respect, the ongoing resistance of many landowners to granting their lands to the state, and the state's own policies favoring large agricultural holdings at the expense of peasant claims for land, are rooted in the belief that many small plots can be dangerously inefficient. Some experts have presented evidence to support this argument; others have refuted it wholeheartedly. The record shows that the regime sided with the proponents of a land reform program, but only a moderate one.

The pace of the land distribution program slowed following President Miguel Alemán's introduction in 1946 of two legal provisions to protect large landowners from expropriation measures. The first was the limit on the extension of land exempted from public expropriation, which was set at 100 hectares (247 acres). The other was the introduction of the judicial remedy known as *juicio de amparo*, which gave landowners the right to contest in court expropriation orders by the Ministry of Agrarian Reform. Most of these legal processes lasted for decades, much to the disadvantage of frustrated peasants. Thus, 37 million hectares (91 million acres) were distributed between 1916 and 1946, but the amount for the period 1947 to 1976 was substantially lower, roughly 20 million hectares (49 million acres).[8]

It seems that about 2 million heads of family have benefited from the agrarian reform program, and a similar number are still claiming their right to land. Land reform has been one of the most effective tools used by the regime to maintain political control over the peasantry. President López Portillo, however, committed his administration to end the distributive phase of the agrarian reform by 1982. No more land will be expropriated. Still, all past presidential orders are supposed to be effectively implemented. Even this seems to be a formidable if not an impossible task: It has been estimated that more than 50 percent of lands legally distributed—more than 27 million hectares (66 million acres)—have never reached peasant hands.[9] And viewed from a historical perspective, the struggle for land is unlikely to come to an end as a result of an executive order, even though peasant participation has been largely controlled by the state.

Ever since President Cárdenas incorporated the peasantry into the official party, efforts at achieving independence from the state have been either repressed or co-opted. For example, Rubén Jaramillo led a movement in Zapata's region, pursuing some old land claims, but he and his family were killed by soldiers in 1962. Notably, some peasants formed the Independent Peasant Confederation (CCI), in 1963, but the organization was soon divided, and by 1974 it had joined the state-controlled peasant movement. The CCI formalized its alliance with the National Peasant Confederation (CNC) during signing ceremonies at Ocampo. But in spite of the political stability that has resulted from the effective control and co-optation of the peasantry, and from continual repression, land invasions are still a common feature of life in rural Mexico. Usually, landless peasants conduct these invasions. But on other occasions, cattle raisers and large landowners illegally occupy peasant property. The issue of landownership, therefore, remains unsolved.

Peasants will continue to leave the countryside because of the lack of opportunities there. They will continue to migrate to urban areas or to the United States, the political consequences of which are discussed in subsequent chapters. As long as these channels for social mobility remain open as a safety valve, they can be counted (more than satisfaction of the peasants' material demands) among the factors that have contributed to the overall stability of rural Mexico. Of course, there is one last option, given the long struggle of the peasantry for its own survival, that should not be discounted. Mexican peasants could organize themselves independently from the regime in order to bargain from a position of greater strength for their desired role in society. The ongoing unrest in rural Mexico is a signal that difficult years lie ahead for everyone involved. But just as in the case of labor, the establishment of an independent powerful peasant organization at the national level still remains an unfulfilled objective.

We have argued that effective political participation by workers and peasants has generally been limited. More decisive, though less visible, participation comes from another actor—the business community.

The Business Community

Despite many legal provisions and much rhetoric to the contrary, the Mexican economy has remained essentially capitalist. Confusion among foreign observers in this respect has stemmed partly from the fact that the Constitution reserves for the state the exclusive rights of ownership and exploitation of underground natural resources. This places an important constraint on private property, a constraint pointedly uncharacteristic of many capitalist nations. In addition, there is a very large public sector in Mexico. The state controls oil, electric power, communication systems, railroads, fertilizers, much of steel output, a large share of credit sources, and other strategic inputs for production. And yet, state control has been used more in support of than in competition with the private sector. For example, oil has been provided abundantly and at subsidized prices to the private sector ever since the 1938 nationalization of the industry. The strong state that grew out of the revolution has played a very important role in the process of economic growth while it has maintained political stability. The private sector, nonetheless, has often voiced complaints against the state.

What are the origins and evolution of the participatory organizations representing the private sector? And how do these relate to the state? One of the first acts of the new constitutional regime of 1917 was to encourage businessmen to organize themselves and to participate in the process of economic reconstruction. On November 3, 1917, the Confederation of Chambers of Commerce of Mexico, today known as CON-

CANACO, was born. Less than a year later, industrial producers formed the Confederation of Industrial Chambers (CONCAMIN). These institutions, together with the National Chamber of Manufacturing Industry (CANACINTRA), which was founded in 1941, received initial support from the state. However, CONCANACO and CONCAMIN became autonomous and very critical of governmental policies over time. Other organizations came to life independently of state actions and have always been critical of the government when they have considered their interests injured by government action. The Mexican Bankers Association, the Confederation of Employers of the Mexican Republic (COPARMEX), the Mexican Council of Businessmen, and the Association of Insurance Institutions have all fit into this important category, although the first association is obviously jeopardized by the 1982 government takeover of private banking.

Another channel through which the private sector expresses itself has emerged as the economy has grown more complex. We are here referring to the combinations of industrial, commercial, financing, and investment firms resulting from the concentration of capital in fewer hands. The origins of the proliferation of what have been labeled *grupos* date back several decades in some cases. For example, the oldest and strongest of these grupos is based in the northern city of Monterrey. It has grown from a beer industry in the nineteenth century into an economic empire including steel, electronics, mass media, banks (at least until 1982), and many other enterprises controlled by the four grupos into which the original one has been divided. One of them, the Grupo Cervecería Cuauhtémoc, controls a large share of the national beer-exporting industry and, again until 1982, the Banco de Londres y México. Grupo Alfa controls steel production and a television channel (eight), among its other properties.[10]

Finally, some foreign investors have been able to exercise important influence on domestic politics affecting their interests. They do so by negotiating the terms under which new foreign investment comes into Mexico or the terms on which to continue investing within Mexico. A celebrated case concerns the role played by the U.S. Chamber of Commerce in Mexico City. By incorporating Mexican businessmen into its ranks, this association has been able to present the views of its mainly U.S. investors—publicly and on a continuous basis.[11]

Of course, the private sector is not homogeneous. There are competing interests among organizations—and the government exploits this competition to its advantage. In general, however, the private sector is the actor that has best organized itself independently of the regime. Its interests have been favored by the regime to a greater extent than those of labor, peasants, or sectors of the middle class—even though each of these three is a formal constituency of the official political party! There is also a continuous interaction between government agencies and the various representatives of the business community, both during meetings of business organizations and within the framework provided by formal structures set up by the government to discuss certain economic policies. To be sure, there have been some conflicts, such as business skepticism in regard to the nationalization of the electric industry in 1960 and business opposition to the support given Cuba, Chile, and Nicaragua in recent years. But never in the previous few decades had relations between the private sector and the regime been so severely strained as they were during Echeverría's administration. Both in rhetoric and in practice, each attacked the other to a point unknown in recent Mexican history. Because of its implications for the relations between the state and the business community, a brief account of this conflict follows.

Carlos Arriola has written a very well-documented analysis of the confrontation from 1973 to 1975 over labor and fiscal policies and over the central issue of the limits on public intervention in the economy.[12] In a context of rising inflation, the leaders of all major labor organizations, represented by their Congress of Labor, presented Echeverría with a series of demands in early 1973. These included a proposal for price controls, wage increases, and a forty-hour working week. Following months of unsuccessful bargaining with business organizations, labor announced that it would resort to a general strike in support of a 33 percent increase in salaries by October 1. Echeverría supported labor. To further complicate the picture, the coup d'etat in Chile on September 11 had led to massive leftist demonstrations, which were wholeheartedly disliked by the business community. In addition, Eugenio Garza Sada, the leading figure of the Monterrey Group, was killed on September 17, allegedly by an extremist organization of the left. According to Arriola, Echeverría assured himself of the army's support, took the offensive, and called for a "popular alliance" to face mounting pressures on his government by the business community, which only then cooled down its rhetoric. Tensions eased further in the aftermath of a huge demonstration organized by the PRI in Mexico City. It led some weeks later to an agreement to raise wages by 20 percent, thus ending the threat of a general strike. Politicians who have become in some measure alienated from the private sector apparently need to rely increasingly on the army and on mass-based working-class organizations (within the PRI) to legitimize their rule. This last resort, however, has been generally unnecessary because of the formal and informal ties that most politicians have with the business community.

Even after the 1973 crisis eased somewhat, tensions continued during the next few years. In 1975, all business organizations (with the exception of CANACINTRA, which withdrew from the conflict), formed a common front to face what they perceived as "a threat to the free enterprise system," establishing the Coordinating Business Council (CCE). The CCE delivered a document to the president expressing its positions on several critical matters. For example, it declared private property to be a natural right, called on the state to sell some of its enterprises to the private sector, and claimed that direct foreign investment with a majority interest should be permitted in some cases. (By law, any firm must now have at least 51 percent Mexican capital.) These positions were so opposed to principles commonly accepted in Mexican society that the document was condemned even by such traditional allies of the private sector as sectors of the Catholic Church and the rightist National Action party (PAN)!

Toward the end of Echeverría's term (1976), events led to a renewed crisis. The president announced, during his State of the Union address on September 1, that the government had decided to devalue the peso. This measure had last been taken in 1954. A capital flight ensued, facilitated by the impossibility of implementing foreign exchange controls in a country with such a long border with the United States. Further, inflation was rampant, at more than 20 percent for 1976, and the gross domestic product grew by only 2.1 percent over the previous year. The overall crisis confused large sectors of the population as well as domestic and foreign observers of Mexican politics. There were wild rumors of a coup d'etat planned for the twentieth of November.[13] Perhaps the most interesting aspect of the confrontation was that as the economic growth model became strained, different perspectives held by several groups within the PRI and the private sector, and those in control of state institutions, on the proper course for Mexico to follow came to light. Naturally, not all individuals and groups stress the same priorities or favor similar policies, an issue that will be discussed at greater length in Chapter 8. Nevertheless, flexibility and compromise have generally characterized relations between the state and the business community because they have shared some basic goals for Mexican society. Most important, they share an interest in self-preservation; this is why their competition for power has been kept within limits.

THE PARTY SYSTEM

One distinctive form of political participation involves the competition of political parties for power through elections. Because in Mexico the official party has never faced a serious challenge at the polls, many analysts have tended to downgrade the importance of electoral participation. However, recent reforms aimed in general at providing a freer political environment and in particular at encouraging a larger sector of the population to vote make it necessary to include elections in our discussion of political participation. The major provisions of the most important laws governing elections will be discussed first. Further, political parties are the main actors in the electoral arena, and for this reason we will provide a brief sketch of their background, key principles, strategic objectives, and constituencies.

First we should put the present party system into historical perspective. Once the revolutionary warfare was over, a comprehensive federal electoral law was passed by the new Congress in 1918. Voting rights were restricted to literate, married males at least eighteen years old and to literate, unmarried males at least twenty-one years old. Political parties could be formed easily, with only minimal requirements, such as holding a constitutive assembly of at least one hundred people. Also, political parties were forbidden to be affiliated with religious denominations. When a new federal electoral law was approved in 1946, it reflected some of the important changes that the Mexican political process had undergone during the preceding three decades. In particular, the official political party had been formed in 1929. The party was bent on monopolizing the electoral process, so the new law tried to avoid challenges by independent candidates to the party's presidential nominee, as had occurred in 1940 and in 1946. It included provisions giving the government and the party absolute control over the electoral process. For example, the Federal Electoral Commission could hardly be considered an impartial body. It has always been headed by the minister of the interior and has included a representative of the Chamber of Deputies and a representative of the Senate; such provisions have given the regime practical control over the commission. Furthermore, the formal confirmation of electoral results is reserved to both chambers of Congress, where the PRI is not seriously challenged. This phenomenon of self-certification, which has precedents dating back to colonial times, hardly guarantees impartiality in reviews of the electoral results. Finally, the 1946 law made it difficult for new political parties to emerge, requiring certified registration of at least 30,000 members nationwide, with 1,000 or more distributed in at least two-thirds of the total federal entities in Mexico at the time.[14] Until recently, the minister of the interior also had the right to decide whether or not a political party should enjoy legal status.

During the thirty years following the 1946 law, electoral reform was sporadic and limited. Three of the more important openings were the 1954 law that granted women the right to vote, the 1963 law that guaranteed the opposition minimum representation in Congress, and the 1973 law that lowered the minimum voting age to eighteen years, irrespective of gender and marital status. The new age requirement is particularly relevant in a country where most of the population is very young.

In 1977, a substantial political and electoral reform was enacted. From the electoral standpoint, its main thrust is the establishment of a mixed voting system in the Chamber of Deputies, which is more powerful than the Senate. The latter, which is composed of 64 members elected for a single six-year term, has been left untouched. There are 300 seats in the Chamber corresponding to the electoral districts into which the country is divided. All candidates who win a simple majority in these single-member districts win the election for a single three-year term. In addition, there are 100 seats to be assigned on the basis of complex mathematical formulas of proportional representation. All parties that win fewer than 60 seats under the majority system and that have run candidates in at least one-third of the districts under this system are entitled to a share of these 100 seats. This allows even small opposition parties a place in the federal Congress. The Federal Electoral Commission— still dominated by the government—decides on the legal status of political parties. The commission is headed by the minister of the interior. It includes one representative of the Chamber and one of the Senate, as well as a notary public who, amazingly, rather than holding a disinterested position, has been granted voting rights. Opposition parties that have been granted full legal recognition also have voting rights in the commission, so it is conceivable that government control of this body could diminish in the future if the opposition takes unified positions.

There are currently two procedures available for parties seeking legal status. One is to apply for *conditional registration*, which allows any party to participate in elections. Such registration would become "permanent" upon attainment of at least 1.5 percent of the total votes cast nationally; failure to attain that minimum in any single national election results in the loss of legal status. All parties that chose this option reached their minimum during the 1979 elections, although their fate would probably have been different had the abstention rate been lower. In the 1982 presidential elections, the Social Democratic party failed to attain this minimum 1.5 percent of the total vote and thus lost the opportunity to be granted legal status on a permanent basis. The older Authentic Party of the Mexican Revolution (PARM) also failed to attain that minimum and consequently lost its legal status. By contrast, the new Revolutionary Party of the Workers (PRT) attained permanent registration by gaining 1.8 percent of the presidential vote. The second option involves presenting the Federal Electoral Commission an official copy of the party's statutes and principles and proof of a minimum of 65,000 members distributed as follows: either 3,000 or more in at least one-half of Mexico's states, or 300 or more in at least one-half of the 300 electoral districts. Upon fulfillment of these requisites, the commission is supposed to decide within 120 days on the application. Only one party, the Mexican Workers party (PMT)—which did not participate in the 1979 and 1982 elections—has sought legal status under this provision.

Finally, it is interesting that all parties enjoy free radio and television time every month to broadcast their programs and activities. This may have encouraged many voters to become involved in the 1982 elections by supporting the parties that appeal to them. Which are the major political parties in Mexico today? What do they stand for? Which are the social bases of support of these parties?

Institutionalized Revolutionary Party (PRI)

The background of the official party was discussed in Chapter 2. Here we will discuss only the PRI's role in the electoral process. The PRI is headed by a president and a secretary-general, who are directly responsible to the party's national executive committee. Members of this committee are elected by the national assembly, which provides a meeting point for representatives of labor, the peasantry, and the "popular sector." During presidential elections, the selected candidate appoints a close associate to coordinate all activities related to his actual campaign, which usually lasts about ten months. The campaign's chief oversees the organization of mass meetings throughout the country to support and legitimize the candidate. In addition, the Institute of Political, Economic and Social Studies (IEPES), the PRI's planning branch, organizes endless seminars involving professionals, intellectuals, and other groups. The purpose of these meetings, the PRI declares, is to provide the candidate with some sense of what different sectors of society consider to be the major problems the new administration should address. An occasional outcome of these meetings has been the establishment of the party's electoral platform and plans. Such plans, however, have been shelved once the candidate has been elected.

The PRI has exercised such a monopoly over the electoral process that its candidates have seldom lost an election, as is indicated in Tables 3.1 and 3.2. And when they have, the government, through its control of electoral bodies, frequently has seen to it that the PRI would fill the positions anyway. That many of the electoral results have been based on fraud, as is often charged, is almost uncontestable, although we may never know the specifics of each case. At the same time, it seems that the PRI would have retained an overwhelming majority in most cases even if elections had always been fair. For example, the results of the 1979 and 1982 elections, although plagued with many shortcomings, probably were among the cleanest of Mexican history, with representatives of the opposition participating in overseeing the voting. The PRI none-

TABLE 3.1
Presidential Electoral Results, 1934-1982

Year	Percentages of Votes Cast			Total Votes Cast
	PRI	PAN	Others	
1934	98.19	--	1.81	2,265,971
1940	93.89	--	6.11[a]	2,637,582
1946	77.90	--	21.80[b]	2,293,547
1952	74.31	7.82	17.85[c]	3,651,201
1958	90.43	9.42	0.13	7,483,403
1964	88.81	10.97	0.20	9,422,185
1970	85.82	14.00	0.17[d]	13,892,624
1976	98.69	--	1.31	16,925,880
1982[e]	71.63	16.41	11.96	22,539,272

Sources: Pablo González Casanova, Democracy in Mexico (London:
Oxford University Press, 1970); and Robert Furtak, El partido de la
revolución y la estabilidad política en México, 2nd ed. (Mexico City:
Universidad Nacional Autónoma de México, 1978).

[a]The main opposition candidate was General Almazán (5.72 percent
of the vote), whose Revolutionary Party of National Unity was short-
lived. Some claim he really won the election.

[b]Ezequiel Padilla's Democratic party got 19.33 percent of the
vote.

[c]This challenge by General Henríquez was better organized than
Padilla's was, but it failed too. Henríquez was supported by the
Federation of Mexican People's Parties (15.87 percent of the vote).

[d]López Portillo ran an uncontested election. The then legally
unrecognized Communist party nominated labor leader Valentín Campa;
it claimed one million votes.

[e]The 1982 figures are preliminary ones from the Federal
Electoral Commission.

Note: PRI = Institutionalized Revolutionary Party; PAN =
National Action party.

        Total percentages may not add to 100.00 because of
nullified votes.

theless got more than two-thirds of the national vote in both years, even
though its share diminished significantly (from 85 percent in 1976 to
slightly under 70 percent in 1979 and 1982) in the elections for the
Chamber of Deputies. And the PRI still attained 72 percent of the 1982
presidential votes; this might appear to be a significant decline from
1976, until we remember that abstentionism, itself a rejection of the PRI,
also declined from 1976 to 1982. While PRI's de la Madrid received over

TABLE 3.2
Electoral Results for the Chamber of Deputies, 1961-1979 (in percentages)

Year	PRI	PAN	PPS	PARM	PCM	PST	PDM
1961	90.26	7.57	0.95	0.49	--	--	--
1964	88.35	8.51	0.55	2.59	--	--	--
1967	83.86	12.36	2.17	1.42	--	--	--
1970	83.25	14.14	1.40	0.83	--	--	--
1973	77.37	16.32	4.00	2.01	--	--	--
1976	84.88	8.97	3.18	2.67	--	--	--
1979[a]	68.35	11.06	2.82	2.16	5.10	2.26	2.13

Sources: Same as for Table 3.1, but for the 1979 electoral results
see Secretaría de Gobernación, Diario Oficial (Mexico City, July 31,
1979).

[a]In the 1979 elections, 6.12 percent of the votes were declared
invalid or void. Totals for other years may not equal 100.00 because
of such votes.

Note: PRI = Institutionalized Revolutionary Party; PAN =
National Action Party; PPS = Popular Socialist Party; PARM = Authentic
Party of the Mexican Revolution; PCM = Mexican Communist Party;
PST = Socialist Workers Party; PDM = Democratic Mexican Party.

16 million ballots in capturing more than seven of every ten presidential votes cast in 1982, his closest competitor, PAN's Pablo Emilio Madero, trailed far behind, receiving only 3.7 million votes, or 16.4 percent of the total. The only other presidential candidate to garner a sizable share of the vote, with roughly 1 million ballots, was Arnaldo Martínez Verdugo of Mexico's Unified Socialist party. PSUM's 4 percent of the vote represented a disappointing showing for this new leftist coalition challenging the PRI. While PAN did considerably better, these two parties still looked very much like also-rans next to the PRI's continued dominance.

The PRI has also dominated all elections for the Chamber of Deputies. Table 3.2 shows that its share of the total vote diminished significantly following the 1977 political reform, but it also shows that the opposition—both on the left and on the right—is still too divided to mount a serious challenge to the PRI. The PAN's 11 percent and the Communist party's 5 percent are just unimpressive compared to the PRI's 68 percent of the vote in the 1979 elections. In the 1982 elections for the Chamber of Deputies, the PAN increased its share to 17.5 percent, but the new Unified Socialist party and other smaller parties registered some losses, while the PRI held its own. The 1982 elections also illustrate, as does Table 3.2, that the official party's most consistent challenger at the polls has been the National Action party, to which we now turn our attention.

The PRI organizes campaign support for its candidate, Miguel de la Madrid. However sure the candidate's victory, the campaign is still important. (Photo courtesy of Rodolfo Romo de Vivar)

National Action Party (PAN)

The PAN was formed in 1939 with initial support from the Catholic Church, some businessmen, and other groups that felt alienated by the radical reforms of President Cárdenas. In effect, the PAN has assisted the PRI to legitimize the electoral process. Except in 1940 and 1976, it has nominated its own presidential candidate every six years. In the presidential elections in 1976, it abstained from nominating a candidate (following a very divisive and acrimonious national convention). Probably as a result of that decision, it lost 40 percent of its voting strength, which had been at its peak—2.2 million votes—in the 1973 elections for the Chamber of Deputies. The results of the 1979 elections (shown in Table 3.3), however, confirmed the PAN's status as the principal party of opposition. The PAN won more than 1.5 million votes (11 percent of the total), four Chamber seats under the system of the simple majority, and thirty-nine seats on the basis of the new system of proportional representation. Results for the 1982 elections again show the PAN to have been the major opposition winner. It increased the number of its deputies elected under the proportional representation system to 50,

As the legitimizing machine for the "revolutionary" regime, the PRI promotes mass participation in the 1982 campaign. The banners represent the PRI's official peasant, youth, popular, middle-class, and bureaucratic constituencies. (Photo courtesy of Rodolfo Romo de Vivar)

TABLE 3.3
Party Affiliation of the 400 Deputies, 1979 Elections

Elected Under the Simple Majority System		Elected Under the System of Proportional Representation	
PRI	296	PAN	39
PAN	4	PCM	18
Total	300	PARM	12
		PPS	11
		PST	10
		PDM	10
		Total	100

Source: Secretaría de Gobernación, Diario Oficial (Mexico City, July 31, 1979).

mostly at the expense of the now defunct PARM. The other four opposition parties maintained roughly the same number of deputies they had attained in the 1979 elections under this system.

The PAN is particularly strong in Nuevo León, the Federal District, Sonora, Puebla, and Jalisco—most of Mexico's wealthiest regions. Its supporters are mostly from cities in these regions and from the middle class. In fact, its relatively privileged class composition is what is most significant about this party. It has failed to gain the backing of large labor unions and other working-class organizations. Nearly two-thirds of its votes in 1979 came from urban areas. In comparison, the PRI got only one-third of its total from the 128 urban electoral districts in Mexico.[15] Like the PAN, the Communist party also got more than 60 percent of its votes from urban areas. Thus, the major challenge to the PRI's electoral strength is found in the cities, especially the big cities. Ironically, even though the regime has done less for rural than for urban areas, it is electorally stronger in the countryside. This is probably because the official party has exercised greater control over the peasantry, a sector of the population that has had less access to independent political organizations. Another problem faced by the PAN is that, despite its conservative bent, it does not do well with the upper class, which long ago realized that its best bet is to work with the PRI in order to influence public policy.

The PAN is likely to continue playing its traditional role of loyal opposition. In general, it has reacted positively to the strengthening of other opposition parties, with which it can now join forces against the PRI.[16] Issue-oriented coalition politics were previously unknown in the Mexican party system, but recently the PAN has found itself voting together with other parties—even with the Communists! In contrast to the situation of six years earlier, the PAN's national convention in 1981 took a unified stand behind its candidate for the 1982 presidential elections, Pablo Emilio Madero. A nephew of Francisco Madero, he is a conservative politician with special appeal among the urban middle class. As a member of the business community, he led the CANACINTRA in 1969. He was a member of the Chamber of Deputies from 1979 to 1982. One of his major achievements was to confirm PAN as the second largest electoral force in Mexico. The candidate of the former Communist party finished third in the 1982 presidential race. The Communist party recently engaged in a pro-united-left campaign, leading to the establishment of the new Mexican Unified Socialist party.

Mexico's Unified Socialist Party (PSUM)

The Mexican Communist party (PCM) was the third largest electoral force in 1979, and again in 1982. Founded in 1919, ten years before the PRI began to evolve, it is the oldest political party in Mexico. It has lived through internal strife and governmental repression. In 1978, after more than thirty years of being denied legal status, the Communist party applied for conditional registration under the new electoral law. It then received a permanent registration, and thus full legal status, following its success in the 1979 elections. The PCM participated in 1979 together with three other minor parties, the Mexican People's party, the Action Movement for Socialist Unity, and the Revolutionary Socialist party (a faction of the Popular Socialist party [PPS]). In the aftermath of the elections, it called upon all the parties of the left to form a united front in the 1982 presidential elections. Following extensive consultations with other leftist parties, the PCM merged with some of them to form a new party with its own identity, statutes, and objectives. But the Communist party failed to convince the PPS, the PST, and the PMT to sacrifice their individual organizations in favor of the new party. Some leaders charged the Communist party with being more interested in forming an electoral coalition for its own ends than with establishing a new, more moderate party with greater public appeal. Others complained that the Communist party has not devoted enough of its attention and resources to establishing links with mass-based working-class organizations, which remain affiliated with the PRI. (In reality, none of the small leftist parties can claim a large following among working-class organizations.)

The Communist party was formally dissolved on November 4, 1981, during a PCM party congress, and three days later, Mexico's Unified Socialist party was born. It nominated Arnoldo Martínez Verdugo, the former PCM secretary-general, as its presidential candidate for 1982.[17] Under his leadership, the Communist party had identified itself with the unorthodox, relatively moderate positions of the Italian Communist party of Enrico Berlinguer.[18] This moderate posture, together with the PCM's critical view of the Soviet Union's foreign policy and some aspects of its domestic system, probably helps explain its new appeal. We now analyze the three leftist parties that did not agree to join the new Unified Socialist party.

Popular Socialist Party (PPS)

The PPS was formed in 1948 by Vicente Lombardo Toledano, the founder of the PRI's labor organization, when he became disaffected with some of the PRI's conservative tendencies. Although the PPS formally seeks the establishment of socialism in Mexico, it has gradually allied itself with the PRI, endorsing many of its candidates. The rationale for this strategy is that the PPS considers (U.S.) imperialism to be Mexico's worst enemy, and the PRI has ostensibly stood up to this challenge by pursuing whatever nationalistic and revolutionary policies have been possible, given political realities. Like the Communist and other parties of the left, the PPS supports greater state intervention in the economy and nationalization of private banks, mass transportation, minerals, and other economic areas.

Today, the PPS is a party in electoral decline. In 1979, the majority (led by Gazcón Mercado) left the party to join the growing Communist party. Later that same year, the leader of the faction that had spurned the Communists, choosing instead to perpetuate the PPS, became the first opposition member ever to gain a Senate seat. This illustrates how the regime and the PRI may tolerate and even reward "trustworthy" leftists who pose no significant challenge, especially when such arrangements undercut potentially more serious challenges. The PPS got fewer than 400,000 votes in 1979 (2.8 percent of the total), and 450,000 votes in 1982 (2.2 percent of the total), continuing the trend leading gradually toward its probable political death.

Socialist Workers Party (PST)

The PST was founded in 1974 by some former leaders of the 1968 political movement who split away from the leadership of Heberto Castillo. The PST has received the support of the PRI and, some allege, of former President Echeverría. Both seem interested in filling in the vacuum left by the declining electoral strength of the PPS. The PST could take a large share of the voters disenchanted with PPS policies and with its poor electoral showing. However, the PST failed to reach its goal in 1979. It lost the opportunity to capture the PPS's votes and finished poorly at the polls (2.2 percent). The same happened in 1982, when it received only 2.0 percent of the vote. It does not seem to have a bright future.

Mexican Workers Party (PMT)

Heberto Castillo has been a well-known professor at the school of engineering of the National University of Mexico. More important, he has been a well-known political leader for some time. Upon completing a jail sentence imposed for his part in the 1968 political movement, he convinced a group of university people and old opposition leaders, such as Demetrio Vallejo (who had led the 1958–1959 railroad workers' strikes), to form a new political party. The PMT claims today more than 25,000 regular members, primarily of working-class background and distributed mainly in the Federal District, Puebla, and Sinaloa. As it did not participate in the 1979 and 1982 elections, however, we do not know its present strength. It decided against participation because it considers the recent electoral reform law to be antidemocratic. In particular, it opposes the government's control of the Federal Electoral Commission and the fact that there is no right to appeal decisions by that body. The

PMT sought registration in 1981, but the commission denied it. Castillo, as we shall see later, led the way toward the opening of a public debate on López Portillo's oil policy; Castillo has charged that for this reason the commission succumbed to presidential pressure not to grant his party legal status. Then the PMT entered negotiations with the Communist party, and for several months Castillo was considered the most viable presidential candidate of the emerging party of the left. By changing its mind at the last minute, the PMT lost an opportunity to measure its true appeal among the electorate. The PMT supports nationalizations, price controls, indexing wages to price increases in order to protect the purchasing power of workers, and the use of oil resources for domestic consumption.

Democratic Mexican Party (PDM)

The PDM is an outgrowth of the fascist National Union Against Anarchy (Unión Nacional Sinarquista) founded in 1937. It struggled for many years, without success, for legal status. But it has endured nonetheless. It claims 86,000 members, most of them conservative Catholics (from rural areas) and small businessmen. It is particularly strong in San Luis Potosí, Guanajuato, Jalisco, and Querétaro. The PDM is critical of Mexico's mixed capitalist economy. It gives special attention to the rights of individuals and considers the family the center of society. To the right of PAN in the political spectrum, PDM is the most overtly conservative electoral option in Mexico. It got only 2.1 percent of the vote in the 1979 elections for the Chamber of Deputies and a similarly small share of the votes in 1982.

Authentic Party of the Mexican Revolution (PARM)

Little can be said of this rather obscure party. It was founded in 1952 by retired army generals alienated from the PRI. Like other parties, it soon began receiving public funds to conduct its activities on a regular basis. Like the PPS, it has supported most of the PRI's programs and candidates. Its ideology parallels the main principles of the PRI. The PARM received fewer than 300,000 votes in 1979 (2.1 percent of the national vote). In 1982, it failed to receive the minimum 1.5 percent of the national vote, thus losing its legal status. Its limited electoral support has come mainly from Tamaulipas, Veracruz, and Jalisco. It now appears to be following the PPS into oblivion.

CONCLUSIONS

The 1977 political reform law formalized a number of changes that had in fact already occurred during the previous two decades. A central question is whether, in formalizing these changes, Mexico has established a plural party system open to positions of the right and left, or whether it has only bolstered a *modified one-party system*, legitimizing it today with the presence of the PSUM, PST, PDM, and other emerging small parties, as it did yesterday with the PAN, PPS, and PARM. The reform has been instrumental to the regime in several ways. For example, it has given the regime some breathing space in the current environment of popular discontent over inflation and other economic problems; the regime may in fact find it easier to control the activities of an open than of a more repressed opposition. In addition, the reform has enhanced the perception of Mexico's stability at a time when substantial funds and investments are needed for the country to proceed with its ambitious oil and other industrial development plans. Finally, the reform has provided the official political party with an incentive to modernize itself and its methods of political control in order to continue its successes in the face of a strengthened opposition. Although in 1979 abstentionism remained a critical problem, as more than 50 percent of registered voters did not choose to vote, the abstention rate fell significantly (to 30 percent) in the 1982 elections.

Whether the wide political spectrum represented by the various parties will trigger a greater polarization of Mexican party politics is anyone's guess. There are confusing elements in the positions of many parties. And there are many objections to those parties, such as the former PCM, in which positions are more clearly defined. Furthermore, there are no clear indications that issue-oriented coalition politics will take hold in Mexico. Some alliances have been formed in the Chamber of Deputies, but mostly to oppose the PRI. Finally, an increase in public participation may depend on the political education the public receives from the political parties. If other parties succeed, the PRI may feel compelled to work more closely with its own supporters in order to expand their political education and participation.[19]

In addition to discussing the characteristics and the record of political parties and electoral participation, we have identified in this chapter the most important institutions and actors in the Mexican political system. We have reviewed the extraordinary concentration of power in the hands of the president and the competition for influence between key government agencies. Additionally, the background and the most important features of organizations representing labor, the peasantry, and the business community, as well as some of their interactions with the government and the official party, have been analyzed. Such interactions have been a form of political participation of far greater importance than elections. With variable degrees of effectiveness, the actors here identified make demands upon the political system. In the following chapter we analyze how this variable political effectiveness, along with variable political freedoms and policy changes, have affected political stability.

NOTES

1. For voting records of Congress, see Pablo González Casanova, *Democracy in Mexico,* trans. Danielle Salti (London: Oxford University Press, 1970), p. 201.

2. See the interesting analysis of the new role and powers of the Ministry of Programming and Budget by John Bailey, "Presidency, Bureaucracy, and Administrative Reform in Mexico: The Secretariat of Programming and Budget," in *Inter-American Economic Affairs,* 34, no. 1 (1980):27–59.

3. His remarks are taken from an interview with Mexico City's weekly *Proceso,* September 22, 1980, pp. 6–8.

4. Reported in *Uno Más Uno,* December 10, 1980.

5. Marlise Simons, "US Said to Approve Jet Sale for Mexico's Military Buildup Plan," *Washington Post,* February 24, 1981; and Sadot Fabila, "Miembros de las fuerzas armadas acudieron a felicitar al presidente," *El Día,* January 3, 1980.

6. Philippe Schmitter, "Still the Century of Corporatism?" in *The New Corporatism. Social-Political Structures in the Iberian World,* ed. Frederick Pike and Thomas Stricht (Notre Dame, Ind.: Notre Dame University Press, 1974), p. 86.

7. José Luis Reyna et al., *Tres estudios sobre el movimiento obrero en México* (Mexico City: El Colegio de México, 1976); and Raúl Trejo, "El movimiento obrero: Situación y perspectivas" in *México, hoy,* ed. Pablo González Casanova and Enrique Florescano (Mexico City: Siglo XXI, 1979), pp. 121–151.

8. Shlomo Eckstein et al., *Land Reform in Latin America: Bolivia, Chile, Mexico, Peru and Venezuela,* Staff Working Paper 275 (Washington, D.C.: World Bank, April 1978), pp. 16–21; and Gustavo Esteva, *La batalla en el México rural* (Mexico City: Siglo XXI, 1980), pp. 230–231.

9. Esteva, *La batalla en el México rural,* p. 230.

10. Salvador Cordero and Rafael Santín, *Los grupos industriales: Una nueva organización económica en México.* Cuadernos del Centro de Estudios Sociológicos. 23 (Mexico City: El Colegio de México, 1977), appendix.

11. An interesting study is by Angella M. Delli Sante, "The Private Sector, Business Organizations and International Influence: A Case Study of Mexico," in *Capitalism and the State in US–Latin American Relations,* ed. Richard R. Fagen (Stanford, Calif.: Stanford University Press, 1979), pp. 337–381.

12. Carlos Arriola, "Los grupos empresariales frente al estado," *Foro Internacional* 16, no. 4 (1976):449–495.

13. Soledad Loaeza, "La política del rumor: México, noviembre–diciembre 1976," *Foro Internacional* 17, no. 4 (1977):557–586.

14. There were twenty-nine states, two territories, and the Federal District. Subsequently, Baja California and Quintana Roo have become states, for a total of thirty-one.

15. Rafael Segovia, "Las elecciones federales de 1979," *Foro Internacional*

20, no. 3 (1980):397–410. We have drawn heavily from Segovia's work in our analysis of the 1979 elections. He is one of the few with direct access to government information, and he is an expert on elections in Mexico.

16. Partido Acción Nacional, *A propósito de la reforma política* (Mexico City, 1977). For further reference, see Donald J. Mabry, *Mexico's Acción Nacional: A Catholic Alternative to Revolution* (Syracuse, N.Y.: Syracuse University Press, 1973).

17. The political views of Arnoldo Martínez Verdugo are presented in his *Crisis política y alternativa Comunista* (Mexico City: Ediciones de Cultura Popular, 1979).

18. See Partido Comunista Mexicano, *Declaración de principios, programa de acción y estatutos del Partido Comunista Mexicano* (Mexico City, 1979).

19. For further analysis of the political reform, see Kevin Middlebrook, "Political Change in Mexico," in *Mexico–United States Relations*, ed. Susan Kaufman Purcell (New York: Academy of Political Science, 1981), pp. 55–66. Two books dealing broadly with Mexico's political institutions and actors, and therefore appropriate as suggested reading beyond this chapter, are Richard R. Fagen and William S. Tuohy, *Politics and Privilege in a Mexican City* (Stanford, Calif.: Stanford University Press, 1972); and Merilee S. Grindle, *Bureaucrats, Politicians, and the Peasantry in Mexico* (Berkeley: University of California Press, 1977).

4

The Politics of Stability

This second chapter on the political system shifts from a "micro" analysis of the system's actors and institutions to a "macro" analysis of the system as a whole. Its central concern is with regime stability. We have already discussed how extraordinary this stability appears in both cross-national and historical perspectives. But on what political terms has stability been achieved? Recent experiences of extended military rule in other major Latin American nations illustrate that political order may exact a substantial cost in terms of other political goals. Critics of the Mexican political system charge that it furnishes signal proof that long-term stability per se is no promoter of desirable politics, that it may in fact be an obstacle. This chapter analyzes the extent to which Mexico reconciles political stability with political freedom, political equality, and political change. In so doing, it considers some of the central paradoxes of a political system that has been variously characterized as free and repressive, inclusive and elitist, continually changing and remarkably unchanging, pluralist and authoritarian.

POLITICAL FREEDOM

Most prominent definitions of democracy focus on elections in which the citizenry selects its leaders. Mexico falls short of democracy on this count—but so do the overwhelming majority of nations, including nearly all in Latin America. Thus, Daniel Moynihan, as U.S. ambassador to the UN in the early 1970s, could accurately remind democracies that their club is a limited one. Such evaluations, however, often leave the misleading impression of considerable homogeneity among the world's nondemocracies. They do so by raising elections beyond the true importance they hold, both intrinsically and in promoting other freedoms. Elections do not in fact determine the extent of all other freedoms. Political systems without free elections vary enormously in how free they are.

81

Within the nondemocracies, the Mexican system is comparatively free, but we are obviously hedging with the term "comparatively free." One way to make the phrase meaningful is to identify salient patterns of freedom and limits to freedom, assisted by comparisons with other political systems. The purpose is neither to depreciate nor to legitimize the Mexican political system, but to gain a broader understanding of it.

Individual Expression and Organizational Action

Very different rules hold in Mexico for individual expression and organizational action. As Daniel Cosío Villegas has described it: "Complete personal freedom has existed" and "public freedom [has been] almost equally ample," but there has been a "failure of personal and public freedom to find an outlet in political action."[1] Some responsibility for this failure may lie with dissidents who do not take proper advantage of available opportunities, but most observers attribute the failure to repression by a regime that does not tolerate organized action that threatens its stability. Of course, no regime complacently tolerates such threats. The difference is what threatens them. Democratic regimes are not characteristically threatened by independent critical organizations, and competition is open for government leadership positions. These regimes usually deny freedom of organizational action only to groups advocating their overthrow. By contrast, the Mexican regime does not allow strong independent organizations to challenge the basic development model even if they support maintenance (or expansion) of existing freedoms.[2]

In this context, the Mexican regime's careful restrictions on the electoral process make perfect sense. Elections are inherently organizational or group processes, not simply vehicles for individual expression. Political parties are organizations that bring people together, and voting itself represents an aggregation of individual expression. Thus, Mexican elections must be steered outside the democratic process so that they do not determine who will rule.

Mexico's elections do serve certain purposes, however. The citizenry has a chance to acquaint itself with its future leaders, who campaign as vigorously as if the results were in doubt. Candidates use campaigns to build personal and regime strength by visibly distributing promises and ultimately resources to the loyalists and the co-opted. In the best cases— the Cárdenas campaign is the most frequently cited—candidates may learn something about the citizenry. But perhaps the campaign's main purpose is to promote stability through the illusion of popular sovereignty.

A similar analysis of limits on organizational activity could be made of the party system, and of the PRI in particular. Free parties generally try to aggregate and organize individual expression, bringing them to bear on the policy process. Mexico's party system does not fundamentally function on such a basis. Nevertheless, both the electoral and party processes are freer in Mexico than in most Latin American nations (where there are no elections whatsoever, or just plebiscites or elections without competition between parties, and where campaigns do not offer possibilities for free expression, let alone government change). Mexico's greater freedom could be increased significantly if the 1977 political reforms take hold.

Whatever the qualifications, freedom is still restricted in Mexico's electoral and party systems. The picture is very different, however, if the focus shifts to freedoms dependent less on organizations, more on individuals alone. The Mexican regime does not feel threatened by personal freedoms that many authoritarian regimes would not tolerate.

Religious freedom is an excellent example. It may seem a bit of an odd choice at first glance. After all, the revolutionary regime attacked the church, stripping it of much of its power. But therein lies the key factor. Churches are organizations and they bring individuals together. The regime would not tolerate the church *as a political organization*, capable of influencing political events and even challenging the regime. The modus vivendi meant that the church surrendered this political power in return for guarantees, legal and tacit, of its legitimacy as a religious organization. Today the church has the freedom to function as it sees fit, within this context.

Religious freedom for the individual is substantial. Mexicans have the right to worship freely, in whatever religion they choose, and they have the freedom not to worship at all. There are disquieting incidents, of course, and some would argue that the regime's pointed secularism in effect represses the church even as a religious organization, but by and large Mexico presents a contrast to the restrictions placed on religious freedom in some authoritarian countries. Nor is there any attempt, as sporadically occurs elsewhere in Latin America, to extol Catholicism as the official religion of the nation. Moreover, the Mexican regime supports religious freedom not only by its own lack of repression but also by strength. This strength helps protect citizens from the sort of persecution by fanatical or vigilante groups that has stalked Argentine Jewry, for example. And religious freedom in Mexico means more than the absence of active persecution. It means the opportunity to practice one's religion and to maintain vibrant religiously oriented institutions such as private schools.

Other individual freedoms exist; some are flourishing. Mexicans travel freely outside the republic, often more freely than their U.S. counterparts. Banned from visiting Cuba in the 1960s and 1970s, U.S. citizens bound for the island would most often make their way via

Mexico. Nor does the Mexican government tell its citizens what jobs to take, just as it does not tell university students what careers to pursue. Allowing for exceptions, there are protections for property and for legal rights. Yet Mexico's "human rights" marks have not been exemplary. There has been increasing concern over missing persons, irregular detentions, forced confessions, and tortured political prisoners. As in the far more abusive Argentine case, it is often difficult to pinpoint the extent of government complicity in actions by hired thugs.

A troubling issue arises even regarding the personal freedoms that do exist. Many are gratuitous freedoms for most Mexicans—what critics might call "bourgeois" freedoms, available only for those who can afford them. Recent party and electoral reforms may not mean much to most peasants. Few Mexicans will ever exercise their freedom to travel to Havana, New York, or Paris. Few will attend the university or send their children to private schools. Few will have a wide choice of jobs; the issue will often be work or no work. Few own much. Few will hire lawyers to take their grievances to court, where many legal provisions purposely protect privilege. Of course, similar questions could be raised about the extent of bourgeois freedoms in the United States, but there many more do have the means to exercise those freedoms.

Furthermore, if the range of individual freedoms is expanded, Mexico does poorly. What Franklin Roosevelt spoke of as the "freedoms from" are not usually included in the U.S. concept of political freedom; the line between political freedom and socioeconomic freedom is thinner elsewhere, however, and the Mexican Constitution gives testimony to the overlap. Yet so many Mexicans do not enjoy freedom from want, hunger, and disease. Without those freedoms, the more purely political ones may seem hollow. Critics can interpret Mexico's religious freedom in this light, arguing that the regime ceased its antagonism toward religion as the regime itself ceased being revolutionary; when it failed to deliver on its material promises, it once again encouraged the flow of "opium" to the people.

Up to this point we have divided political freedoms into more organizationally and more individually or personally oriented ones. Obviously, however, the distinction is not always clear-cut. Freedom of speech, for example, has significant elements of both. There is wide latitude for individual expression. A Mexican can stand on the proverbial street corner and say almost anything without government reprisal. He can say whatever he wants at the dinner table and to a friend on the bus or at a bar. Freedom of speech in Mexico becomes less certain as it becomes a less individual act, when more people are interactively involved. In the cases of freedom of assembly and freedom of the media, freedom of speech ceases to be a fundamentally individual act, yet it does not lie in as directly sensitive an area as electoral or political party freedom. Neither inherently raises an organizational alternative to the government.

There is ample freedom of assembly—up until such point as demonstrations are no longer ad hoc and instead develop a stronger organizational base. Demonstrations occur daily in Mexico. Not all are predominantly political in nature, and not all of the political demonstrations express dissent, but many do. Harassment comes in many forms, ranging from the organization of counterdemonstrations, to infiltration, to the hiring of thugs, to outright use of police or even the army. Restrictions on the freedom of assembly come from government and they come from bullying by opposing groups. Freedom of assembly is neither fully respected nor dormant.

An interesting test of the freedom to assemble came in September 1980.[3] On the first of the month President López Portillo commented that constant demonstrations wreaked havoc with Mexico City's traffic and asked aloud what solutions might be found. Mexican presidents do not ask questions idly. The interior minister immediately "asked" Mexico City's mayor to talk with leaders of political organizations and registered parties, and on the fourth of the month an ambiguous but ominous communiqué was released by the city. It raised doubts about the legality of demonstrations outside the Plaza of the Republic, emphasizing that demonstrations caused "the disruption of normal life in Mexico City." Demonstrations should therefore restrict themselves to the plaza—but they should not feel deprived, because a sound system would be available and there would be access to officials in nearby government buildings! Many interpreted the government's statement as an attempt to restrict freedom of assembly. Not everyone accepted it. Some political parties expressed opposition, and demonstrations continued in the ensuing days, although police blocked some of them. Television channels dutifully interviewed irate drivers caught in traffic jams, eager to curb demonstrators.

Then, as quickly as the crisis had arisen, it subsided. On September 11 Mexico City announced that no constitutional guarantees had been altered. The announcement tacitly ended what had been called "The Battle for the Streets." If the government had been trying out a quiet, indirect way of restricting the freedom of assembly, the experiment had failed. Demonstrators in effect challenged the government to back down or enforce a clear policy through active repression. The government backed down. By not making its initial policy explicit, it could retreat without making its new policy explicit; it did not have to lose face by formally retracting any statement. It could have moved toward active repression but, apparently, only at the risk of considerable opposition, including violent opposition, and a loss of legitimacy.

Why then did the government act in the first place? One cannot overlook the truth in its stated premise: Demonstrations do aggravate the city's abominable traffic situation, and there were roughly 300 demonstrations in the previous year! But most demonstrations are not protests. They are symbolic political acts organized by the government or government-controlled institutions, and they are carried out in order to support policies or to greet a domestic or foreign dignitary. It lies well within the government's power to quarantine these demonstrations. Furthermore, the government's transportation policy belies a paramount concern for traffic, as it encourages automobiles while devoting insufficient resources to public transportation. Another possible explanation for the government action is that officials underestimated the opposition that would be engendered by their move. Yet another is that they planted the seeds for future action by drumming up widespread motorist resentment of demonstrators. But for now at least, the right to free assembly has been reasserted.

Freedom of the Media

Like freedom of assembly, freedom of the media attracts our attention for lying ambiguously between Mexico's ample individual freedoms and its restricted organizational freedoms. Moreover, freedom of the media is basic to a free society, certainly in the modern world. This section considers three principal issues: (1) general factors supporting or restricting media freedom; (2) variation in degrees of freedom; (3) substitutes for freer news coverage.

1. *General factors supporting or restricting media freedom.* At first glance, Mexico would appear to have many of the requisites for media freedom. There are, for example, multifarious sources. Many newspapers enjoy a national circulation. Mexico City's residents can choose among *El Día, Excélsior, El Heraldo, Novedades, La Prensa, El Universal, Uno Más Uno,* and numerous minor newspapers. By contrast, the U.S. capital city has been reduced to one major newspaper, and even New York City has but a few. Mexico also boasts an impressive number of news magazines, radio and television stations, and publishing houses. There is no government or official party vehicle, such as Radio Havana or the newspaper *Granma* in Cuba, although the government is *one* media owner. In fact, the great majority of all the media forms are privately owned. Beyond this, overt government censorship is exceptional, and freedom of the press is widely and constitutionally proclaimed.

On the other hand, there are significant sources of government influence. One lies in regulation of the resources necessary for media production. Significantly, the government controls, distributes, and subsidizes all newsprint. PIPSA (Producer and Importer of Paper) is a virtual government monopoly, with private interests supplementing the government's controlling stock. Established in 1935, it purchases newsprint and sells it to periodicals wholesale. Almost all periodicals buy their newsprint from PIPSA, and to shop elsewhere, often abroad, means higher costs and less competitiveness. PIPSA can also provide excellent credit terms or it can be tough.[4]

Another specific source of government control is advertising revenue. Mexican newspapers depend heavily on the government to buy space for its announcements. Unprofessional and often corrupt advertising practices contribute to government influence and adversely affect independent news reporting still further. Gacetillas (publicity stories) can be bought and not labeled as advertisements. Insertions may be devoted to commemorative events, inaugurations, appointments, or government statements. Some of those working at Mexico's newspapers, often not satisfied with their salaries, have second jobs with firms sending in gacetillas. Similarly, they may collect igualas, monthly gratuities from business or government organizations involved in policy areas covered by them, to insure favorable reporting. Clearly, then, government interference is not the only obstacle to media freedom.

The patronage of private businesses could provide a buffer against government economic pressure, but it also carries its own strings in terms of not reporting certain kinds of news. Even where private ownership may be a hedge against government control, it does not necessarily imply free coverage of the news by competitive organizations. First, there is less competition than the plurality of media might imply. For example, while some newspapers are independents and some are cooperatives (owned by the employees), many belong to commercial chains, and a few big chains dominate. Second, those who own the media rarely believe in an independent line. Their generally conservative interests are served pretty well by the development model. It would be easier to identify the bounds of freedom and repression if more of the private media identified themselves with the opposition or at least with the value of strict independence from the regime. The media would then attempt to act in conflict with the regime and we would see how far they could go. In fact, however, the question may be less one of regime censorship, whether imposed ex post facto by the regime or a priori by media too frightened to criticize, than one of interest overlap. Freedom requires individuals and organizations devoted to exercising it, a generalization that may be especially relevant in mixed authoritarian-free settings. There is less opportunity in more authoritarian settings; there is less danger in freer settings. Of course, it is not easy for a strong professional ethos based on free expression and integrity to arise in the Mexican setting. For instance, as Mexican politics is group-oriented, so media cliques may be closed to news stories written by those from other cliques.[5] Media cliquishness provides another illustration of the fact that restrictions on media freedom in Mexico do not all emanate from the government.

2. *Variation in degrees of freedom.* As media freedom in Mexico is not an all-or-nothing concept, so it is not a constant. We can identify certain variables that determine when media freedom is stronger or weaker. One is the disposition of any particular administration. Echeverría, despite one jolting confrontation (analyzed below), clearly allowed greater freedom than did his predecessor. The media could take a more critical look at Mexico's general development model and its results. Government money actually supported cinematic efforts to depict poverty, corruption, and even political injustice. Of course, all this could be linked to Echeverría's own effort to alter the development model, but there was also greater latitude than before for criticism of ongoing government policies. Under López Portillo, who labored to revitalize the development model, media freedom progressed still further. Reforms paralleled those made in the political party arena, and in fact, there are some direct links; since 1977, all parties have been allowed monthly television time to air their views.

Freedom also varies according to the particular medium in question. A key factor is audience size. The government generally places more stringent limits on those media that reach more people; printed media are generally freer than "action" media. All this makes sense in terms of the greater limits placed on freedoms that involve greater organizational or interpersonal interaction. Cinema, for example, comes under a measure of regulation by the Interior Ministry. But it is television that is probably the major action medium, especially important in urban areas.

By 1973, television already had a potential audience of roughly 25 million.[6] Private interests dominate, and they buttress the status quo. Most of Mexican public television is educationally oriented, attracting limited audiences. When Echeverría bought an ailing private channel and made it into a public channel (thirteen), the powerful Monterrey Group of industrialists countered this perceived threat to the private sector by merging their channel eight with Mexico's major network system, thus forming Televisa. But private ownership (with government representation on Televisa's governing board) implies no fountain of dissent. In fact, compared to public television, Televisa has generally been a more ardent proponent of a conservative line within the stable development model. When, for example, public television took an anti-Somoza position in covering the insurgency in Nicaragua, Televisa tended more to emphasize the dangers of revolutionary Marxism. Probably the major point about television news coverage overall is that it very rarely covers events that are embarrassing to the government or criticizes government policies.

Moreover, aside from restricted news reporting, television upholds the political system by transmitting the soap operas, comedies, and variety and other shows that often portray the social values of the privileged; such programs do not question the status quo.

Radio also mixes restricted news coverage with "safe" programming, conscious of government watchfulness. The government has the authority to regulate broadcasting in the "public interest." More directly, the government can require that radio stations allot a considerable amount of time for government programming, although the government exercises such authority less than it holds it in reserve. Yet there are pockets of dissent. University Radio, for example, speaks freely and even critically of the government, reflecting the general freedom exercised by the National University. Thus, it is difficult to assess the actual limits on broadcast freedom; rarely are they boldly approached, let alone transgressed, by radio or television.

If the broadcast media give less critical coverage than daily newspapers, news magazines give more. The magazines range from very conservative, such as *Impacto*, to rather conservative, such as *Tiempo*, to more liberal, such as *Proceso*. Some, such as *Siempre*, have been open to divergent orientations. Mexico is not unusual in permitting weeklies to publish material that no daily would or could. Illustratively, Mexico's human rights abuses have received much more prominent mention in magazines such as *Razones* than in any newspaper.

Two special kinds of journals present probably the most critical view of official Mexico. One, a popular one, is the comic book. Most comic books are rather conventional and nonpolitical, but a few have vigorously attacked government policies on an array of issues. Drawn in typical cartoon fashion, these magazines are scathingly satirical. The two most famous have been *Los Agachados* (literally the stooped ones) and *Los Supermachos* (super-machos). Eduardo del Río ("Rius") was their guiding light. With his freewheeling socialist bent, Rius did not go unmolested. But by the time he had to leave *Los Supermachos* the comic book claimed a circulation of roughly 200,000. Although *Los Supermachos* has not been the same since Rius's departure, Rius reactivated his challenge with *Los Agachados*, where he remained from 1968 to 1977; the new comic book achieved a peak circulation of roughly 150,000.[7] Like *Los Supermachos*, *Los Agachados* used Mexico's provincial towns for backdrops. There, the apparently simple and definitely beleaguered peasant asked the apparently simple questions that in fact cynically interpreted why he was beleaguered. U.S. imperialism was a favorite target, but the Vatican, private enterprise, *and* the Mexican government were also treated irreverently.

A second special kind of periodical is the scholarly journal. Several factors sustain its critical orientation. One is its relatively limited audience; another is its association with the university. The *Revista Mexicana de Sociología*, published at the National University, and *Foro Internacional*, published at El Colegio de México, are good examples.

Book publishing, with generally limited sales, also ranks closer to the freer than the more restricted end of the Mexican media spectrum. Surely self-censorship has existed, and interesting voids result. One, of special interest here, is that although many first-rate, incisive books by Mexicans are available on Mexican *history*, far fewer penetrating analyses are found on contemporary *politics*. Still, it is some indication of freedom that translations of nearly all books on Mexican politics by foreign authors have been available, and many of these have been critical of Mexico's political system. Translations of more general works, from Karl Marx to Milton Friedman, have also been available. Additionally, if domestic "political science" has been relatively weak, prominent Mexican historians have dealt critically with contemporary affairs. Venerable figures such as Daniel Cosío Villegas and Jesús Silva Herzog have repeatedly denounced restrictions on party, electoral, and press freedoms. Essayists, novelists, and poets have written very sharply on political themes. Recently, there has even been a surge of political gossip books. Thus, for example, Irma Serrano, allegedly the mistress of former President Díaz Ordaz, has written luridly of her experiences. Serious works of political criticism have been published not only by prominent private companies such as Siglo XXI and Nueva Imagen but also by government-financed ones such as the Fondo de Cultural Económica.

3. *Substitutes for freer news coverage.* Clearly, the latitude for freedom varies with the medium in question and is potentially greatest when audiences are small; a related question is what content is produced in the absence of wider freedom. As book publishing cannot substitute for ongoing news coverage, and as little may be expected of the broadcast media, our attention focuses here mostly on the printed news media.

Readers find woefully little information on how and why political decisions are made. They will quickly see that the government raises wages, but not that the increases are inferior to the inflation rate; nor will they find specifics on the decision-making process. They read the story of the PRI's congressional leader adjourning a legislative session, claiming that there was no quorum, and of opposition members yelling "antidemocratic," but they do not learn whether there really was a quorum.[8] With rare exceptions, investigative reporting is not a major part of news coverage. Limited news reporting reflects the limited degree to which the ruled hold their rulers accountable. Mexico's government does not often forthrightly address citizen questions about why one policy is favored over another. After surprising the nation by firing those thought to be his most important and loyal cabinet ministers, President López Portillo "explained" his action as "for the national good." Lightly prodded for elaboration, he made it clear that he was the president in a presidential, not a parliamentary, system and therefore did not have to account for his decision. "At least tell me the latest rumors!" one columnist satirically pleaded. In practice, because officials rarely discuss intragovernment policy debates, even ambitious reporters are handicapped by government secretiveness. A cycle develops in which Mexican newspapers become both perpetrators and victims of the lack of news.

Filling page after page without addressing the most important news of the day becomes an art. Popular or "human interest" stories, indeed most nonpolitical stories, receive ample coverage. Entertainment, sports, fashion, medical news—there is no problem once one gets beyond section one, or basic news. The crux of the matter is what happens within section one. Publishers find many substitutes for critical coverage of Mexican politics. International news gets considerable space. The high ratio of international to domestic news in Mexico, higher than in the United States, reflects Mexico's lesser parochialism or at least lesser self-sufficiency, but it is also true that restrictions on domestic coverage leave greater latitude for international coverage.

Proclamations capture prominent space. These are grand statements, usually by government officials, that characteristically just repeat what is already well known. President López Portillo declares, "I will defend the Revolution," and newspapers have a headline piece. "I do not recommend a change" (in the six-year presidency), López Portillo declares; readers can only wonder who did. Some proclamations may be subtle or symbolic policy indications—the government's verdict on some matter under consideration. "Mexico Will Defend Its Independence" may suggest that Mexico is rejecting a U.S. proposal—but it also may be a cover for actual acceptance of a proposal. One might subscribe to what has been called a "mirror" approach to understanding Mexican government proclamations: Prepare yourself for the opposite. Most often, however, proclamations are mere banalities: If believed, they help legitimize the regime; if not, they just fill space. Among those continually used as slogans during López Portillo's administration were "To Justice by Liberty," "The Only Dogma in Our Constitution is Liberty," "The Program of My Party Is My Program," "We Are All the Solution," "To Love Mexico and Understand the World."

Banalities are used as if there were a constant political campaign. And indeed there is one of sorts, not against any specific opponent but against a feeling that the government has not satisfied its revolutionary promise. *Triunfalismo* (proclaiming triumphs) becomes especially intense in the last years of each *sexenio* (six-year presidential term). Mexicans see that a certain amount has been spent on expanding health facilities, for example, but they are rarely given a basis for evaluation. How does the amount compare in inflation-adjusted terms to what the last administration spent? How does it compare to what other nations spend? What real impact has it had? That such information does not flow from the government itself is one thing. That it is not provided by the media is another.

Mexican politics are rich in commemorations and these receive extensive media coverage. Heroes are extolled, holidays are celebrated. In fact, the proliferation of holidays is often cited as an economic liability. Coverage of commemorative events not only fills media space with empty news; it also serves symbolic purposes. When Mexican leaders pay homage to Zapata's peasant revolutionaries they reaffirm their allegiance to contemporary peasants and make it more difficult for dissidents to mobilize around Zapata's image. A few thoughtful columnists seize the opportunity to raise some doubts about the regime's true faithfulness to Zapata's cause, but most simply publicize the government line.

Far removed from news trivialities and nonsense, readers can also find serious commentaries decrying the fundamental structure of the social-political-economic system. Unprepared observers may indeed be startled at the profound, sweeping criticisms, often neo-Marxist criticisms, repeatedly leveled against the status quo. Of course, such critiques are more likely to be found in books and journals with small readerships, but they also appear in some newspapers. Why does a system sensitive to less profound criticism readily tolerate more profound criticism? The apparent paradox is rather easily unraveled. One type of criticism is dangerously policy-relevant; the other is not.

It might help to think in terms of a distinction between "regime" and "state."[9] The state would be the broad "pact of domination" of the ruling classes, the very general guidelines within which privilege is assured. The regime would be the particular political and governmental configuration by which the pact is implemented. There is much less variation among states (at similar levels of development) than there is among regimes in Latin America. Short of revolution, the Mexican state will not basically change. Columnists can elaborate the failures of Mexico's "dependent capitalist state" and the power of the high bourgeoisie and foreign interests. Government officials, far from clamping down on such broadly radical critiques, may even join in the moaning, skillfully portraying themselves battling the state. The high bourgeoisie and foreign interests are denounced in rhetoric, even as they are gratified in policy. Officials solemnly pledge to fight poverty and inequality, while they prudently attribute such evils largely to the nature of the state, immutable. Alas, little can be done to change the state. And so, profoundly sweeping commentaries are much more acceptable than specific, policy-relevant ones. Columnists can heatedly write what they choose, in general terms, about dependency, capitalism, and imperialism, but let them advocate specific tax or wage policies at odds with actual government decisions and press liberty will get a truer test. "Profound" criticism may even be *encouraged* insofar as it siphons off energy from policy-relevant specifics. So media freedom, like other freedoms discussed earlier, may well be belittled as bourgeois freedom, freedom for expression that does not directly address—much less change—material policies.

In sum, Mexicans can follow the news media regularly and still have little idea of how policies are being made, what are the pros and cons, who supports each side, and what are the ultimate results. Instead, the news is covered ("covered" in the sense of hidden as much as in the sense of reported) with omissions, masks, mirrors, and metaphors. In nations with vibrant news media one may associate diverse headlines in different papers with free expression of multiple viewpoints. But in Mexico the fact that one newspaper features some stories and a second paper features others may reflect the lack of hard news coverage in both.

Case Studies in Media Dissent

Despite all the restraining factors on hard, especially critical, news reporting, there have been bold exceptions. After a brief look at two such exceptions, we focus on the major exception—the *Excélsior* case.

Kenneth Johnson has described how *¿Por Qué?* (literally, Why?), a leftist weekly journal, functioned from its inception in 1968 to its forced demise in 1974.[10] *¿Por Qué?* strongly attacked the status quo, even supporting guerrilla activities. Alleged government harassment included supply and price pressure from PIPSA, bullying potential advertisers out of doing business with *¿Por Qué?*, and imprisonment without trial of the journal's most prominent figure (who was implicated in guerrilla actions). Yet in 1972 *¿Por Qué?* still claimed a circulation of 100,000. One can emphasize either the harassment or the fact that such a radical publication as *¿Por Qué?* could function for as long as it did.

For a second example, occurring during a different presidential sexenio, consider the fate of *El ABC de Tijuana*. The newspaper began in January 1977, attracting dissidents from newspapers that would not publish their columns.[11] *ABC* quickly became a strong voice for the anti–status quo left. Critics charged that *ABC*, like *¿Por Qué?* for that matter, was highly sensationalistic. But also like *¿Por Qué?*, *ABC* was an independent political voice. Mediocre journalism did not make *ABC* unusual; independent journalism did. With the notable exceptions of a few journals, Mexico's provincial press does not report extensively or critically on such issues as the violent repression of peasants. It comes as no surprise, then, that the state government of Baja California repressed *ABC*.

Framing the issue was very important. No official credence could be given to an image of a leftist, independent newspaper fighting a nonleftist, U.S.-oriented state government over substantive issues, certainly not over freedom of the press. So the government encouraged a labor strike at *ABC* and, under the cover of the strike, helped oust the paper's director. Using its "official left wing," the government brought in the PRI-affiliated peasant and worker unions to rally around labor's cause against *ABC*'s management. Although the government identified this as a labor problem it belied its own posture by adding that newspapers should merely give the news, not judge it. The government received extensive support in the non-*ABC* media throughout the crisis. In the aftermath, the government offered only a withered olive branch, as *ABC*'s director was invited to open a new but definitely transformed paper. The *ABC* one could find on the newsstands a few years after the confrontation was quite different from its fiery predecessor, and its daily circulation would be only about 10 percent of the previous 35,000–50,000.

The events at *ABC* sensitize us to another important variable in patterns of freedom and repression. This is the factor of federalism. Chapter 3 established that ultimate authority lies with the national government, which can assert its will over any state government. But that does not mean that it always does. Ultimate authority cannot be invoked too often without diluting itself. The president makes a commitment to only so many issues, often leaving governors or other officials to bear the responsibilities of—and the resentment for—government repression. Freedom of the press as well as other freedoms vary according to the political situation in particular states.

Turning to the national scene, no single episode in recent years has attracted more attention to the issue of media freedom in Mexico than the *Excélsior* case in 1976.[12] Its importance stems from several factors. More than any other major newspaper in Mexico, *Excélsior* exercised the freedom to dissent. Progressively oriented (since 1968), it criticized Mexico's domestic and foreign policies and continually called for increased political freedoms, broader distribution of the national wealth, greater worker participation in economic decision making, and more serious attacks on corruption. It also sold space to dissidents for their advertisements. *Excélsior* naturally angered many businesses, which proceeded to withdraw their advertising. Initially, however, the Echeverría government backed up its rhetoric on press freedom with concrete actions and even picked up some of the advertising slack.

Excélsior provided a shining example not only of press freedom but of press quality. It counted among its columnists such well-known intellectuals as Daniel Cosío Villegas, Gastón García Cantú, Ricardo Garibay, Pablo Latapí, Vicente Leñero, and Rodolfo Stavenhagen. It earned a reputation for avoiding corrupt practices, for not selling headlines. In fact, *Excélsior* earned an international reputation. Its reports were used as evidence in U.S. congressional hearings on Latin America, and it established links with many of the world's finest newspapers. The London *Times* called *Excélsior* the most influential daily in Latin America. One prominent U.S. observer even called *Excélsior*, somewhat exaggeratedly, "probably the last bastion of intellectual and press freedom in Mexico."[13] Thus it becomes especially important to take a careful look at just what the *Excélsior* case shows and does not show.

First question: *Why* did the government repress *Excélsior*? There is no single, definitive answer, but probably the main factor was the perceived degree of dissent. Not just in frequency but in type and tenor of criticism, *Excélsior* went far beyond anything seen in other dailies. This was true of *Excélsior*'s editorials, and it was truer of many of the articles written by its columnists, including some that came close to direct criticism of the president—a serious violation of the unwritten rulebook on political dissent in Mexico.

More frequently, *Excélsior*'s criticisms touched another sensitive nerve. They questioned the regime's progressiveness. The *Excélsior* case has this factor in common with the *¿Por Qué?* and *ABC* cases. Here, then, lies another clue to variable patterns of regime tolerance of dissent. The regime is especially sensitive to criticism from the left because such criticism challenges the myths of its revolutionary legitimacy, of its commitments to political and economic equality. Criticism from the right may actually lend support to those myths and therefore even please the regime. What better way to appear progressive than to be accused of pandering to peasants or workers or Cuba? Also, insofar as the right rather than the left is truly represented within the system, its criticisms do not suggest an independent alternative to the system. Even if leftist, more than rightist, administrations allow a wider range for leftist speech, they may be just as sensitive to leftist criticism.[14]

Other motivations also emerge for the action against *Excélsior*. One widely circulated rumor was that Echeverría was trying to preserve his influence after his official term expired and that a strong tool would be a loyal press. Additionally, Echeverría reportedly had an economic interest in an expanding editorial organization, a competitor of *Excélsior*. Others argue, however, that the economic motivation could have been only marginal and that surely Echeverría understood Mexican political history too well to suppose that he could preserve power beyond his presidency. The best guess remains that the government moved against *Excélsior* mostly because of the paper's unusual independence.

Second question: *How* did the government act? Again, although there is no definitive answer, there are strong likelihoods. No open repression based on a straightforward statement of government dissatisfaction with *Excélsior*'s dissent would be forthcoming. That would be uncharacteristically direct, and it would undermine the government's progressive image. Methods would be far more subtle—and insidious. Mexico's most progressive daily would have to be turned upside down for being too conservative!

Excélsior was depicted as an enemy of peasants and slum dwellers. On June 10, 1976, scores of landless Mexicans invaded land owned by *Excélsior* on the outskirts of Mexico City. *Excélsior* had purchased the land in 1959 precisely to insure itself a secure economic base, a base that could help sustain political independence. In 1976, *Excélsior* was seeking needed revenues by building a middle-class housing development on the land. Surely, the Mexican regime is not known for siding with peasants against the middle class. Standard procedure might be to expel the peasants or to seek some sort of accommodation. Instead, the squatter movement was led by a PRI candidate from the agrarian sector of the party, a sign of official backing. The government helped bring more peasants (in trucks, modern buses, and luxury cars), sheltered them, and staunchly rejected *Excélsior*'s legal effort to expel them. Soon the squatters numbered more than a thousand. *Excélsior* had hoped that the initial invasion was a maneuver by a single governor or a mischievous trial balloon against dissent; perhaps Echeverría ultimately might repudiate it in the face of courageous *Excélsior* resistance. After all, the president had previously gotten along well with the paper's editor, Julio Scherer García. More important, the president had established a laudable record of permitting dissent, and many thought he would have to nurture it to pursue what were thought to be two of his fondest dreams—the Nobel Peace Prize and the UN secretary-generalship. But Echeverría publicly joined with the minister of agrarian reform in pressuring *Excélsior* to reach a compromise with the squatters. Involvement by the Agrarian Reform Ministry provided a nice touch, posing the problem as one of land reform rather than property rights and press freedom.

Simultaneously, the government orchestrated a strong media campaign. It withdrew its advertising from *Excélsior*, and it increased its financial support of competing dailies, in part by purchasing advertisements attacking *Excélsior*. Such attacks were not restricted to the printed press. In fact, the major media assault came through television's campaign against *Excélsior*'s "lack of patriotism." The news program, "24 Hours," waged nightly warfare. *Excélsior* gamely tried to defend itself by reporting on the campaign against it. Its columnists even finally published a joint declaration on the need for a free press, especially in a society that lacked freedom in so many other institutions! Before that, however, the paper tried to mix independence with discretion. However reluctantly, editor Julio Scherer compromised principle by participating in the annual Liberty of the Press Day with colleagues he regarded as hypocritical enemies and with Echeverría himself. The day was filled with all-too-ironic declarations about how freedom of the press was respected.

In addition to its squatter, financial, and media offensives, the government also penetrated *Excélsior*'s internal labor operations, another procedure reminiscent of the *ABC* case. *Excélsior* was a cooperative, owned by the workers; editor Scherer was not the paper's owner, but an employee. Although he was greatly admired by the editorial staff and columnists, he did not enjoy smooth relations with many of the rank-and-file workers. Many at *Excélsior* believed that the government exploited this opening to finance a dissident minority.

Early on the morning of July 8, 1976, came the coup, the culmination of the six-month anti-*Excélsior* campaign. Scherer and his supporters were strong-armed out; the printing presses were seized by the paper's minority (which cited Scherer's ineffective management of the squatter issue). The government insisted that the cooperative itself had legitimately changed its leadership. In any case, it was a conventional Mexican newspaper that came out the very next day. Its new directors congratulated themselves for restoring *Excélsior* to the mainstream of Mexican media. As happened at *ABC*, the periodical kept its name but lost its personality. Almost all the previous columnists resigned.[15]

The meaning of the *Excélsior* episode must be judged in light of not only the precipitating but also the ensuing events. While the international press (*Le Monde*, the *New York Times*, the *Washington Post*, and so forth) was predictably outraged, the Mexican press was predictably low-key, giving the coup only scant coverage. There were a few notable exceptions among magazines, such as *Siempre*. Some intellectuals expressed chagrin. Octavio Paz wrote of the triumph of "grey," the "color of conformity and passivity."[16] Reaction was also sharp in segments of the university community. On the other hand, author Carlos Fuentes offered a qualified defense of Echeverría. Echeverría himself predictably and bitterly denounced the prevalent foreign view as "anti-Mexican." Less predictable, at least for those who saw repression at *Excélsior* as clear evidence of the impossibility of press freedom in Mexico, was the nearly immediate stirring to reestablish an independent outlet for the ousted *Excélsior* team. Much to Echeverría's chagrin, the *Excélsior* episode was not over.

Scherer loyalists established a weekly magazine called *Proceso*, which Echeverría could not appear to repress without a legitimizing pretext. More important, Echeverría's presidential term would end within a month, and his further threats were backed by diminishing power. One Echeverría minister warned that a new independent journal could be considered unpatriotic, given Mexico's political-economic crisis. Echeverría himself strongly urged Scherer not to accept invitations to discuss the *Excélsior* case in the United States, as the United States was not truly interested in press freedom but only in attacking Mexico's anti-imperialist government. PIPSA made access to paper difficult, and *Proceso* had to buy what it needed at high black-market prices. Nonetheless, valor and freedom triumphed when *Proceso* appeared on November 6.

Outgoing President Echeverría continued to threaten *Proceso*, but incoming President López Portillo was now the key figure with whom to reckon. As PRI candidate, López Portillo had played the proper role of regime loyalist, agreeing that the crisis was internal to *Excélsior*. Yet he also gave Scherer a sympathetic ear and promised full press liberty starting December 1. As president, he allowed *Proceso* to flourish freely and critically (although it has not maintained its original quality). But however pleased they were with their success at *Proceso*, *Excélsior*'s dispossessed leaders realized they had come only halfway around. Weeklies simply do not have the impact of dailies. They wondered how the government would react to a new independent daily. Moreover, because there was no chance to get private-sector funding, the group was forced to seek government funds, despite the all-too-obvious risks of accompanying restrictions on press freedom.

López Portillo's response seemed to go beyond the Scherer group's imaginings. Why establish a new daily, the president asked, instead of simply returning to *Excélsior*? The president's possible motivation ranged from embarrassing and weakening Echeverría, to forestalling creation of a truly new and financially dependent daily, to upholding press freedom. With a mixture of hope and trepidation, Scherer's group accepted the president's offer and returned to *Excélsior*. Their hopes seemed confirmed when the Mexican press, perhaps signaling a new climate of tolerance, covered Scherer's acceptance of a prominent journalism award in New York City. But at this point the *Excélsior* saga took a sudden and bizarre turn. The *New York Times* broke the developing story of Scherer's return to *Excélsior*. Many Mexicans thought they smelled Yankee involvement, and Scherer's successor at *Excélsior* played his hand to the hilt by covering the *Times* piece on the front page. Scherer's plans to return to *Excélsior* soon fell apart.[17]

In assessing the ramifications of the *Excélsior* case for Mexican press freedom, the negative side is clear. A uniquely independent, quality daily had been assaulted and transformed. On the other hand, a major newspaper had exercised considerable freedom for several years prior to the repression. The *Excélsior* case suggests the limits on dissent but also the latitude for it. It mocks the pious rhetoric of a free press but also indicates that such freedom can far exceed what is found in some Latin American nations. The fate of Mexico's independent periodicals, subsequent to the *Excélsior* coup, also illustrates the mixed picture. Until 1982, *Proceso* labored in the *Excélsior* tradition, without significant government interference. Then, stung by criticism amid economic crisis and his own tarnished political image, López Portillo cut off government advertising revenue to *Proceso* and one other periodical, declaring that the government could permit dissent without having to subsidize it. Still, the López Portillo administration avoided any full-scale parallel to the 1976 repression of *Excélsior*. Moreover, *Uno Más Uno*, a daily with many former *Excélsior* figures on its staff, had become the most important heir to the *Excélsior* legacy. The *Excélsior* case reminds us that repression lies within the regime's logic, but it does not prove that such repression is inevitable or constant. It also illustrates the regime's adeptness at acting in insidious fashion to accomplish ends that it would not openly declare.

POLITICAL EQUALITY

Rarely does a political system function equally freely, or equally effectively, for all its citizens. Yet Mexico appears unusual in the extent to which inequality characterizes the political system. We can speak meaningfully, if with qualification, of a free British political system, compared to an unfree Soviet system, whereas the contrasts within Mexico are so great as to constitute not qualifications but the essential characterization itself. "The" Mexican system is really (at least) two systems. Some Latin American political systems allow more freedom to their citizens and most allow less, but few, if any, allow more freedom to a sizable minority while allowing so little to the majority.

An analogy to Mexico's economic system is appropriate. Many nations are richer, many poorer, but few distribute wealth in the same unequal way as Mexico. Extremes of wealth and poverty usually coexist in countries in which only a very few enjoy the wealth while all but the few are impoverished. Although Mexico has the extremes, it also has a substantial middle class and lower middle class (including many workers). Rarely does such relatively widespread wealth coexist with abject poverty for perhaps one-fourth of the population (see Chapter 5). The political/economic parallel is of course no accident. Economic resources contribute to political resources and political resources contribute to economic resources.

The concern here is with inequality in political *power*. One valid definition of political power is the ability to get others to do what they would not otherwise do. A corollary is the ability to prevent others from doing what they would otherwise do, forcing "nondecisions" where decisions might have been injurious. Power and freedom do not always go together; one may be free to express himself, yet gain little power. In practice, however, there is great overlap, so that this section on power relates to the previous section on political freedom. The most common explanation for the correlation between freedom and power is that freedom brings power as groups have the opportunity to advocate, act, and influence. Accepting that, it is also true that power creates its own freedom, as power implies the means (influence, finance, expertise) to act (positive freedoms) and the ability to resist others' actions (defensive freedoms). Potential antagonists, including the regime itself, must pay a price to suppress the freedom of powerful groups.

The Less Powerful Sector

If we start by dividing the Mexican political system into two parts, one more powerful than the other, then most Mexicans find themselves in the less powerful part. The largest blocs within this subsystem are the workers (with exceptions) and peasants. Also included are the unemployed, grossly underemployed, squatters, marginals, and Indians; some individuals in these groups may also be workers or peasants. Our comparison of less and more powerful groups thus builds on the analysis in Chapter 3. There, we analyzed workers and peasants as political actors who have generally enjoyed little freedom or effectiveness in making demands on the state. Instead, these groups characteristically have had to accept the results afforded by a corporatist system, realizing that organized dissent carries strong risks of outright repression.

One of the great paradoxes of Mexican worker and peasant politics has been incorporation without power. In fact, few Latin American nations make equally strong claims to widespread incorporation. The Mexican revolution brought many workers and peasants "into" a political system that could no longer simply ignore, exclude, or repress them. The PRI became the chief vehicle for incorporation, and that is one reason that the PRI—despite its limited role in policymaking—may be the most important political party in any nondemocratic Latin American nation. Yet (at least within the Western world) few if any systems that incorporate so many groups also give them so little freedom of action and so little material reward.

Two major qualifications are warranted. The first, elaborated in Chapter 3, is that a significant sector of organized workers has managed to bargain effectively with the state, reaping material benefits and thereby at least partly escaping the "less powerful" category. The other qualification is that even the less powerful are not necessarily powerless. In fact, some agricultural policies have respected the political power of the peasantry.

The regime has generally regarded small plots (*minifundia*) and communal holdings (*ejidos*) as much less productive than large commercial farms. Yet it has been wary of the political costs inherent in repudiating the principle that every peasant is entitled to land. Finally, López Portillo partially abandoned revolutionary rhetoric by disavowing *further* land distribution, thereby frankly elevating production based on economic rationality above distribution based on political concessions.

Yet even López Portillo's conservative policies did not imply the demise of peasant power. Instead, there have been continual examples of independent organizational initiatives by peasants. Compared to urban workers, peasants protest more frequently and strongly outside official organizations, which is one reason that they are more often repressed. Sometimes this repression is tempered by concessions; less often, tacit concessions may actually substitute for outright repression. Peasants who "invade" and squat on land, often defying legality in the name of revolutionary justice, may be ruthlessly evicted, even slaughtered—or they may be permitted to stay. Going still further, the regime has been known to provide squatters with money and tools, at the same time perhaps placating owners by paying compensation for their lost land. Urban squatters often pin their hopes on a similar sort of something-for-everyone solution. Some squatter movements even get away with brandishing radical ideology. For example, there are Marxist communes, such as the largely self-governing Tierra y Libertad (the zapatista slogan of "Land and Liberty").

On the other hand, the illegality of squatting often provides a handy standby weapon for the government to wield against dissident organizations. Thus, in March 1981, Mexico City police suddenly engulfed the Second of October Encampment, established in 1975 and named in commemoration of the dissident students slaughtered on October 2, 1968. As one leftist leader saw it: "The government didn't move against them because they were squatters. There are squatters all over the city. It acted because it cannot tolerate an independent organization that doesn't follow the political rules of the system."[18] Yet, it is also true that the government did tolerate the encampment from 1975 to 1981, mixing its tolerance with harassment and attempted co-optation.

Were nearly all groups to enjoy only the limited power and freedom characteristic of the less privileged groups, then the Mexican political system could properly be labeled authoritarian. There would be qualifications, of course, as there are for most inclusive system labels. But considerable concentration of power would reside in a regime relatively autonomous of society's rather powerless groups. Pluralism, the dispersion of power to various political actors, would be a grossly misleading characterization of such a system.

The More Powerful Sector

The rules are different, however, for the middle class and business groups (including industrial, commercial, agricultural, insurance, manufacturing, and importing and exporting concerns). These groups have much more independent political power, much more freedom to chart their own policies, even in opposition to regime policy.

Even within the state apparatus itself, middle-class employees have formed "bureaucratic enclaves that are relatively distinct from and independent of presidential authority."[19] Naturally, because the bureaucracy is part of the government, and because the president enjoys strong policymaking and appointive powers, there are important limits to bureaucratic independence. Nonetheless, other factors have encouraged some independence. These include the very size and intricacy of the bureaucracy, the prevalence of personal rather than systemwide loyalties (discussed later in the chapter), and the growing role of technocrats reluctant to subordinate their special expertise to political commands.

An example involving greater structural autonomy from the state is the university, which offers a good opportunity to analyze the degree of freedom and autonomous power possible in a middle-class institution. In fact, there is no more middle-class institution in Mexico than the public university.[20] There are strong reasons to expect only limited freedom and autonomy. Dissent, usually from the left, is endemic at the university, and it has a potential organizational base there. The government invests substantial finances in the university, and the university is a leading center of national thought, as well as a socializing organization for most of the nation's budding political leaders. Furthermore, several authoritarian regimes elsewhere in Latin America maintain considerable repressive control over university policy. And, indeed, the Mexican government does not tolerate organized political dissent that moves beyond the campus and challenges the regime. The most notorious incident occurred in 1968, when some 300 protesting students were killed by the government. This incident serves as a sobering reminder that the middle class is not exempt from brutal repression.

Yet a pluralist or reconciliation model more than an authoritarian model characterizes Mexican government-university relations. The middle class, compared to the lower class, is usually given a wider area for dissent and even then punished less harshly for stepping outside this area. As Lorenzo Meyer has written: "When the opposition came from groups such as students, the intelligentsia, and the middle class in general, the response was much less violent and repressive."[21] In regard to ongoing political issues, the regime does not typically impose its will on the university. There is great autonomy in academic affairs, such as curriculum. University leaders, like business leaders, are much less likely than peasant or labor leaders to be appointed by the government. The university itself basically decides how to distribute the block grants it receives from the government, and the size of these grants is determined much less by university compliance with government guidelines than by the size of the student body, which the government does not control, and by the university's ability to block government attempts to impose tuition. The tuition issue epitomizes the contrasting political power of privileged and unprivileged Mexico. Middle- and upper-middle-class students receive free public higher education, but the government dispenses scant resources to its woefully inadequate primary and secondary schools, especially in rural areas.

The relative autonomy of (middle- and upper-class) business groups has been more widely documented than the autonomy of any other group. Because the regime's economic policies are basically favorable to business, it is often difficult to evaluate business power to oppose the regime. The conflict with the Echeverría administration (see Chapter 3) provided a vivid example of business power. Of course, business frequently holds a veto power over government policy in nations where market economics dominate.[22] Mexican business appears even more powerful because of the relative lack of power and autonomy of most other Mexican groups, including labor. Naturally, just as the less powerful groups are not powerless, so the more powerful ones are not omnipotent. Even during the López Portillo years, business was dissatisfied with the restrictive credit policy, high interest rates for borrowers, and increased government control over certain areas of the economy. Tensions obviously increased markedly with the 1982 government takeover of all domestic private banks, a startling assertion of the regime's political power to make public policy even against business interests. Barring crises and certain other exceptions, however, the regime has generally seen benefits outweighing costs in pursuing pro-business policies.

Basic comparisons between more privileged and less privileged groups lead us to the conclusion that there is a great disparity between constitutional provisions and the realities of political power. The Mexican government has more legal authority over business than it uses,[23] and Mexican business has more political power than a reading of the Constitution might suggest. Mexico's masses, on the other hand, wield less power than the Constitution would suggest.

Differences in the blends of repression, co-optation, partnership, and accommodation characterizing relations between the Mexican regime and various groups are essential to the ways the regime pursues political stability. Because of its development model, the regime has more in common with privileged than unprivileged groups. Only rarely, then, would privileged groups act to destabilize the regime. Partnership best characterizes the relationship between privileged groups and the regime, and when disagreement arises it is usually narrow enough to be bridged through accommodation. Regime repression is less frequently contemplated, and the costs would be high, given the power of these groups. The comparative powerlessness of mass groups, by contrast, makes the costs of repression and co-optation much lower. There is a vicious cycle. Mass groups lack power and therefore are vulnerable to regime policies—which make them less powerful. Furthermore, the costs of regime accommodation to independent mass movements would be high, given the grievances they could raise about the development model. If the regime is to get along peacefully with underprivileged mass groups, co-optation is a more suitable relationship than true partnership. As a very general rule, it costs the regime more to repress than to accommodate powerful groups and more to accommodate than to repress less powerful ones.

The stability of stable democratic regimes is generally based on greater equality. For example, the working class is freer in democracies than in Mexico. The democracies' policies are generally more favorable to it, and when disagreements do arise the working class can exercise independent political power. Blatant repression is unlikely, partly because interest conflict does not run that deep, partly because the costs would be high. Elsewhere, political stability may be compatible with great political inequality, but usually with more widespread repression than is found in Mexico. Co-optation is a partial substitute for repression of Mexico's less powerful groups, while partnership and accommodation are substitutes for repression of the more powerful groups.

The Mexican regime has pursued political stability through discriminating behavior patterns. There is one political subsystem for the freer and more powerful groups and a second subsystem for the less fortunate groups. Mexico's political stability has not been incompatible with political inequality; rather, it has rested on pragmatically different relationships based on that inequality. This should not imply that Mexico has two political systems that exist independently of one another. In fact, more powerful Mexico can often mobilize or otherwise use less powerful Mexico politically just as it does economically.[24] But such integration does not generally narrow the power gap between the two systems. Finally, to conclude that it is more appropriate to think of two political systems, rather than one, is not to overlook that more precision could come from a three-, four-, or eight-way discussion, sensitive to differences between, for example, well-organized and unorganized labor, the lower middle class and the upper middle class, and small and big business.

POLITICAL CHANGE

A crucial challenge for the Mexican political system has been the reconciliation of stability and change. Stability, after all, implies some continuity. Yet change may be necessary to prevent continuity from deteriorating into stagnation, ineffectiveness, and ultimately, instability. Many normative values also are frequently associated with political change. Some, such as progressivism and representation of competing ideas, relate principally to *policy* change. Others, such as personnel mobility and protection against extended tyranny, relate principally to *leadership* change. There is obvious overlap between these two types of political change, but the distinction facilitates discussion of the Mexican case. Although leadership change proves to be more compelling and is therefore the object of greater attention here, we explore both types of change and their interrelationships.

Choosing the President

The great political event in Mexico, unrivaled in importance, is presidential selection. Mexico changes its top leader every six years without fail. Much is at stake, especially given the president's power and also given policy variation among administrations. Excitement is heightened by the way in which the selection process is publicized, like a great sporting or gambling event.

Few political events anywhere combine so much interest, even media coverage, with so much secrecy. The coverage is excessive, given the paucity of reliable information. Thus journalists and politicians alike repeatedly denounce *futurismo*, speculation about future political candidates, yet they themselves promote it. Already in 1979, newspaper headlines fequently quoted politicians explaining that it was too early to discuss what they were discussing, the 1982 elections. U.S. citizens may have become upset over their own system, in which more than a year passes with attention riveted on the presidential campaign; Mexico's gestation period is much longer. And it is more secret, less openly competitive. Futurismo diverts attention from present-day policy problems.

Futurism can be quite puzzling, as politicians play subtle games, sometimes through the media. Governor Rubén Figueroa of Guerrero suggested to the press in 1979 that Emilio Múgica Montoya would make a fine president. Any such "nomination" is "bad form," a blow to the nominee's chances, if he ever had any. When a journalist therefore asked Figueroa why he had spoken publicly, Figueroa responded cryptically that he had his reasons, that "politics is a scientific art that not everyone understands. If you understood it you wouldn't be a journalist but a governor, at least a senator. Well, the truth is that there are several messages, but I will not tell you them. You, the journalists, who are always bragging about your political expertise, should have sufficient talent to decipher them."[25] In sum, there is implicit disdain not only for the press but also for the public in the way that the nation's most important political event is handled. No single political event in Mexico provides more empty news.

Incumbent presidents are the most important figures in appointing their successors, although it is uncertain how much they consult or even negotiate with their inner circles or with interest groups. Mexico's best-known scholar of sexenio politics sardonically dismissed claims of U.S. scholars to have discerned further rules.[26] The interior minister has been selected frequently, but by no means automatically. The closed nature of the selection process is reflected in words like *tapadismo* (the process of keeping the nominee under wraps or hidden, until formally "uncovered" to the public) by the *gran dedo* (the great finger). The PRI's *tapado* always wins the general election. Certain parallels might be made with the way U.S. *vice*-presidential candidates are chosen by the presidential nominee. The gran dedo is the U.S. presidential candidate, choosing a vice-presidential tapado; he makes his decision in varying consultation with power brokers; factual secrecy is combined with wild excitement and speculation; public campaigning by U.S. vice-presidential candidates is considered bad form; the tapado will be the convention's vice-presidential choice, even though the convention could theoretically nominate a different running mate.

Echeverría spurred speculation about making Mexico's selection process less secretive. He discussed the process more openly than had any of his predecessors. Through a spokesman, he revealed in April 1975 the names of seven possible candidates, inviting an open evaluation of them. The press, he said, should investigate their personal fortunes and behavior. Others should comment on the candidate's qualifications. Some did. The right, for example, probably communicated its preference for Mario Moya Palencia or Hugo Cervantes del Río and its disapproval of Porfirio Muñoz Ledo, Gómez Villanueva, or Gálvez Betancourt. But such communications were nothing new, and most were still made privately. Representatives of private enterprise (as well as those of the United States, for that matter) repeatedly declared publicly that they would not interfere in any way whatsoever. And, if the Echeverría–López Portillo transition suggested some modification of the secrecy surrounding tapadismo, the López Portillo–de la Madrid transaction reversed the process. Typically cryptic preference signals from several groups hardly filled the information gap left by the tight silence of the front-running candidates right up until de la Madrid was selected. López Portillo issued no "short list" for public reaction. In fact, he "sprung" his decision early, perhaps to short-circuit any building interest-group pressures, perhaps to begin sharing the burdens of economic crisis, perhaps to reassure business interests (thereby slowing capital flight), perhaps to detract attention from leftist attempts to form a coalition, perhaps to show personal decisiveness, perhaps partly to avoid appearing too predictable. Speculation is easy, definitive answers impossible. Ironically, whereas Echeverría had opened the process a little bit and then selected a dark horse, López Portillo kept the process tightly closed and then made a much more predictable choice.

The secretiveness of the selection process obviously limits our understanding of it. But that very secretiveness is suggestive. It shows, for example, that public opinion does not play a central role. Mexico's most important leadership change is not based on a public dialogue concerning either policy issues or even competing aspirants. No matter how obscure the details, at least one important result of the selection process is clear—its contribution to political stability. (Of course, the process is also a reflection of that stability.) Among the factors that we will consider are the certainty about the timing and wide range of leadership change, the ample opportunities available within the system, the periodic renewal of hope, the periodic policy adjustments, and the subordination of policy considerations.

Continuismo

Continuing in office beyond one's legally prescribed term (continuismo) has been frequent in Latin American politics. Instability often results at these times, as incumbents face challenges from aspirants suffering the denial of legality or opportunity. Mexico, however, has overcome the problem. First, the revolution brought the principle of "free suffrage, no reelection."[27] There were attempts, in the early years, to defy the principle or to circumvent it—and leadership transitions were generally violent. Since 1935, however, when President Cárdenas turned back his predecessor Calles's attempt at maintaining power, continuismo has not been a major problem. If an ex-president holds political office, it is likely to be some relatively minor position, not a leadership post. Ex-presidents are neither generally seen in important places nor heard on important issues. The new president assumes a strong hand. Many have attributed the stability of the political system largely to the concentration of legitimate authority in the hands of its leadership.

If the principle of orderly and significant leadership change recently needed reaffirmation, López Portillo provided it. Many factors suggested some effort by Echeverría to perpetuate his own power—not actually to stay in office, of course, but to influence his successor. Of the seven possible candidates presented to the public, López Portillo was considered among the least likely. Perhaps as president, the relatively unknown López Portillo would therefore owe a special debt to Echeverría. Furthermore, López Portillo lacked his own strong personal following, a cadre of loyalists who could immediately dominate a new administration. Echeverría, by contrast, had been a energetic president, developing a strong personal following and trying to mold a long-range PRI program. In addition, he had economic holdings in the press and television and a claim to mass support based on progressive policies. Moreover, Echeverría was what his supporters might call a crusader, his detractors a fanatic; all would call him ambitious. Finally, he and his successor had been friends since childhood.

Yet López Portillo immediately established his independence, appointing many of his own associates and promoting the trend to elevate more *técnicos* (technical experts) over *políticos* (politicians)—and reversing some of his predecessor's policies. Echeverría consecutively became ambassador-at-large, representative to the United Nations Educational, Scientific and Cultural Organization (UNESCO), ambassador to Australia, and director of his own Institute of Third World Studies. Ex-presidents are suitable as ambassadors because ambassadors merely carry out presidential policy and because they are kept outside Mexico. By the time Echeverría returned home in 1979 he was greeted by headlines, perhaps purposeful, perhaps gratuitous or even vindictive, proclaiming his inability to influence the 1982 elections.[28]

Sharing Opportunity

By restricting the time span of one administration, the political system leaves open the way for another. Sexennial (six-year) change involves the presidency, first and foremost, but it also involves widespread turnover. Most stable political systems combine change at the top with continuity below; Mexican officials come and go in groups, although individuals may reappear in new positions. A typical sexenio may draw on the previous one for roughly 20 percent of its important personnel and on the two before that for 15 percent more, therefore counting mostly on new faces.[29] Nor is turnover restricted to six-year intervals. Few in López Portillo's cabinet at the beginning were in the same place at the end.

Lack of peaceful elite circulation contributed to violent power transfers in nineteenth-century Latin America, and certainly to the rebellion against Porfirio Díaz in Mexico. For all the parallels that may be drawn between the porfiriato and the present regime, this difference is crucial. A major contributing factor to political stability since 1929 has been political opportunity born of elite circulation. Aspirants to power need not change the system when they have reasonable chances for upward mobility within it. Another major difference is that there is no single power elite today as there was before the revolution. Instead, the political and economic elites are relatively distinctive. This gives the political system some autonomy to make the effective decisions that buttress its own stability, and it opens two relatively *separate* routes to advancement.[30]

The circulation of political elites provides opportunities not just for power but also for personal profit, as such opportunities are available to holders of Mexican political office. Naturally, corruption is a tricky matter to analyze. Governments do not publish data on the subject. There do seem to be unwritten rules on permissible corruption, however, in terms of both amounts and methods. Some administrations, such as Alemán's, earn reputations for excessive greed, others, such as Ruiz Cortines's, for unusual integrity. Corruption is also difficult to assess because no fine line distinguishes it from legitimate politics. Most corruption comes not from blatantly taking money out of public coffers but from peddling influence. Awarding public contracts to firms in which one has a personal interest is a typical method.

As we saw in Chapter 3, one factor contributing to corruption is that political actors need flexibility to see their demands gratified within an otherwise rigid bureaucracy. Another possible factor is the relatively small number of trained, professional civil servants, as opposed to political appointees. Yet another is the inadequate salaries of bureaucrats. Of course, the expectation of corrupt income can then become a rationale for inadequate salaries. Besides, there is always sheer greed. Whatever the causes of corruption, the personalistic nature of Mexican politics promotes it, and once corruption pervades a system, it feeds on itself.

Mexicans adopt all sorts of judgments on official corruption. Some will not begrudge one ex-president his houses in Acapulco, Cuernavaca, indeed "everywhere in the world," because "at least he invests in Mexico," while another ex-president is berated for allegedly investing most of his money outside Mexico. Some Mexicans excuse officials who steal if, at least, they also "do things." But there is increasing concern over corruption and continual discussion of curbing it. López Portillo declared an official attack on corruption, and although this would not be the first publicized anticorruption campaign, and although there are conflicting views of its profundity, some important officials have been disciplined. Sometimes, however, the battle against corruption is also a tool for political jockeying. The arrest of Echeverría's last minister of agrarian reform was widely seen as a slap at the ex-president. And the right has often attacked bureaucratic corruption in order to discredit the public sector in general.

Even if it proves technically feasible, diminishing Mexico's widespread corruption could actually undermine political stability. Aspirants to political office now peacefully await their turn at corruption as well as power. Leaders who have taken care of themselves are more likely to leave office satisfied than to plot comebacks. And corruption decreases the chances of serious attempts at radical policy change insofar as political leaders have to work their way up by playing skillfully within the system as it is. If everyone is hostage, no one can rock the boat with impunity. Thus de la Madrid undertook a supremely difficult task when he dedicated his new administration to a frontal attack on corruption and to the "moral renovation" of society. Perhaps his two major assets, beyond the commitment of his strong public rhetoric on this subject, are his own reputation for integrity and his comparatively few political debts to various interest groups.

System Renewal and Policy Change

As leadership change promotes stability by offering opportunities to aspiring elites, it also promotes stability by providing hope for policy change to the nation as a whole. As one observer put it: "We Mexicans are given to live on hope, since we lack a good reality."[31] Sexennial change appears so dramatic that it offers new promise, partly by blaming present woes on the *last* leaders. Of course, continually frustrated hopes frequently turn to cynicism, but leadership change does promote system renewal.

Echeverría could disassociate himself from Díaz Ordaz's repression, even though he had been his right-hand man as interior minister. López Portillo was Echeverría's last finance secretary but that did not stop him, as president, from disassociating himself from his former boss's economic policies. More important, Echeverría himself helped out, intentionally or not, by devaluing the peso before leaving office, thus saving the incoming president a politically onerous but necessary task. President-designate López Portillo lost no time making it clear that the consequences of devaluation were Echeverría's responsibility. He could subsequently justify his conservative presidential policies as necessary to put the house back in order. The idea was that irresponsibility and inefficiency had left Mexico in a position in which major reforms or even salary maintenance was impossible. Disassociation from his predecessor also let the new president wipe the slate clean and court key groups alienated by Echeverría. One of López Portillo's early actions was to meet, dine, and be photographed with the Monterrey Group in order to reassure the business community and, in turn, to secure its pledge to invest heavily during the ensuing years. The changeover itself seemed to revitalize a shaky Mexico. The peso began to recover, peasants in various parts of the country agreed to postpone disruptive actions, and industrial and agricultural producers, like foreign investors, were reassured and reassuring.[32] The new president would have his honeymoon period. Without the prospect of *institutionalized renewal*, the Mexican political system might have had more difficulty surviving the crises of Echeverría's tenure. Another severe test of the ability of sexennial change to revitalize the system came with the 1982 López Portillo–de la Madrid transition amid renewed economic crisis. The fact that so many politically unpleasant responses (e.g., repeated devaluations and cuts in subsidies to consumers) to the economic crisis were made while López Portillo was still president would help de la Madrid to assume office in December 1982 without having to initiate those decisions. As López Portillo did with the economic crisis of 1976, de la Madrid could defend further unpleasant policies as necessary to combat an inherited crisis.

More than just hope or symbolism is involved. As the Echeverría–López Portillo transition shows, renewal may encompass real policy changes. There is even a "pendulum" theory that sexennial politics involves swings between left and right, giving each side a chance. Outgoing presidents restrain themselves, or are restrained by others, from appointing like-minded successors, instead fulfilling an unwritten obligation to system renewal and stability. The theory has some validity, but it is exaggerated. Policy variation occurs from the left to the right only *within the establishment*, not over the entire political spectrum. Nor has the pendulum swung each time from one extreme to the other even within establishment limits. Another pendulum theory postulates swings between activists and consolidators. After activists shake things up a bit, consolidators placate consequently alienated groups, insuring that political change will not endanger system stability.[33] Of course, this pendulum theory does not rule out incidents of ideological policy change.

Whatever its contours, policy change across administrations probably has less to do with a president's personal inclinations than with the system's needs. Labor Minister López Mateos had earned a reputation for liberalism and compromise, but President López Mateos, concerned over increased unrest, repressed labor. Minister Echeverría earned his reputation as a hard-liner tolerating little dissent, but President Echeverría, seeing the system's legitimacy in question after 1968, was relatively tolerant. Policy also changes within administrations because of similar factors. The Echeverría administration, by necessity at least as much as choice, pushed less actively for reform during the second half of its tenure than it had during the first. Thus, a new president's personal political background does not necessarily presage his policies, and even when outgoing presidents (e.g., Díaz Ordaz) try to choose like-minded successors (e.g., Echeverría), the pendulum may swing.[34] In this light, President de la Madrid's politics cannot safely be predicted. Because of his personal background, he is widely expected to follow López Portillo's conservative economic policies. Indeed, beyond being Mexico's first president to hold an advanced degree (a master's degree from Harvard in public administration) from the United States, de la Madrid had worked in the Bank of Mexico and the treasury ministry before heading the Ministry of Programming and Budget. Like López Portillo and unlike most of their predecessors, de la Madrid came up through the technical, not the political, ranks, which helps explain the apparent consternation within sectors of the PRI itself over his selection as president. Notwithstanding his own record, however, de la Madrid could choose to disassociate himself from some of his predecessor's policies and their deleterious social and economic effects.[35] Moreover, he would be constrained to shape his initial policies so as to confront the pressing economic difficulties he inherited.

Policy change across and within sexenios is limited by the system's subordination of policy to personnel politics. For example, leadership change is so extensive that many officeholders are inexperienced. It often takes some time before new administrations get under way.[36] Additionally, incumbent "lame ducks" often lose some power in some areas during their last year in office, once everyone knows who the next president will be. On the other hand, an outgoing executive may feel free of interest-group pressures and take bold actions. In 1982, López Portillo devalued the peso, as Echeverría had done in his last year in office. In fact, it is frequently difficult to determine the point at which the president-elect may become more powerful than the incumbent, or how much is decided through consultation. For example, considerable speculation surrounded de la Madrid's role in the September 1982 decision, forcefully proclaimed by President López Portillo, to take over Mexico's private banks. Whatever the degree of power transfer prior to the official end of any presidential term, power surely passes from individual to individual, sooner or later. The point is that, on the whole, the political compromises on which the system rests simultaneously maximize the extent of personnel change and may limit the extent or impact of policy initiative and change.

Personnel and Policy Compromises

That personnel change is more extensive than policy change does not necessarily mean that it is more important to political stability;

scholars have debated the relative importance of compromises based on shared opportunities and compromises based on issues. In fact, however, these are not mutually exclusive possibilities, and leadership change is designed to bring some policy change. Even so, the politics of leadership change demand that policy considerations be carefully circumscribed. *Personnel coalesce and advance mostly on nonpolicy criteria. Camarillas* are crucial. These are cliques built around central political figures, *not* policies. Members must pledge their first loyalty to the leader, not to whatever ideology they themselves may hold.

Loyalty provides organizational glue, and for good reason: Most political officeholders, even at lower levels, owe their jobs to someone. An individual's mobility depends on his camarilla. Here then is a critical link to the issue of elite circulation. One maintains loyalty to his camarilla and waits for it to get its chance. If the leader moves up, the group is likely to go with him. Camarillas clearly are based on hierarchy, on vertical relationships. An *Agachados* cartoon (October 29, 1975) depicts a puzzled peasant asking his impoverished friend why he personally congratulated López Portillo on his selection as PRI candidate, when the friend did not even know him. "Well, so he'd throw me a bone and in a year I'd stop being poor." Personal connections are important in politics almost anywhere; they are especially important in Mexico.[37]

Mobility is based on skillful bargaining and exchanging favors. It is not based on genuine and popular public policy records. Such appeals might in fact brand the politician as unreliable. The importance of personnel bargaining has even led to a reassessment of the traditional view that Mexican stability is based on strong institutions.[38] On the other hand, personnel mobility occurs within a well-developed set of structures and rules, and one does not get to the top in politics through uninstitutionalized routes. Suffice it to say here that Mexico's stability is based partly on institutions that facilitate the compromises, concerning policy and especially personnel, on which stability surely rests.

PLURALISM AND AUTHORITARIANISM

The Mexican political system has been extraordinarily stable. There is no serious disagreement about that. But whether that stability has coexisted with democracy or with authoritarianism has been hotly debated. Less provocatively and more profitably put, the issue is really a matter of degree. Prior to the late 1960s, most major works emphasized the system's democratic inclinations. If Mexico was not yet democratic, it was evolving in that direction. Subsequent works, however, began to depict ostensibly democratic inclinations as but the trappings of a fundamentally authoritarian system. It now seems appropriate to offer a different interpretation, rejecting some important tenets of the authoritarian interpretation while affirming that it has come much closer to the mark than has the democratic interpretation.[39]

The Mexican political system is not democratic insofar as leadership change is not effected through a free, competitive process, and this, if we use but two categories, makes it authoritarian. But we have seen that there are great differences in political freedoms among "nondemocracies." Variation is necessarily great in a category that encompasses most of the world's systems. Only Colombia, Costa Rica, and Venezuela, among the twenty republics of Latin America (excluding most of the Caribbean), might reasonably be said to fit in the democratic more than in the authoritarian category for most of the 1970s and early 1980s. All authoritarian systems place limits on pluralism, participation, and mobilization, but they differ significantly in the extent of these limits. Moreover, they differ significantly in terms of repressiveness, human rights and freedoms, political equality, political mobility, civilian-military balances—in short, on most important aspects of politics. Even in the electoral process, where the authoritarian label for Mexico has been much more apt, recent reforms offer the possibility of increased competition and choice.

Recognizing the breadth and consequent imprecision of the authoritarian category, scholars increasingly tied Mexico to the mode of authoritarianism found in most of Latin America's relatively developed nations. A key feature of this authoritarianism is the regime's ability to dictate its will, regardless of, or even against, the will of once powerful political groups.[40] With that goes the political exclusion of many groups and the widespread and intense repression of their political freedoms.[41] Another feature is extended rule (usually military) with little or no provision for regular changes of political leadership.

Fortunately, however, the tendency to overidentify Mexico with such authoritarianism now appears to be waning.[42] The previously cited distinction between "state" and "regime" is helpful here. State "pacts of domination" favoring capitalist-dependent development and benefiting the upper bourgeoisie and industrial and urban interests—to the detriment of popular (especially rural) interests—may not be that different in Mexico, Chile, and Venezuela; nonetheless, the political regimes are fundamentally different. While those who see "who gets what" as the core of politics may emphasize fundamental similarities among states, those who also care about degrees of political freedom, human rights, participation, inclusiveness, civilian rule, regularized political change, and blatant repression may emphasize fundamental differences among regimes. The Mexican state has more in common with the Chilean and Venezuelan states than the Mexican regime has with their regimes.

Just as the breadth of the term "authoritarian" poses analytical problems, so does the restrictiveness of the term "democracy." Granted that Mexico is not democratic, the relevant question becomes the extent to which it is "pluralist."[43] Pluralist systems may or may not be democratic, but they require distribution of power and freedom of political action beyond the central government officials. Pluralist policymaking and leadership selection depend largely on the demands and interests of various groups, on bargaining and conciliation among them.

Although no single, simple characterization of Mexican politics emerges, *our analysis of political freedom, political equality, and political change suggests mixed and variable patterns of authoritarianism and pluralism.* It also shows how the Mexican political system has struck its own balances, neither typically authoritarian nor pluralist, in reconciling stability with freedom, equality, and change. Thus, this chapter concludes by summarizing its analysis of central paradoxes in Mexican politics.

There is a complex, subtle, variable, and imperfectly defined degree of *political freedom* in Mexico. Imprecision stems not just from the difficulty of figuring out where the dividing line between freedom and repression lies. It stems also from actual variability. Two similar challenges may evoke two different responses. Some independent newspapers or squatter settlements or demonstrations may be repressed while equally independent ones may be tolerated. It is presumptuous to interpret specific cases of repression or tolerance as proof that either always occurs under certain given circumstances. All we can establish are probabilities and patterns. Thus we have considered variables such as individual expression versus organizational activity, the nature and source of criticisms, the size and composition of the participating groups, the specific issues involved, and the posture of given national and state administrations. The individual versus organizational dimension has received the greatest attention. Comparisons of freedoms with major (e.g., electoral), limited (e.g., religious), and intermediate (e.g., media) organizational bases show respectively limited, major, and intermediate ranges of freedom. To formulate the issue in a rational calculation: The regime permits freedom and dissent up to the point at which tolerance causes it less trouble than repression, and that point is different for different freedoms. Moreover, different officials see different dividing points. Of course, judgments are not always rational, let alone precise. Personalities and emotions make the picture less predictable.

Political freedom in Mexico clearly falls short of pluralism, let alone democracy, because of severe restrictions on organizational freedoms. But most personal freedoms are not simply tolerated; they fall logically within a system that is as "open" as it is "closed." Compared to most authoritarian systems in Latin America, Mexico allows more latitude even for organizationally oriented freedoms, but especially for individually oriented freedoms.

The Mexican regime obviously runs the risk that the considerable freedom and dissent it allows may undermine its stability. Thus, it responds in repressively authoritarian kind when it perceives itself threatened. That it does not feel threatened by many freedoms, however, means that it need not maintain ceaseless vigil or repression to maintain stability. It does not incur the costs of repression for that dissent which does not really pose an organizational alternative. Furthermore, Mexican freedoms have actually buttressed stability by enhancing the regime's image, legitimacy, and support base.

In terms of *political equality*, both freedom and power vary notably according to socioeconomic status. The personal freedoms cited above are exercised far more in privileged than in humble Mexico, while restrictions on independent organization apply far more to humble than to privileged Mexico. Pluralism better than authoritarianism characterizes the political subsystem for privileged Mexico. The regime responds to interest-group demands more than it molds or controls them. Or it refrains from making policy that would offend powerful interests, that is, it makes "nondecisions." Examples include not imposing tougher taxes on business and not imposing tuition at the public universities. The regime is not an omnipotent center of power or policy initiative and it does not select or control group leadership. Indeed, these groups are relatively autonomous of the government. In sum, there are plural centers of power.

Authoritarianism better characterizes the political subsystem for less privileged Mexico. The regime generally initiates policy, bringing affected groups into the policy process only for legitimizing support. Nondecisions in this subsystem usually concern issues on which potentially affected groups would like to see action but on which the regime prefers not to act; examples would include a much stronger government role in economic production and a radical reorganization of rural opportunities. Leaders of the less privileged groups are tied more to the regime, less to their constituencies. Of course, important qualifications could properly be made for both the pluralist and authoritarian subsystem characterizations, but far fewer than if either characterization were generalized to the system as a whole.

Surely, continual discrimination against the less privileged, especially as relative deprivation increases, poses a threat to political stability. Nonetheless, for decades that threat has not materialized. In fact, the discrimination, whatever else one thinks of it, probably has promoted stability. Because the system assumes only a minimal burden for the less privileged, resources are left for the privileged, who are not constrained to share either their political power or economic well-being. And whatever the threat of popular revolution by less privileged groups, Latin American regimes more often fall to revolts inspired by privileged groups—often fearing the rise of those less privileged groups that, in Mexico, are kept in place. If Mexican business, for example, had less power within the system than it does, it might well oppose the system more strongly. Furthermore, by satisfying the demands of more privileged Mexico, the regime generally needs to incur the costs of repression only in dealing with less privileged Mexico, where, almost by definition, the costs are lower.

That *political change* is carefully and secretively controlled by a small elite mocks not only democratic but also pluralist criteria. Groups do not bargain openly over policies and candidates. Yet neither does political change follow patterns typical of authoritarian Latin America. It involves more contact with the populace, even if elections ratify more than they determine. More important, group interests are taken into account in changing both personnel and policy. Mexico's process is more regularized, yet more flexible. It is a civilian, not a military process, and it systematically allows for more personnel and even policy change. Turnover is not only greater but also smoother than it is in most authoritarian systems.[44]

Mexico has found its own solution for reconciling political change with political stability. Pluralist democracies generally meet this challenge through regular, competitive elections, based at least partly on public policy issues. Dictatorships generally have more difficulty with leadership changes. This applies not only to the Third World; communist systems too have notorious problems with orderly succession. Latin America has long suffered from continuismo and from instability, and many of the region's recent military governments have tried to forestall instability by proclaiming their intentions of ruling unchallenged for long terms. These intentions are backed by force, often leaving few opportunities for peaceful policy change through leadership change.

By contrast, political change in Mexico has promoted political stability. Orderly rules have become institutionalized. There is little room for disruptive conflict over the timing of leadership change or for challenges by incumbents to the new leadership's policymaking authority. Regular and extensive turnover provides widespread opportunities for power and wealth, encouraging ambitious Mexicans to compete peacefully *within* the system. The system, in turn, can purge itself peacefully of the potentially destabilizing excesses born of leaders' unlimited tenure. Leadership change provides a fresh start, partly by supplying scapegoats for ongoing policy problems. It also provides real opportunities for policy adjustments based on the system's varying needs—unburdened by accountability to the populace according to *its* perception of needs. Symbolic and psychological as well as policy renewal are thus provided within the system. Yet the potentially volatile politics of policy are subordinated to the carefully monitored politics of personnel. By restricting the role of policy choice, openness, and public accountability in leadership change, the system protects itself against victory from within by any proponent of radical policy changes in the system. The system has not, therefore, fallen under leadership that would promulgate policies considered populist, leftist, irrational, or irresponsible enough either to change the system fundamentally or to provoke a harshly authoritarian backlash takeover to prevent such change. Foregoing a more truly pluralist process, the regime has also avoided the politics that sometimes help produce political regimes far more authoritarian than Mexico's.

So to call Mexico's political system authoritarian is accurate, but only in such a broad and vague way as to risk misleading characterizations. The same could be said of a pluralist identification. Extensive pluralist freedoms coexist with significant authoritarian restrictions in more sensitive areas. Pluralist dispersion of power in a subsystem for more privileged Mexico coexists with authoritarian concentration of regime power in a subsystem for less privileged Mexico. Pluralist compromises in effecting political leadership and policy change coexist with authoritarian denial of public influence and accountability. The Mexican political system is neither authoritarian nor pluralist—because it is both.

The very complexity of Mexico's hybrid authoritarian-pluralist political system, defying any single inclusive characterization, has a good deal to do with its extraordinary stability.[45] Stability is based on neither authoritarianism nor pluralism alone. Nor is it even fundamentally based on authoritarianism, allowing for mere pluralist trappings or marginal features, or on pluralism, allowing for authoritarian imperfections. It misses the mark to say that Mexico's political stability has been achieved *despite* significant political freedom and dissent or despite repression, despite the relative autonomy and power of privileged groups or despite political inequality, despite extensive leadership change, or despite the limited scope of policy change. All these factors, and the complex interplay among them, have in some identifiable ways actually promoted stability.

NOTES

1. Daniel Cosío Villegas, *American Extremes*, trans. Américo Paredes (Austin: University of Texas Press, 1964), p. 93.

2. The reforms of the 1970s in the party and electoral systems might qualify this assessment.

3. Our account draws on Miguel Angel Granados Chapa, "La democracia en la calle," *Razones* 19/22 (September-October 1980):10–12, and the editorial in the same issue.

4. Thomas E. Weil et al., *Area Handbook for Mexico* (Washington, D.C.: Government Printing Office, 1975), pp. 244–249.

5. For more details on the media, see the chapter on censorship and the media in a forthcoming book by Roderic Camp, *Intellectuals and the State in Mexico.* Also see Evelyn Stevens, *Protest and Response in Mexico* (Cambridge, Mass.: M.I.T. Press, 1974), pp. 12–13. For a comparative view see Marvin Alisky, *Latin American Media: Guidance and Censorship* (Ames: Iowa State University Press, 1981).

6. Weil et al., *Area Handbook for Mexico,* p. 254.

7. Charles Tatum, "Rius: Comic Book Writer as Social Critic and Political Gadfly," paper presented at the Sixth Conference of Mexican and U.S. Historians, Chicago, September 1981. Also see Alan Riding, "Humorist Tickles Mexico While Tweaking Official Noses," *New York Times,* August 19, 1979.

8. We are thinking here even of the better reports, such as José Ureña's "Escándalo panista," *Uno Más Uno,* December 5, 1979.

9. This is the distinction elaborated by Fernando Henrique Cardoso, "On the Characterization of Authoritarian Regimes in Latin America," in *The New Authoritarianism in Latin America,* ed. David Collier (Princeton, N.J.: Princeton University Press, 1979), pp. 33–60.

10. Kenneth F. Johnson, *Mexican Democracy: A Critical View,* rev. ed. (New York: Praeger Publishers, 1978), pp. 156–171. A recent study of press freedom has ranked Mexico in the top four (in both 1970 and 1975) among twenty Latin American republics. Kim Quaile Hill and Patricia A. Hurley, "Freedom of the Press in Latin America: A Thirty-Year Survey," *Latin American Research Review* 15, no. 2 (1980):212–218.

11. Our account of the *ABC* episode is based mostly on Carlos Monsiváis, "El ABC de Tijuana," *Proceso,* no. 164, December 24, 1979.

12. It is difficult to be sure about all the details in a sensitive case involving conflicting claims and considerable maneuvering and secrecy, but our principal sources are good ones, supported by our numerous conversations with other involved parties. The principal sources are Armando Vargas, "Coup at Excélsior," *Columbia Journalism Review* 15, no. 3 (1967):45–48; Vicente Leñero, *Los periodistas* (Mexico City: Editorial Joaquín Mortiz, 1978); Alan Riding, "Mexico: Reinstating Editor Ousted by Former Regime," *New York Times,* May 14, 1977; other Riding articles in the *Times* and written correspondence with Riding, winter 1980; "Mexico: The Right to Edit a Paper," *Latin American Political Report* 10, no. 29 (1976):2229–2231. Our analysis focuses on the regime-*Excélsior* confrontation. As we mentioned, however, a private sector-*Excélsior* confrontation also occurred, starting before the regime itself attacked *Excélsior.* The role of U.S. subsidiaries in Mexico was especially noteworthy. For this aspect of the *Excélsior* case see Angela M. Delli Sante, "The Private Sector, Business Organizations, and In-

ternational Influence: A Case Study of Mexico," in *Capitalism and the State in U.S.–Latin American Relations*, ed. Richard R. Fagen (Stanford, Calif.: Stanford University Press, 1979), pp. 370–377.

13. Johnson, *Mexican Democracy*, p. 54.

14. López Portillo, inevitably concerned with criticisms of his conservatism, reacted angrily when some journalists seized the 1979 midpoint in his administration as an opportunity to give midterm report cards. Although virtually all gave high marks on many counts, some hinted very strongly that his administration was rightist. "Unfair: I am not moving to the right," headlines featured the president's denial. "It offends my consciousness as a committed Mexican revolutionary to argue that I protect businessmen and therefore that I lean toward the right."

15. *Excélsior* did still have some good columnists and, after a few more years, even some relatively independent ones.

16. Quoted in Leñero, *Los periodistas*, p. 232.

17. Although Scherer was angry at *Times* columnist Alan Riding, Riding claimed that Scherer had approved the story.

18. We draw the quote and details from Alan Riding, "Mexico, Crushing a Maverick," *New York Times*, March 19, 1981.

19. Rose J. Spalding, "State Power and Its Limits: Corporatism in Mexico," *Comparative Political Studies* 14, no. 2 (1981):149, 150–151. For further reading on bureaucrats, see the work of Merilee Grindle and Roderic Camp. For example, Grindle's "Power, Expertise and the 'Técnico': Suggestions from a Mexican Case Study," *Journal of Politics* 39, no. 2 (1977):399–426; and Camp's "The Middle-Level Technocrat in Mexico," *Journal of Developing Areas* 6, no. 4 (July 1972): 571–582.

20. The summary of university, student, and middle-class power comes from Daniel Levy, *University and Government in Mexico: Autonomy in an Authoritarian System* (New York: Praeger Publishers, 1980), pp. 16–17, 43–63, 138–154.

21. Lorenzo Meyer, "Historical Roots of the Authoritarian State in Mexico," in *Authoritarianism in Mexico*, ed. José Luis Reyna and Richard Weinert (Philadelphia, Pa.: Institute for the Study of Human Issues, 1977), p. 8.

22. See, for example, Charles E. Lindblom, *Politics and Markets* (New York: Basic Books, 1977), pp. 170–188. Specifically on Mexico, see, for example, Robert Shafer, *Mexican Business Organizations* (Syracuse, N.Y.: Syracuse University Press, 1973).

23. Dale Story, "Entrepreneurs and the State in Mexico: Examining the Authoritarian Thesis," Technical Papers Series no. 30, Institute of Latin American Studies, University of Texas, Austin, 1980, p. 2 and passim. Also see Susan Kaufman Purcell's account of how regime autonomy and business privilege sometimes blend, "Business-Government Relations in Mexico: The Case of the Sugar Industry," *Comparative Politics* 13, no. 2 (1981):211–232.

24. Larissa Lomnitz has shown how many of the urban poor or "marginals" (urban "hunters and gatherers"), by offering cheap and ready labor, may actually buttress the position of privileged Mexico. *Networks and Marginality: Life in a Mexican Shantytown* (New York: Academic Press, 1977), p. 208 and passim.

25. Quoted in Ignacio Ramírez, "No me lancé por amor," *Proceso*, no. 163, December 17, 1979.

26. Daniel Cosío Villegas, *La sucesión presidencial: Desenlace y perspectivas* (Mexico City: Cuadernos de Joaquín Mortiz, 1975), pp. 9–36.

27. The proscription of reelection is of interest primarily for political systems plagued by continuismo, but the idea of a single-term, six-year presidency has attracted considerable interest in the United States. Some recent presidents, most forcefully Lyndon Johnson, have spoken in favor of it. Despite the dangers of diminished accountability, the hope is that the president could more often place the national interest above personal political interest. López Portillo himself was not bashful in recommending the Mexican model to others who might likewise look beyond petty politics to substantive policymaking and to history. "No recomiendo reformas," *Excélsior*, December 4, 1979. Yet Mexico may not serve as a good model of decisive, rational policymaking.

28. See Froylan M. López Narváez, "El retorno de Echeverría," *Proceso*, no. 163, December 17, 1979. Echeverría became more visible again in 1981, writing newspaper and magazine articles, and official spokesmen again reacted by saying that Echeverría had had his chance—and had not done too well with it.

29. Peter Smith, *Labyrinths of Power: Political Recruitment in Twentieth Century Mexico* (Princeton, N.J.: Princeton University Press, 1979), p. 165. Roderic Camp has written extensively on political socialization, recruitment, and mobility in Mexico. His most recently published book is *Mexico's Leaders: Their Education and Recruitment* (Tucson: University of Arizona Press, 1980).

30. Smith, *Labyrinths of Power*, pp. 191–216. However much these routes to top positions have opened for men, they have not significantly opened for women. Women in high political office remain a decided rarity.

31. Leopoldo Mendívil, "Lo malo es dejar de trabajar en el presente," *Impacto*, no. 1553 (1979), p. 14.

32. The Echeverría–López Portillo renewal is usually discussed in terms of reassuring business, but the middle class, disturbed over inflation, urban deterioration, and Echeverría's brand of populism, also needed reassurance. Alan Riding, "Middle Class Asks Fair Deal in Mexico," *New York Times*, November 28, 1976.

33. Susan Purcell and John F. H. Purcell, "State and Society in Mexico: Must a Stable Polity be Institutionalized?" *World Politics* 32, no. 2 (1980):194–227.

34. The inability of outgoing presidents to influence their successors was captured twice over in a clever remark attributed to ex-president Díaz Ordaz, asked to give his opinion on outgoing President Echeverría: "He is more intelligent than I am; he knew how to choose his successor."

35. One anecdote circulating before de la Madrid was nominated, and before the economic crisis deepened, may be illustrative. It holds that Díaz Ordaz solved the problem of public opposition but left a problem of political legitimacy, whereupon Echeverría solved the legitimacy problem but left an economic problem, whereupon López Portillo solved the economic problem but left a social problem; hence the next president must solve the social problem.

Although an apparently unlikely choice for the task, de la Madrid has expressed his view that Mexico has already embarked on "a new strategy of development, that is transforming mere economic growth into effective social development." "Medidas de política presupuestaria," *Comercio Exterior* 31, no. 8 (1981):923. The problem is that, unlike the political crisis of 1968 or the economic crises of 1976 and 1982, the social crisis has been chronically characteristic of Mexican development. Also, measures to fight the 1982 economic crisis are likely to aggravate the social crisis.

36. Most new leaders, given the personal more than policy base of allegiance and action, feel compelled to trumpet their own "new" policies. Thus personnel changes may stimulate policy *changes*, but they may also simply mean scuttling predecessors' policies and continually limiting the chances for effective, sustained policy, planning, and implementation. For two recent examples of these problems see Merilee Grindle, *Bureaucrats, Politicians and the Peasantry in Mexico* (Berkeley: University of California Press, 1977), pp. 166–175; and Miguel S. Wionczek, "On the Viability of a Policy for Science and Technology in Mexico," *Latin American Research Review* 16, no. 1 (1981):57–78.

37. Smith, *Labyrinths of Power*, pp. 247–277, formulated twenty-two "rules of the game" for "making it" in Mexican politics, rules that emphasize personnel over policy concerns. Probably both the importance and obscurity of personnel politics are reflected in the special interest that the works of Camp and Smith have generated among Mexico's politicians and political observers. Furthermore, much of what we have said about personnel politics with regard to the presidency and national politics also applies to various other political arenas, from governorships to public university rectorships.

38. Purcell and Purcell, "State and Society," pp. 194–227.

39. For a review essay on the major characterizations, see Lawrence E. Koslow and Stephen P. Murnane, "The Evolution of the Mexican Political System: A Paradigmatic Analysis," in *The Future of Mexico*, ed. Lawrence Koslow (Tempe: Arizona State University Press, 1979), pp. 47–98. For another recent review essay on contemporary politics, see Judith Adler Hellman, "Social Control in Mexico," *Comparative Politics* 12, no. 2 (1980):225–242. Recent works that reject democratic evolutionary hypotheses, or even pluralist ones, while also emphasizing the limits on authoritarianism and regime power include John F. H. Purcell and Susan Kaufman Purcell, "El estado y la empresa privada," *Nueva Política* 1, no. 2 (1976):229–250; Spalding, "State Power"; Story, "Entrepreneurs and the State"; and Levy, *University and Government*. Also see Daniel Levy, "Comparing Authoritarian Regimes in Latin America: Insights from Higher Education Policy," *Comparative Politics* 14, no. 1 (1981):31–52. Reyna and Weinert's *Authoritarianism in Mexico* is now the single most prominently cited example of the authoritarian interpretation.

40. A major issue of scholarly debate has been the degree of presidential power in Mexico. Chapter 3 showed that presidential power is virtually unchallenged within the government; Chapter 4 broadens the assessment by adding that presidential power can be no greater than government power, and therefore the president is not as nearly omnipotent as often portrayed.

41. Our discussion, like most on Mexican authoritarianism, focuses mostly on repression by the government. Other forces, of various political persuasions, also restrict freedom in important instances. It may in fact be argued that political authority and stability are necessary, though insufficient, conditions for freedom.

42. See, for example, most of the references to Mexico in Collier's *New Authoritarianism*.

43. Our definitional juxtaposition of authoritarianism and pluralism (or reconciliation) borrows from Levy, *University and Government*, pp. 8–13.

44. Smith, *Labyrinths of Power*, pp. 182–183.

45. Naturally we want to avoid automatically interpreting every feature found in a stable system as necessarily contributing to stability. For further reading on the political system, see note 39 above, especially Reyna and Weinert's *Authoritarianism in Mexico*. Also see Roger D. Hansen, *The Politics of Mexican Development* (Baltimore: Johns Hopkins University Press, 1971); Johnson, *Mexican Democracy*; Susan Kaufman Purcell, *The Mexican Profit-Sharing Decision: Politics in an Authoritarian Regime* (Berkeley: University of California Press, 1975); Robert Scott, "Mexico," in *Comparative Politics Today*, ed. Gabriel Almond (Boston: Little, Brown and Co., 1974), pp. 366–403.

5

Economic and Social Policy

We have repeatedly stressed the importance of the two-way relationship between Mexico's political stability and its economic growth. In Chapters 3 and 4, we discussed the stability that has contributed to sustained economic growth. This chapter looks at the other side of the relationship. The economic growth experienced during the last several decades has been highly instrumental in bringing about an alliance between the regime and key social groups favored by that process. It has benefited private entrepreneurs for the most part, but it has also touched sectors of the working classes. Partly by providing some opportunities for social mobility, the growth process has assisted the regime in maintaining political stability. This stability has been maintained despite the limited numbers of people who have been able to take advantage of such opportunities. For example, Mexico is characterized by a very uneven profile of income distribution—indeed, one of the world's worst. In this connection, this chapter also examines the social consequences of the growth model.

For decades Mexico achieved rates of high economic growth, coupled with low inflation (below 5 percent annually from the late 1950s through the 1960s), that constituted something of a Latin American economic miracle, paralleling the longer-standing miracle of Mexico's political stability. But closer examination shows the economic record to be mixed. As indicated, growth policies did not address the social problems of widespread poverty and terrible inequalities. Beyond this, economic growth was founded on certain bases that paradoxically contributed to severe economic crises in 1976 and 1982. This chapter tries to analyze the economic successes in such a way as to help explain the social failures and to develop a context within which to understand the economic crises as well.

We focus first on the central features of the economic growth model from 1940 to 1970. While Mexico began to consolidate its political stability in the decades prior to 1940, that year can be considered as the starting point of Mexico's most spectacular period of sustained economic growth. There is wide agreement among experts on the Mexican economy that, throughout the ensuing three decades, the public sector was a major catalyst of economic activity.[1] In particular, the government provided basic infrastructure (e.g., roads and irrigation systems) and policy incentives (e.g., subsidies and protectionism) that have encouraged private investment and supported the growth process. Furthermore, several indicators presented below (e.g., the public sector's accounting today for about one-half of total capital formation) show that there is a very important degree of public involvement in the economy. This situation is rather unusual for a capitalist economy, and it is important to analyze its roots.

Mexico is one of many countries that adopted a strategy of import substitution industrialization (ISI) in the 1940s in order to pursue high rates of economic growth. Many of these countries previously had relied on exports of a few raw materials, using their export revenues to purchase all other products that they needed. The main objective of ISI has been gradually to replace imported products with goods produced locally. Entrepreneurs have been encouraged to concentrate their investments in order to fulfill that objective. The strategy worked well for many years, generating high rates of economic growth. Along with economic growth, however, several problems have emerged. These problems have concerned agricultural and industrial production, the disequilibria of the external sector, and the distribution of new wealth in society. Such problems, if not properly dealt with, may become important constraints on growth. The Echeverría and López Portillo administrations were faced with several of the problems associated with the pursuit of an ISI strategy; we analyze the manner in which their respective administrations attempted to deal with those problems.

This chapter includes several tables with data on Mexico's economic performance from 1940 to 1980. We first use the tables in discussing the 1940 to 1970 period and then, later in the chapter, we refer back to the same tables in discussing economic and social policy under Echeverría and López Portillo. One inescapable qualification is in order concerning the data. Acknowledging problems with the data's reliability, the Mexican government, in cooperation with several international organizations, has engaged in a continuous effort to improve official records. Thus, we can claim only to try to analyze the best *available* data.

THE GROWTH MODEL, 1940-1970

The Mexican economy underwent a fundamental transformation in the period between 1940 and 1970, bringing about a number of no less dramatic changes in the nation's social structure. The average annual rate of growth for the whole period was more than 6 percent, which is comparable to that of only a handful of highly successful economies (e.g., postwar West Germany, Japan, Taiwan, and South Korea). In the process, Mexico turned into a semi-industrial country as people steadily migrated away from rural areas. Agriculture's contribution to total production diminished from 21 percent to 11 percent, while industry's contribution increased from 25 percent to 34 percent. Whereas two-thirds of the labor force was employed in agriculture in 1940, the figure dwindled to only a little more than one-third by 1970.[2] Thus, many people moved to urban areas where they worked in industry and in the service sector.

The engine of economic growth has been an industrialization strategy supported by various governmental policies and institutions. The creation of the Central Bank in 1925, the National Development Bank (NAFINSA) in 1934, and the nationalization of the railroads and the oil industry in the 1930s were all indications that political elites were committed to building a strong public sector that could play an important role in the economy. Government investment expanded the economy's infrastructure and productive capacity. The government also provided private investors with a series of policy incentives. Let us first analyze how (i.e., to what targets) the Mexican government has allocated its investments.

Government Investments

The government has invested much of its resources to facilitate the movement of raw materials and goods throughout the country, thereby helping to integrate the national market. The building of roads, airports, railroads, and ports has improved transportation and communication (both important to the economy) between large and small towns. In addition, the government has invested heavily in agriculture and industry to promote the nation's productive capacity.

Gross fixed capital formation is a common measure of the national commitment to expand infrastructure and productive capacity. It tells us how much of the resources of the public and private sectors is invested to increase production facilities. In Mexico, capital formation has increased steadily, representing only 8.2 percent of gross domestic product (GDP) in 1940, but 18.9 percent between 1965 and 1970. The latter compares well with ratios found in some of the most advanced industrial nations. Table 5.1 shows that the public sector has been very active in this respect, providing more than one-half of total capital formation during the initial years and an average of 40.5 percent during the 1940–1970 period overall. The public sector's share of capital formation fell from 56 to 42 percent during the Alemán administration (1946–1952). It then remained near the new level during most successive administrations. Therefore, this

TABLE 5.1
Gross Fixed Capital Formation, 1941-1980 (in percentages)

Years	Average Share of Gross Domestic Product	Public Sector	Private Sector
1941-1946	8.2	55.5	44.5
1947-1952	13.7	42.1	57.9
1953-1958	17.2	31.6	68.4
1959-1964	16.4	38.9	61.1
1965-1970	18.9	34.3	65.7
1941-1970	14.9	40.5	59.5
1971-1976	20.5	37.5	62.5
1977	20.3	41.0	59.0
1978	21.6	46.0	54.0
1979	23.2	44.0	56.0
1980	25.6	44.3	55.7

Sources: Banco de México, Producto interno bruto y gasto, 1970-1978
(Mexico City, 1979), pp. 43, 49; Nacional Financiera, Statistics on
the Mexican Economy (Mexico City, 1977); and Banco de México, Informe
Anual (Mexico City, various issues).

measure undercuts somewhat the common view that, under President
Alemán, public intervention in the economy was atypically low;[3] rather,
Alemán reduced the public role to what would henceforth be the norm.

Table 5.2 suggests certain tendencies regarding the functional distribution of public investment. Initially, a great proportion of resources
was devoted to improving the communication and transportation systems;
later, the level of investments in these areas stabilized at about 20 percent
of the total. This probably means that many of the facilities that had
been built were not subsequently modernized. As a result, problems have
recently surfaced, revealing inadequate port, rail, and general transportation
capacity. Furthermore, investments in agriculture were unusually high
from 1947 to 1952 because of the great efforts in irrigation. But then
proportional investments in that sector were roughly halved for the
duration of the period in question. This decreasing governmental effort
has been one of several factors contributing to the agricultural output
problems dealt with below.

Industry came to replace both communication/transportation and
agriculture as the most favored recipient of public funds, taking 40 percent
of investment resources from 1965 to 1970. This has reflected the
government's special commitment to industrialization. The bulk of investments in industry has been aimed at securing the supply of various
strategic products such as oil, electric power, and steel.

After years of relative neglect and stagnation, investments in the

TABLE 5.2
Public Sector Investments by Economic Sector, 1941-1980

Year	Total (millions of current pesos)	Percentage of Total					
		Agriculture	Industry	Communications and Transport	Social	Defense and Administration	Unspecified[a]
1941-1946	4,309	15.7	10.2	51.6	12.9	1.8	7.8
1947-1952	14,090	22.0	18.9	40.2	13.3	0.2	5.4
1953-1958	29,673	13.0	30.2	36.3	14.3	3.0	3.2
1959-1964[b]	67,180	10.6	37.5	24.9	24.2	2.8	--
1965-1970	128,439	11.0	40.0	22.0	25.0	2.0	--
1941-1970	243,691	14.5	27.4	35.0	18.0	2.0	--
1971-1976	374,728	15.6	40.0	21.7	19.0	2.8	0.9
1977	140,102	18.5	45.2	19.0	13.8	2.8	0.7
1978	221,700	19.8	59.0	11.0	8.3	1.4	0.6
1979	315,000	20.1	55.0	13.9	9.4	1.3	0.5
1980	465,000	20.6	53.1	16.3	8.6	1.1	0.3

Sources: For 1941 to 1964, Nacional Financiera, 50 años de la revolución mexicana en cifras (Mexico City, 1963), p. 133. For 1965 to 1976, Nacional Financiera, Statistics on the Mexican Economy (Mexico City, 1977), pp. 370-371. For 1977 to 1980, Banco de México, Informe Anual (Mexico City, various issues).

[a]In most cases this category refers to investments to expand tourist facilities.

[b]Figures were available for authorized rather than for actual investments during this period.

social sector (e.g., hospitals, schools) accounted for 25 percent of the total from 1959 to 1970. Finally, the low level of defense-related investments (referred to as "defense and administration" in Table 5.2), averaging only 2 percent between 1940 and 1970, supports our earlier point that the external dimension of national security has not been a major source of concern to civilian leaders. Otherwise—as is the case in many Latin American nations—public investment for the expansion of the military industry would have been greater, putting additional pressure on the finances of the public sector.

Public Revenue Problems and Incentives for the Private Sector

The public sector has been less and less able to finance its investments from its own resources. Starting in the early 1960s, it had to borrow increasingly from creditors (domestic and foreign), because its role in the economy expanded substantially while little was done to secure additional revenue.[4] To be sure, some efforts have been made to increase the public sector's intake of available economic resources. Thus, for example, although the relation of public-sector income to gross domestic product remained stable (at about 10 to 12 percent) between 1940 and 1960, it had increased significantly (to 19 percent) by 1970. However, such an increase was not enough to compensate for the growth of total public-sector expenditures, which rose at a faster pace. By 1970, the ratio of public-sector expenditures to gross domestic product had risen to 24 percent. And these trends have intensified since 1970.[5]

Why have officials done so little to prevent the deterioration of the public sector's financial position? For one thing (in addition to building a relatively adequate infrastructure), the government has showered private investors with several policy incentives. These incentives have included the provision of goods and services at substantially subsidized prices, a low level of taxation, and protection from foreign competitors. Such policies have involved high economic costs, borne by a relatively unremunerated public sector.

The government's generosity in providing these kinds of incentives very likely has reflected the general conception of Mexican society held by many politicians and their advisers. While they have encouraged the development of a strong public sector, their primary objective has been *to support rather than to compete with private investors.* Ironically, many private investors have been very critical of the government's role. Public enterprises are often accused of inefficiency and corruption, and the government is viewed as being responsible for the ills of the economy. More important, private investors fear that the government is becoming too involved in the economy at the expense of the private sector. The figures above may lend some support to these fears. But the government has also gone a long way to facilitate capital accumulation in the private sector, and that sector's position has thus been strengthened.

That government policy has promoted the private sector is also seen in Mexico's taxation and subsidization policies. Mexico's low level of *taxation* can be explained by the fact that its tax system has sought to encourage investments more than to keep the government financially fit. Thus, in order to promote private investment, the government has sacrificed its financial health as well as resources that it could have used for income redistribution purposes. According to Robert Looney, the ratio of tax revenues to gross national product in Mexico at the end of the 1960s was 9.9 percent—one of the lowest in the world.[6] This low ratio was due in part to problems with the tax collection system, but it was also a consequence of the purposes of that system. For example, contrary to the situation prevailing in most countries at a comparable level of development in 1976, Mexican wage earners and professionals together were contributing as much of total government tax revenues as were *all private entrepreneurs*. This shows the remarkable degree of official support for private capital.[7]

Subsidies constitute another way of encouraging private investment. There are no definite figures on the amount of subsidies granted by the government with the specific purpose of supporting private efforts at industrialization; instead, government reports group such subsidies with subsidies to consumers and with other items. According to experts, however, about one-half of total government subsidies are geared to promoting investments. The figures are impressive. The total value of said subsidies rose from 3.7 billion pesos in 1960, to 16 billion in 1970, to 428 billion in 1980![8]

Given these figures, it is not surprising that the government has had to rely increasingly on credit in order to finance some of its own programs. Initially, domestic creditors were the main source of the public sector's borrowing. For example, the public internal debt rose from 7.2 billion pesos in 1960 to 53 billion in 1970.[9] However, in the 1970s the government began borrowing heavily abroad, driving up Mexico's foreign public debt. Of particular concern to us here is the evolution of foreign public debt over the years, especially because a major indicator of the 1976 and 1982 economic crises was the very high level of foreign indebtedness that the public sector had reached by those years. Analysis of the external sector of the economy provides a broader framework within which to assess the characteristics and implications of this issue.

Public Revenue Problems
and the External Sector

The increased degree of dependence on foreign funds is a corollary to the decreasing ability of the public sector to keep its finances in balance. Up to the mid-1950s, the government had financed its activities primarily through its own savings and through domestic credit, but also by simply printing more money. Because many tensions arose from the resulting high inflation, the government resorted gradually to foreign credit as a complementary means of financing its deficits. Thus, it could pursue a policy of domestic price stability for many years. Such a strategy, however, could be expected to show its own adverse effects in the long run. There is a limit to financing economic growth through foreign credit, just as there is a limit to excessive printing of money.

It should be noted that resorting to foreign credit is not wrong in itself. If used wisely, borrowing abroad can play a positive role, assisting a country in its international transactions. In the Mexican case, foreign funds have aided the government in several critical areas. They have been instrumental in partially financing its investments and its imports of capital goods for public enterprises, and the government has used these funds to adjust Mexico's balance of payments.[10] In addition, foreign funds assisted the government in successfully pursuing a policy of exchange rate stability between 1954 and 1976. During that period, the value of the Mexican peso remained pegged to the U.S. dollar (at 12.50 pesos for US$1). Moreover, a policy of exchange rate stability was compatible for many years with a policy of domestic price stability. The level of inflation from the mid-1950s to 1970 was remarkably low (an average annual rate below 5 percent). The government could not have pursued these policies without relying on foreign credit to finance its deficits and deficits in the current account of the balance of payments. (The current account is a record of the international transactions of goods and services of any one country over a period of one year.)

Given the prevailing rules in the international economic system, however, heavy reliance on foreign funds has some definite limits: Mexico was approaching those limits, that is, it was in danger of defaulting on its foreign debt payments. This danger was seen in the high level that its debt service ratio reached by 1970. The ratio of debt service (which is the sum of annual interest payments plus payments on the principal) to exports of goods and services is one of several indicators commonly used to assess the ability of a given nation to service its debt; therefore this ratio provides a measure of its external financial solvency. Table 5.3 seems at first sight to indicate that, at least until 1970, the problems of increasing foreign public debt and of servicing that debt were kept within

TABLE 5.3
Foreign Public Debt: Structure, Service, and Relation to Gross Domestic
Product, 1946-1980 (in millions of dollars)

Years	Total	Long-term	Short-term	Exports	Service	DE Ratio	DGDP Ratio
1946	485	na	na	395	na	na	na
1960	810	na	na	739	na	na	na
1970	4,262	3,259	1,003	2,933	720	.246	.125
1976	19,600	15,923	3,677	7,371	2,548	.346	.316
1977	22,912	20,185	2,727	8,404	3,837	.456	.310
1978	26,264	25,028	1,236	11,925	6,287	.527	.284
1979	29,757	28,315	1,442	16,131	10,180	.631	.219
1980	33,813	32,322	1,491	24,819	7,681	.309	.195

Sources: Banco de México, Informe Anual (Mexico City, various issues);
and Secretaría de Programación y Presupuesto, Información sobre las
relaciones económicas de México con el exterior (Mexico City, 1979).

Note: na = not available; Long-term = debt contracted for a period
of over one year; Short-term = debt that is due within one year;
DE ratio = debt/export ratio; DGDP = debt/gross domestic product ratio.

manageable limits. When assessed from a broader perspective, however, the situation could be more alarming. The Mexican ratio of 24.6 percent in 1970 was the highest ratio for all of Latin America and one of the highest ratios in the world.[11] In addition, it should be noted that these figures underestimate the total external debt, as they do not include financial obligations contracted by private actors without official guarantee of loans. Servicing the private foreign debt puts additional pressure on a nation's available foreign exchange resources.

As a major concern of any country is to remain financially solvent, the question arises of what, if anything, could have been done to solve the dilemma Mexico was seemingly facing. Mexico had to reduce its reliance on foreign credit to avoid eventual bankruptcy. But for many years it had relied heavily on borrowing abroad to finance public-sector imports and investments (which in turn promoted growth and employment) and to maintain a stable exchange rate, domestic price stability, and ultimately, political stability. In theory, encouraging exports could have been a way out of this dilemma. Greater exports would have meant additional sources of foreign exchange, but the record shows that there has been *a persistent deficit in the current account* since the end of World War II. The fact that imports have been consistently greater than exports has thus had the opposite effect: It has put additional pressure on the government to seek the foreign credit needed to stabilize the balance of payments.

Tables 5.4 and 5.5 provide us with a good perspective on the current account and the composition and evolution of foreign trade. In fact, the export side of the current account has been characterized by a generally

TABLE 5.4
Current Account, 1940-1980

	Amount of Transactions (in million dollars)									
	1940	1950	1960	1965	1970	1976	1977	1978	1979	1980
Balance	22.6	58.7	-300.5	-314.4	-945.9	-3.068.0	-1,623.2	-2,342.3	-4,856.4	-6,596.6
Exports of Goods and Services:	213.9	826.7	1,371.8	1,989.1	2,933.1	7,371.7	8,404.1	11,925.7	16,131.5	24,819.5
Goods	94.4	493.4	738.7	1,213.9	1,281.3	3,315.8	4,418.4	6,217.3	8,798.2	15,307.5
Tourism	17.3	110.9	155.3	274.9	415.0	835.6	866.5	1,121.0	1,443.3	1,670.1
Border transactions	33.0	121.9	366.0	499.5	878.9	1,637.4	1,506.3	2,363.5	2,919.2	3,660.6
Maquiladoras	--	--	--	--	80.9	535.7	524.7	714.3	637.6	773.4
Other	69.2	100.5	111.8	100.8	277.0	1,046.6	1,088.2	1,509.6	2,333.2	3,407.9
Imports of Goods and Services:	191.3	768.0	1,672.3	2,303.5	3,879.0	10,439.7	10,027.3	14,268.0	20,987.9	31,416.1
Goods	132.4	596.7	1,186.4	1,559.6	2,326.8	6,029.6	5,889.8	8,143.7	11,985.6	18,572.2
Tourism	8.0	9.3	40.5	119.1	191.4	423.1	395.0	519.0	713.6	1,010.8
Border transactions	20.0	76.5	221.0	295.2	563.3	1,192.7	786.4	1,751.5	2,241.2	3,056.4
Remittances	25.3	47.5	131.0	174.8	357.5	813.3	171.8	215.5	284.0	422.3
Interest on public debt[a]	--	11.2	30.4	62.2	229.2	1,266.0	1,542.3	2,023.1	2,888.4	3,957.6
Other	5.6	26.8	63.0	92.6	210.8	715.0	1,241.0	1,615.3	2,875.1	4,396.8

Sources: Nacional Financiera, Statistics on the Mexican Economy (Mexico City, 1977); Secretaría de Programación y Presupuesto, Información sobre las relaciones económicas de México con el exterior (Mexico City, 1979); Banco de México, Informe Anual (Mexico City, various issues).

[a]These figures refer to interest payments on public debt only. They do not represent amounts comparable to those in Table 5.3, where figures refer to total debt service (interest payments plus amortization).

TABLE 5.5
Composition and Evolution of Foreign Trade, 1956-1980

Year	Imports						Exports			
	By Sector		By Type of Goods				By Economic Activity			
	Public	Private	Consumer	Raw Materials	Capital	Other	Agricultural[a]	Extractive Industries	Manufacturing	Other
1956	na	na	16.6	36.6	46.8	--	54.2	31.8	7.4	6.6
1960	na	na	17.8	34.2	48.0	--	52.7	21.3	18.2	7.8
1966	17.2	82.8	17.9	35.9	46.2	--	52.7	16.9	20.4	10.0
1970	24.0	76.0	7.0	39.7	39.2	14.1	45.2	7.6	33.2	14.0
1976	35.7	64.3	5.8	43.3	41.1	9.8	34.8	20.7	27.4	17.1
1977	37.3	62.7	9.5	44.7	35.1	10.7	32.1	27.0	25.1	15.8
1978	37.6	62.4	7.3	49.0	33.6	10.1	26.1	34.6	23.8	15.5
1979	31.8	68.2	8.3	61.6	30.0	0.1	19.9	46.1	34.0	--
1980	36.6	63.4	13.1	59.2	27.5	0.2	10.1	67.8	22.0	0.1

Sources: Same as for Table 5.4.

[a]Mexican government statistics usually include in this category fishing, livestock, and beekeeping.

Note: na = not available

favorable performance. Thus, the value of total exports (in current dollars) rose from US$214 million in 1940 to about US$3 billion in 1970. Furthermore, although the share of agricultural exports fell somewhat between 1956 and 1970, the export shares of the extractive and manufacturing industries increased greatly during the same period. Hence, by 1970, manufactures accounted for 33 percent of total exports, indicating the trend toward industrialization. Services, tourism, and border transactions have always been pluses—bringing into the country more foreign exchange than the corresponding amount of Mexican expenditures abroad related to those activities. On the other hand, only since 1970 have the *maquiladoras* had an effect worthy of consideration when assessing the external sector of the economy. Maquiladoras are U.S. firms operating on the Mexican side of the border (since 1965), assembling products for the U.S. market. The goods processed in Mexico return to the United States, paying import duties only on the value added in Mexico. The process benefits from cheap Mexican labor in exchange for provision of some jobs and payment of taxes to the Mexican government. Maquiladoras were intended to alleviate the problem of workers' migrating to the United States in search of jobs not found in Mexico by providing employment opportunities on the Mexican side of the border; they have had this effect, but the number of jobs involved is small.[12]

Increased export revenues, however, have been overshadowed by the much faster growth in imports. The current value of imports rose from US$191 million to nearly US$4 billion dollars between 1940 and 1970. While Mexico began importing fewer consumer goods (which were being produced domestically), it increased its imports of raw materials and capital goods necessary to resupply local firms or to establish new industries. The public sector has been partly responsible for the higher deficit in current account, due to the combination of its greater imports of goods and higher interest payments on foreign public debt. Table 5.5 indicates that, by 1970, the public sector accounted for 24 percent of total imports. It also shows that foreign investors have been sending out of the country more foreign exchange than they have brought in (remittances).

Despite some obvious problems, the relatively good export performance of the economy during the 1960s, particularly in manufacturing exports, created the illusion in some circles that Mexico was attaining self-sustained economic growth. Others were more skeptical and pointed to the broader picture, putting special emphasis on the overall deterioration of the external sector. Such deterioration, it was argued, had been encouraged by government policies that fueled inefficiency on the part of both industrial and agricultural producers. Although industry had developed dramatically, it had done so partly at the expense of agriculture—which was entering a severe crisis. And the strategy of import substitution industrialization, which meant that industrial growth had been largely an inward-oriented effort, was also reaching its limits. Mexico's industry was highly protected, which kept it from developing its full export potential. Therefore, industry did not contribute sufficient foreign exchange resources in order to continue growing with an external sector in relative equilibrium. We have stated that there are some drawbacks associated with the implementation of an ISI strategy, and in addition to the emerging problems in the external sector just discussed, we must analyze the performance of industry and agriculture during the ISI years. Experts have pointed out that unless the government takes appropriate measures to make agricultural and industrial producers more efficient, severe constraints on future economic growth are likely to arise.[13] In what follows, some of the main economic features and problems of industry and agriculture, along with their political implications, are discussed.

Industrial Policy

During the initial stages of import substitution, protectionism is justified on the grounds that emerging local industries need some time to make their products competitive with foreign goods. Protection can take several forms, such as imposing tariffs, limiting the amount of goods allowed into the country (quotas), and raising bureaucratic barriers such as Mexico's complex system of import licenses. Exchange rate policy can also be used for this purpose. At some point, however, it is expected that government incentives will gradually lead producers to cut down their production costs and prices in order to be more competitive and hence to increase their exports. But the Mexican government has long been spoiling domestic producers. Overprotection has been one aspect of the overall governmental strategy to encourage private investors to industrialize the country. It seems that once certain concessions are granted, the government finds it very difficult to take them away from those who have taken advantage of them. A recent example of this situation, discussed below, was the heated domestic debate that followed Mexico's application to the General Agreement on Tariffs and Trade (GATT), an organization dedicated to ending protectionism. López Portillo changed his mind and decided not to join, following protests from sectors of the business community that resist giving up the benefits of protectionism.

In addition to the general problem of industry's export potential, there is the issue of domestic production of capital goods (i.e., production of machinery that is used for producing other goods). Table 5.5 shows that capital goods account for a substantial share of total imports. Ironically, a recent study by the World Bank claims that the low performance of the Mexican capital goods industry has been due, first and foremost, to the low level of protection granted to local producers! The study shows that private-sector importers pay very low tariffs and public enterprises pay no custom duties at all for this type of imports. As late as in 1975, more than 50 percent of total imports of capital goods were not subject to tariffs.[14] Thus, paradoxically, in a situation in which protection would have been justifiable, government action has been lacking. The study also contends that an inadequate exchange rate policy that has kept the Mexican peso overvalued for many years and the lack of credit facilities through which Mexican producers could compete with the more favorable financing offered by foreign suppliers have kept the pace of development of the capital goods industry very slow. In fact, in this respect Mexico lags far behind countries at a roughly comparable level of development, such as Argentina and Brazil.

Substituting imports of capital goods by encouraging domestic production is, according to some experts, one of very few remaining areas justifying protectionism; yet Mexico denies protectionism there even while it readily allows protectionism in other areas. Other analysts contend, however, that the development of a domestic capital goods industry is a very costly and risky enterprise. The generally small size of the domestic market of developing countries and the need for complex technology constitute real obstacles to sustained and sound progress. Instead, it is suggested that developing countries specialize in producing and exporting other types of manufactured goods. In particular, other policies, such as commercial and exchange rate policies, should aim to support the expansion of industries that make efforts to use labor-intensive technologies, thus helping to reduce the unemployment problem that afflicts many developing nations.[15]

In short, there were several options aimed at continuing the process of industrialization. The difficult choices included emphasizing a program to *develop the domestic capital goods industry*, primarily for import substitution purposes, but also for exporting. Alternatively, the government could have pursued an *export-led growth strategy*, which meant that it would cut down import restrictions to induce local industry to be more competitive. Hence, local industry would specialize over time in exporting certain products, and such activity would become the engine of economic growth.

To be sure, there is no way to be certain a priori which policy is most appropriate. One policy might be more efficient in one country than it would be in another. Or a combination of policies would in some cases be both possible and desirable. As an example of the dilemma facing developing countries, Bela Balassa has presented evidence concerning the successful implementation of export-led growth strategies in

Brazil, Taiwan, Korea, and a few other nations.[16] These newly industrializing countries have experienced very high rates of economic growth, expanded their exports substantially, stimulated investments in priority sectors, and achieved a great degree of sophistication in their industrial bases. But in some cases, such as Brazil, more open economies have become very vulnerable to external influences such as high inflation and changing trade patterns, and little progress has been made in reducing social inequalities. It is ironic that the economic fortunes of these countries— which completed most successfully the process of import substitution— have come to depend once again on their export markets. They have come full circle without having achieved self-sustained growth or having greatly diminished their socioeconomic inequalities. Taking into consideration the experience of such countries, Mexico eventually would have to work out a decision about the orientation of its future industrial development effort.

Agricultural Policy

There has been a direct relationship between public investment in irrigation and transportation and the general performance of the agricultural sector of the economy. While investment was high, from the World War II period until 1956, the average rate of growth was an impressive 7.6 percent. Lower investment was accompanied by growth that averaged only 3.8 percent during the following decade.[17] But government investment in irrigation and transportation systems does not tell us the whole story. Earlier, an important factor that accounted for higher agricultural production was the accelerated pace of the agrarian reform program under the Cárdenas administration. Cárdenas provided new lands for cultivation, promoting favorable conditions to meet the growing foreign demand for Mexican agricultural products during World War II. And cheap food and raw materials were also made available to the urban population, permitting the development of the industrial and service sectors. Furthermore, the agricultural sector provided much of the labor force, savings, and foreign exchange that greatly benefited the industrialization process supported by the central government. Shlomo Eckstein and Reyes Osorio have made a rough calculation of the balance of resources taken away from agriculture and channeled to the rest of the economy between 1940 and 1961. They concluded that about US$250 million (1960 prices) was transferred to the rest of the economy by agriculture during those years of relative prosperity.[18]

In addition to both decreasing public investments in agriculture and the transfer of resources, government policy regarding access to good lands and to adequate inputs has favored large landowners for the most part. Their lands are generally the best in the country. These lands are located in northern Mexico and are provided with the best irrigation systems, fertilizers, and modern equipment.[19] These are the truly capitalistic enterprises that form the basis of Mexico's commercial agriculture. They are owned by individuals or by large companies linked to national and multinational firms engaged in the massive production and commercialization of food. A large share of this production is oriented to the U.S. market, which means that more foreign exchange resources have been available to facilitate imports of capital goods and raw materials to further industrialization. For many years, governmental support of these farmers translated into a tacit political alliance that has been instrumental in maintaining political stability. This policy is consistent with our argument in Chapters 3 and 4 that the regime has been particularly supportive of privileged groups and only marginally of more disadvantaged groups. The alliance between government and farmers has seldom been disturbed, in particular when the government has granted some concessions (e.g., land expropriations) to dissatisfied peasants.

What have been the most important government policies toward the peasants? How has agricultural production been affected by these policies? From 1940 to 1970, the peasants who owned lands, but who otherwise had very limited resources, were gradually forced to produce crops for which there was a secure but not very profitable market. They specialized in the production of maize, beans, and other basic foodstuffs, for which the government implemented price controls, and thus subsidized consumers in urban areas. Peasants have been often hurt by these urban-oriented policies. And peasant interests have been affected in other ways. Traditionally, the peasants have had to negotiate with several actors to obtain the resources necessary for production. We discussed in Chapter 3 peasant interaction with the Agrarian Reform Ministry to obtain land; in addition, peasants have been forced to deal with local caciques, who live off the political contacts that are necessary to get fertilizers, credit, and other resources. Furthermore, even when peasants have obtained these resources directly from governmental agencies, they have had to accept conditions in exchange for these inputs. That is, they have had to follow official production policies that, although designed by agricultural "experts," are not necessarily based on accurate knowledge of the environment. This often leads to failures and frustrations, the results of which obviously have adverse effects on peasant families more than on anyone else. Finally, peasants have had to deal with the market, which is largely beyond their control, for selling their products at given prices. They have been at the mercy of tradesmen and the government monopoly, the National Staple Products Company (CONASUPO),[20] which have great resources to influence pricing and other decisions. In short, the peasants have been entrusted with the critical task of providing the basic foodstuffs central to the diet of the Mexican population, but they have not received enough governmental support. The output of their products began to decline sharply in the mid-1960s. By 1970, Mexico, "the land of the green revolution," was no longer a net exporter of cereals. More important, CONASUPO became second only to the state oil monopoly (PEMEX) as the major importer of foreign goods by the public sector. CONASUPO's food imports accounted for about 17 percent of public sector imports in 1970.[21] This was an indication that agriculture, although for reasons other than those prevailing in industry, was also experiencing serious problems.

To summarize, Mexico found itself in 1970 facing several structural problems in the external sector, industry, and agriculture that could constrain future growth. These problems, we have argued, are common to other countries that have followed the ISI strategy. Subsequent administrations would have to address themselves to solving these problems in order to secure steady economic growth—and thus to maximize the prospects for continual political stability. Before we analyze their policies, however, we must more specifically discuss the other social problems that emerged during the years of ISI.

Social Outcomes of the Economic Model

Two aspects of government policy have contributed to a very poor record in distributing the benefits of economic growth. One concerns the government's social expenditures aimed at providing the population with schooling, housing, health care, and other services. The other concerns official policies favoring industrialization; for example, low tariffs on capital goods imports have meant that many firms have preferred to use capital-intensive methods, which in turn have exacerbated the unemployment problem.

Government statistics at the aggregate level are likely to confuse the casual observer of the Mexican scene. Indeed, the government built many schools, hospitals, and other facilities during the ISI period, and Mexico's industrial plant achieved a relatively high degree of sophistication. However, only some sectors of the working classes have benefited from public services, and the social costs of industrialization have been high. The regime, it is true, has proved very capable of maintaining political stability, but generalized poverty still afflicts much of Mexican society. Those who argue that stability has been possible because of official control of the organizations of peasants and workers tell only half the story; strong unions have been able, in some cases, to negotiate agreements that have without any doubt raised the standard of living of their constituencies. But these legal provisions have seldom reached the *unorganized working classes*. One of our central hypotheses is that political stability has resulted in part from the fact that much of the working class has not organized itself to protest the socioeconomic conditions in which it lives. This should be kept in mind when looking at some of the indicators (presented below) of social development in Mexico.

In regard to *government social expenditures*, Mexico's are merely average (despite Mexico's enviable economic growth) when compared to those of other Latin American countries. Most of these expenditures have favored the population in urban areas, particularly near the nation's major industrial centers. Thus, a vast majority of the total population has been kept marginal. As a way of further illustrating this point, consider that the total public sector budget in 1979 was about US$55 billion, only 8.2 percent of which was spent on education, 10.4 percent on health and social security, and but 0.6 percent on housing.[22] On the positive side, these figures seem to have led to impressive achievements. The government provided schooling for more than 18 million and membership in public health institutions for 28 million. However, there are still more than 4 million children annually who do not find a place in elementary schools, 13 million who will never reach the sixth grade, and a national illiteracy rate of 23 percent. In the case of health, even if we assumed that the richest 20 percent of the population received private medical care, we would still be left with roughly 25 million who never receive modern medical care.[23] These figures lend support to our hypothesis regarding the limited number of working-class people who have benefited from state-sponsored social services.

Official policies in support of industrialization have also complicated various social problems. A case in point has been the encouragement given to industry to use capital-intensive technologies when Mexico has a huge labor surplus. Although accurate information about the extent of *unemployment* is very difficult to obtain, some aspects of the problem have been discussed in recent studies released by the Ministries of Labor and of Programming and Budget.[24] Mexico's economy has been growing at rates of more than 6 percent since the 1940s, and the population by an average annual rate of 3.5 percent. But the study by the Ministry of Labor found that the number of new jobs has increased by only 2.5 percent each year. The resulting rate of sheer unemployment could be set at around 7 to 8 percent, yet the major problem is *underemployment:* people have either a part-time job only or are paid less than the national minimum wage. Using such criteria, the underemployment level might reach as high as 35 to 44 percent![25]

Another dimension of the problem is identified in the Ministry of Programming and Budget report. It shows that in 1950 about 32 percent of the population had jobs, but that this proportion fell to 27 percent twenty years later. This means that from 1950 to 1970 proportionally fewer people were providing for the needs of the total population, one of the fastest-growing in the world. These figures also reflect the shifting age composition of the population; youths have increased their share of the total substantially. In addition, the study notes that the ratio of employed women to total population increased from 4.5 percent to 5.5 percent during the same period, suggesting that youths and women are exerting new pressures on the job market, in some ways further complicating the search for solutions to high rates of unemployment and underemployment. So not only has Mexico had a terrible employment problem, it has had a worsening one.

Mexico's large pool of unemployed and underemployed people exerts downward pressure on *wages* and also affects *income distribution*. Information provided by the Central Bank and by the United Nations Economic Commission for Latin America shows a very erratic pattern of evolution of real minimum wages since 1960. An improvement in one year was followed almost systematically by a decrease the next year. And more recently, a steady improvement over the period 1974 to 1976 was followed by four years of uninterrupted decline in real minimum wages. The purchasing power of workers since López Portillo came to office has fallen by an accumulated index of 12 percent.[26] From another perspective, organized workers in certain key industries have attained some fringe benefits over time that probably affected relative factor prices. That is, the marginal cost of labor exceeds that of capital (machines), encouraging entrepreneurs to shift to capital-intensive technologies, thus aggravating the unemployment problem. For example, private employers in the manufacturing sector and the government both pay a 5 percent contribution toward improved housing facilities for their workers, about a 10 percent social security tax, a 1 percent educational tax, an 8 percent profit-sharing levy in some cases, and a bonus of a full month's salary at the end of the year. All such payments have made labor somewhat more expensive, and many entrepreneurs point to this fact in order to justify their adoption of capital-intensive technologies.

In regard to *income distribution*, Table 5.6 shows a steady deterioration between 1950 and 1969. By the latter year, 20 percent of the people garnered a mere 4 percent of national income. At the same time, the top 20 percent disposed of 64 percent! And despite some improvement in the middle income brackets during the Echeverría administration, the World Bank has reported that *Mexico has one of the worst profiles of income distribution of any nation on earth.*[27] The benefits of growth have been maldistributed indeed.

ECONOMIC AND SOCIAL POLICY

TABLE 5.6
Income Distribution in Mexico, 1950-1977

| Income Group | Percentage of Income Earned | | | |
(deciles)	1950	1963	1969	1977
1- 2 (lowest 20 percent)	4.7	3.5	4.0	3.3
3- 5	12.7	11.5	11.0	13.4
6- 8	23.7	25.4	21.0	28.2
9-10 (highest 20 percent)	58.9	59.6	64.0	55.1

Sources: For 1950 and 1963: United Nations Economic Commission for
Latin America, La distribución del ingreso en América Latina (New York,
1970); for 1969: World Bank, The Economy of Mexico: A Basic Report
(Washington, D.C., June 1973); and for 1977: Secretaría de Programación
y Presupuesto, Encuesta nacional de ingresos y gastos de las familias
(Mexico City, 1979).

Social Policy and Private Initiative

There are, naturally, several explanations for Mexico's terrible failure
in the social-welfare field. Many have focused on the regime's role,
claiming that it has clearly favored stability over change and economic
growth over distribution of wealth. Allegedly, while the state plays an
overactive role in support of regressive industrialization policy, it generally
provides far too little by way of resources and opportunities through the
public sector. In fact, most recommendations for dealing with the social
failure have centered on expanding the public sector.

But powerful political and economic factors have worked against
such expansion. First, the regime has indeed placed a much higher priority
on political stability and economic growth than on social change. Second,
as we argue in this chapter, the regime has simply not been able or
willing to extract from the economy the resources necessary to meet even
its present expenditures. Third, the more powerful political groups, such
as business, generally have opposed such public-sector expansion as
either economically unwise or at least not in their interests. This opposition,
in turn, has meant that attempts at expansion, as under Echeverría, have
jeopardized the regime's stability and growth priorities. These, then, are
the major problems with implementing a major public-sector assault on
Mexico's social problems—even if one assumes that the assault would
"objectively" be the most appropriate policy to try. Conservatives, of
course, argue that expanding the public sector, even if it were politically
feasible, would be bad policy.

Despite all the obstacles, the public sector does sometimes expand
significantly and sometimes its benefits do help alleviate social ills. It is

also true, however, that powerful groups often manage to maintain their privileges even under such circumstances. For one thing, they may (through their resources, contacts, and knowledge) reap a disproportionate share of public sector services. For another, they may shun the expanding public sector in order to buy special privileges in the private sector. Among the possible examples from many health and welfare fields, we look briefly at higher education.[28]

We have already seen (Chapter 1) that Mexico spends much more freely on higher education than on primary (or secondary) education and that (until recently) only a small minority enjoyed the privileges of higher education. Thus, the public sector of higher education has served mainly the elite. And when the public sector finally expanded greatly, offering opportunities not just to the elite but to the middle class as well, an interesting pattern developed: Much of the elite bypassed the public sector and established sanctuaries in private institutions. This shift, as in most of Latin America, was a response to changes in the public sector. Elites reacted to the public sector's expanding social class base and to what they perceived as its terrible loss of prestige and quality, all amid rising leftist political activism. Private sector graduates generally receive more prestigious degrees than do their public sector counterparts, and they enjoy privileged positions in the job market. None of this alters the fact that Mexican higher education remains overwhelmingly public, maintaining its roughly 85 percent of total enrollments through the 1960s and 1970s. In fact, enrollments have grown as never before, from roughly 80,000 (1960) to more than 500,000 (1975). But as most groups first gaining access to higher education go to the (free) public sector, the fact that the private sector could hold at 15 percent means that it too has grown in unprecedented fashion and has done so by attracting social groups that once would have attended the public sector. Moreover, the private sector's 15 percent share is significant because Mexico's private sector is at least as private as any in Latin America (indeed, in the world) in terms of finance (virtually no government subsidy), governance (even more autonomy from the government than for public universities), and mission (both ideological and employment orientations toward private enterprise). And the private sector is growing in relative importance. Not only does it far surpass the public sector in job placement for private enterprises, but cracks are appearing even in such traditional public university domains as recruitment to high positions in the public bureaucracy. Critics of the private sector fear rising private penetration of the state.

Thus, as in the economic sphere, the private-public balance raises important policy issues in the social sphere. Critics decry private higher education as elitist. Only the wealthy can afford the tuition, and stiff entrance exams favor those, usually the wealthy, who have enjoyed better educational opportunities throughout their childhood. By attracting top students, the private sector represents a challenge to the quality of public facilities. Any political liberty to "choose" private institutions is seen as bourgeois liberty, only for those who can pay for it. Finally, private universities allegedly foster dependency by copying U.S. academic structures and policies and by encouraging many of their best students to pursue graduate work in the United States.

For others, the private sector represents voluntarism, competition, and superior services. It buttresses political liberty by providing free choice, stability by satisfying powerful groups, economic growth by insisting on both academic quality and practical ties to private enterprise, and even national independence by training top Mexican talent that might otherwise choose study abroad over Mexico's public universities.

However one feels about the desirability of a strong private sector in a field such as higher education, certain facts seem clear. The sector's strength does reflect, simultaneously, a substantial degree of socioeconomic inequality, political freedom, and openness to foreign influence, whether or not it contributes significantly to any of these. It tells us something about the flexibility of the Mexican political system, the ways in which goals such as depoliticization of social groups (such as students) and curbing of public expenditures can be partially achieved outside the public sector, thus lessening the government's felt need to repress the public sector to the degree found in many authoritarian nations. It also reminds us that there can be potent social as well as economic and political reactions to increases in the scope of the public sector. Privileged students can leave the public system just as privileged patients can bypass the public health system and private capital can flee an economy in which the public sector tries to expand its role. Unless the regime expands both its will and ability to impose changes in social policy, privileged groups will retain considerable leeway to shape the social policies not only within but also outside the public sector.

A DECADE OF TRANSITION

Despite three decades of strong economic growth, Mexico entered the 1970s confronting several severe social and economic problems. In structural terms, the ability of the public sector to play a positive role in the economy was being increasingly undercut by its financial problems. The Mexican regime—so often regarded as quite powerful—seemed unable to pursue certain fundamental options to gain the revenue necessary to meet its public-sector responsibilities. Its inability to tax business and wealth sufficiently was crucial. It also seemed unable to cut back on subsidies not just to industry but also to needy consumers. And because of the significance that a strong public sector has had in Mexican politics, selling public enterprises in order to balance the budget was not feasible. Thus, the question arises: Was the public economic posture weak mostly because the regime favored the private sector excessively? Or, perhaps even more important, did the regime really lack the political muscle to extract sufficient resources from society to maintain its powerful position? In addition to the public sector's financial health, other issues included the need to reinvigorate agriculture and industry. From the social perspective, unemployment, poverty, and exploitation of the poor remained salient features. These were the issues that Echeverría and López Portillo faced during the 1970s. Although these two administrations shared the same objective of revitalizing the economic growth model, their policies were different in many respects. We turn to analyzing the evolution of the economy and of the social situation during the 1970s, a decade in which some significant steps were taken to redefine the basic assumptions and the major policies guiding the effort toward further industrialization and growth.

In 1970, a number of prestigious intellectuals and some of their friends in official positions published three volumes (*El perfil de México en 1980* [A profile of Mexico in 1980]) on the desirable evolution of the Mexican socioeconomic and political systems for the new decade. The publication was significant both because it marked the initial steps toward a rapprochement of some sectors of the intelligentsia with the political regime after the 1968 conflict and because some of the contributors would hold very important positions in the Echeverría and López Portillo administrations. For example, David Ibarra became director-general of the National Development Bank during Echeverría's term and from 1977 headed the particularly powerful Ministry of Finance. It is interesting to listen to what a man who would become one of the most influential economic policymakers of the 1970s had to say:

> The old revolutionary guard, in its time, just like the new generation of politicians in our time, congratulated itself on its own achievements. . . . And even some groups of dissidents have endorsed this [laudatory] assessment. . . . Only once in a while have problems surfaced which have called into question the capacity of the nation's institutions to adapt to socio-economic changes.
>
> Unrest is still not generalized within the population, nor has it been so widespread as to force a fundamental and comprehensive reassessment of traditional approaches to economic and political policymaking. However, what would happen to the prospects for development should the major

> forces that have promoted such development during the last decades
> suddenly stall?
>
> It seems necessary, therefore, to begin defining new goals, that is, to
> elaborate clearly the objectives to be pursued and the tools and mechanisms
> necessary to achieve them.[29]

A careful reading of the complete Ibarra essay and of the complete
work indicates a general awareness by intellectuals and by future holders
of cabinet posts of some of the problems associated with the economic
growth model during the previous decades. However, various authors
express different views as to what caused the problems in the first
place, and more important, which policies should be pursued to deal
with such problems.

Naturally, different political actors hold different views as well.
Thus, the left considers the labor unions' lack of autonomy from the
regime a major determinant of the deteriorating standard of living of
the working class. Labor leaders, for their part, put the blame on
"unpatriotic entrepreneurs" who are not concerned with the well-being
of all social sectors. And the business community holds ineffective
governmental policies responsible. By the same token, these organizations
occasionally come forward with proposals to solve their grievances. In
general, however, their input has been rather sporadic and has focused
only on specific problems. That is, dissatisfied groups have not rallied
behind a coherent set of policy proposals to deal with the social and
structural shortcomings of the growth model. Thus, the government has
had a free hand in initiating (or not initiating) actions to correct such
problems. To some extent, this has been due to the lack of freedom
for *organizational* alternatives, as discussed in Chapter 4. But it has also
been due to the fact that key social groups have generally not felt
threatened by the regime's social and economic policies. The evolution
of the economy during the 1970s, however, was influenced to a very
important degree by President Luis Echeverría's loudly proclaimed
commitment to effect a fundamental transformation of the traditional
model of economic growth and by the adverse reaction of the business
community to this proclamation.

The Economic Model Under Echeverría

In the early 1970s, under Echeverría, increasing public intervention
in the economy was a very important factor contributing to continued
economic growth. The number of enterprises in which there was public
participation, with shares ranging from very small to large, increased
from 84 in 1970 to 845 in 1976, while the number of government
employees doubled to more than 1 million.[30] This expansion of the

public sector meant greater investments, imports of capital goods, expenditures for the growing bureaucracy, and so forth. All of the above were provided, *but not as a result of a substantial increase in government revenues following a major tax reform or changes in the amount and allocation of subsidies.*

It is true that some efforts were made to increase government revenues, but they fell short of compensating for the more dramatic increase in government expenditures. Thus, the ratio of public-sector income to gross domestic product increased from 18.9 percent to 27.4 percent between 1970 and 1976. At the same time, however, the ratio on the expenditure side rose from 23.7 percent to 33.9 percent.[31] To make up this gap, the Echeverría administration relied on the same tool used by its predecessors: *deficit financing.* Because of the lack of sufficient domestic sources of credit, the government borrowed abroad, and the level of foreign public debt skyrocketed from US$4.2 billion in 1970 to US$19.6 billion in 1976! The debt service/export ratio increased to the point that in 1976 one out of every three dollars collected from exports had to be used to service the debt (see Table 5.3).

During this period, the poor performance of the current account was no help to the rapidly deteriorating external sector. For example, despite a threefold increase in public investments in agriculture, output growth rates declined steadily and hit a record low of 1.2 percent in 1976. Imports of food in that year contributed significantly to an all-time record deficit in current account of more than US$3 billion.[32] Imports of capital goods continued to account for a significant share of the deficit as well. At the same time, even though the government went out of its way to encourage exports, the rate of increase characteristic of the 1960s slowed. Furthermore, the manufacturing share of total exports actually declined from 33.2 percent in 1970 to 27.4 percent in 1976 (see Table 5.5). Echeverría founded the Mexican Institute for Foreign Trade, and he took many entrepreneurs on his numerous trips the world over, with his government picking up the bill. However, many official policies that actually discouraged exports remained unchanged. Thus, for example, the government artificially maintained a fixed exchange rate for the Mexican peso, a policy that made Mexican goods more expensive in the international market than they would otherwise have been. Had the exchange rate been gradually adjusted to reflect the actual value of the peso, Mexican goods would have been more competitive, and exports could have been greater. More important, little if anything was done to reduce the excessive level of protectionism provided for domestic producers. The complex system of import licenses remained practically untouched, and producers of consumer goods did not feel pressured into becoming more competitive.

To make things even worse, several factors combined to produce rates of inflation of 20 to 25 percent, previously unknown in Mexico. First, there was an upsurge in aggregate demand, partly as a result of greater public involvement in the economy and partly due to gains in real minimum wages and income distribution. The profile of income distribution improved somewhat between 1969 and 1977, favoring mostly people in the middle income brackets, who received 40 percent of the national income in 1977 (see Table 5.6). Because domestic production was insufficient to fulfill the demand for more agricultural and industrial products, some of these products had to be imported. Moreover, as international inflation was widespread, the prices of many of these goods had risen, which also contributed to higher domestic inflation. However, some would argue that inflation would have been even greater had the government imposed import controls: Prices tend to rise when demand is growing and there are fewer goods available.

Most important, the government was losing the trust of key economic actors. For one thing, the government engaged itself in ideologically charged confrontations with the business community, and in the end it did not even stand strongly by its public positions! Government attitudes toward foreign investors provide a good illustration. The government made considerable noise about its efforts to control direct foreign investment through a 1973 law.[33] According to this law, the majority interest (at least 51 percent) in all firms should be Mexican, and some industries (e.g., the automobile industry) are committed to produce locally an increasing share of components. Direct foreign investment usually carries with it a number of positive as well as negative effects. On the plus side, it facilitates the flow of new technology, it creates some jobs, and it brings in foreign exchange. Even socialist countries have sought these benefits. At the same time, however, foreign firms have often created unwanted conflictive situations, especially in developing countries. Politically, they have interfered in domestic affairs, as they did in Chile in the early 1970s. And they have caused economic problems, as even a recent U.S. congressional study shows. It points out that multinational corporations largely dominate the manufacturing sector in Mexico, as they do in Brazil, and that they control more than half the total assets of the 300 largest manufacturing firms in these countries. The study concludes that as a result of very high returns to capital, "resources are misallocated, and the distribution of income and wealth becomes more unequal. Moreover, innovation and growth are likely to be held below the rates attainable under more competitive conditions."[34]

But once it has been acknowledged that the international system exerts important influences over the economies of capitalist nations such as Mexico, we should also look at figures that suggest that the role of foreign capital has been more one of fitting into than of significantly shaping the domestic economic situation. In 1975, for example, foreign capital accounted for only 2.5 percent of total investment resources in the Mexican economy. U.S. firms accounted for about three-quarters of the cumulative US$4 billion of direct foreign investment up to that year. The proportion in 1980 was slightly smaller, about 69 percent of the US$8 billion total for that year.[35] In any event, despite the government's tough rhetoric and the 1973 law, direct foreign investment—which Echeverría blamed for many of Mexico's economic ills—actually increased during his tenure.

Another case in point concerns the domestic business community, which became alienated from the regime. A pointed indicator of this situation was the level of gross fixed capital formation during these years. Despite the unprecedented level of public investments, total gross fixed capital formation fell by 2.7 percent in 1971 and again by 3.5 percent in 1976. That meant that private investors were withdrawing their capital from Mexico. The total amount withdrawn, which was sent primarily to U.S. banks, has been estimated at about US$4 billion.[36] Private investors feared they were being "crowded out" of Mexico's economy. They viewed excessive government spending as a major source of inflation and as a cause of the growing foreign debt. They also disliked wholeheartedly the social reform and foreign policy rhetoric of those years.

It should be noted that the government had its own list of grievances against the business community, some of them well founded. From the government's viewpoint, the crisis in agriculture, the insufficient production of industrial goods, and the capital flight from Mexico seemed unjustifiable. After all, the government had been providing various incentives for private investment—low taxes, huge subsidies, protectionist foreign exchange and commercial policies. Moreover, not all public expenditures were unproductive, despite private-sector claims. For example, 17 percent of the total public investments from 1970 to 1976 were devoted to the expansion of the oil industry alone. This helped end the need for oil imports and laid the basis for the greater production and exports of later years.[37] Thus, what the government expected, at a minimum, was that the business community would share the costs entailed by government policies to promote economic growth. Instead, the further deterioration of the economy during Echeverría's administration scared the political right and entrepreneurs so much that they ended up better organized than they had ever been. The major organizational expression of the 1970s rebellion was the establishment of the Coordinating Business Council in 1975. It became the major forum of private-sector organizations, the place where they form their common policy positions. Beyond all this, some have even argued that certain entrepreneurs control illegal paramilitary groups (primarily in Jalisco, Puebla, and Nuevo León) and that others are funding ultraconservative "independent" labor unions in those and other states in order to strengthen their position in the political system.

Thus, the regime has found itself confronting an intensified paradox, which has been aptly summarized by Douglas Bennett and Kenneth Sharpe: "The national bourgeoisie, in many ways a creation of the state, acts now in ways that limit the power of the state."[38] Roger D. Hansen and E.V.K. Fitzgerald have also contended that the Mexican state's autonomy has been undermined to an important degree by the resistance of the private sector to cooperating to find solutions to the problems associated with the pursuit of economic growth and by its growing capacity to exercise veto power over some of the government's economic policies.[39] Their analyses have been highly influenced by the pattern of events that resulted in the 1976 economic crisis. These analyses obviously square with the assertion in Chapters 3 and 4 that business exercises a more important degree of autonomy from the regime than does any other political actor in Mexico.

In 1976, economic problems and the confrontation between the regime and the private sector reached a climax. By the end of the year President Echeverría had little alternative but to comply with the rules of the international economic system that Mexico has repeatedly accepted in various formal conventions. These rules, for example, discourage excessive reliance on foreign credit to finance a large share of domestic investments and imports. Although there is much debate about what precisely constitutes "too much reliance on foreign credit," the foreign public debt of nearly US$20 billion and the current account deficit of more than US$3 billion in 1976 were considered clearly too much. At the same time, the pace of the capital flight had accelerated, and so Echeverría announced during his last State of the Union address (September 1, 1976) his decision to devalue the Mexican peso. The following month Mexico put into effect some old agreements with the U.S. Federal Reserve and the U.S. Treasury Department, and it got a loan of US$600 million to support the peso. In addition, it signed a stabilization agreement with the International Monetary Fund (IMF), gaining access to as much as US$965 million from the fund's facilities. Mexico accepted in return a number of conditions to improve the economic situation, such as a US$3-billion-a-year ceiling on additional foreign public borrowing during the three years that the agreement was expected to last.[40] Certain major similarities would characterize the 1982 economic crisis and the bitter pills Mexico would have to swallow in order to gain foreign help in combating it.

Echeverría's term in office ended two months after the agreement with the IMF was signed. His successor, López Portillo offered a different project to revitalize the economic model. In 1976, the economy had grown by only 2.1 percent, which meant a 1.1 percent decline in per-capita income, assuming a population growth rate of 3.2 percent. For one thing, a radical change in Mexico's long-standing oil policy was forthcoming. Mexico would become once again one of the world's leading oil producers and exporters. The expectations raised by this prospective change in oil policy probably explain how López Portillo could afford to remain largely silent during his campaign for the presidency. With oil, the new president-elect did not need to expound rhetorical promises to restore confidence in the Mexican government and economy. Furthermore, recent events had shown that any efforts to revitalize the economic model would have to be supported by a reassured business community.

The Economic Model Under López Portillo

Soon after López Portillo became president, he reaffirmed that his government was bound by the agreement with the IMF. He also expressed his determination to use oil as a means to improve the ailing economy. Expansion of the oil industry was expected to trigger the reestablishment of high growth rates. And growth could take place with an external sector in equilibrium, thanks to foreign exchange resources provided by oil exports. The government could count on an additional source of revenue, so that it could lower the public deficit and reduce the need to borrow money abroad. These and other problems would be solved as PEMEX, the state's oil monopoly, increased its production of crude oil from 0.9 to 2.25 million barrels per day by 1982, half of it for export. It will be shown in Chapter 7 that this and other production and export targets were reached earlier (mid-1980) than originally planned. And high economic growth rates were reestablished during 1978–1981, until Mexico fell into a new economic crisis toward the end of the López Portillo administration.

Other broad economic policy objectives were never fulfilled. In fact, as Mexico entered the 1980s, *several of the structural and social indicators of the ills of the growth model that were the focus of attention during the 1976 crisis had deteriorated even further.*[41]

Using traditional evaluative standards, one could compile a long list of problems with the troubled economy of Mexico today. Take, for example, some of the indicators used earlier in this chapter to present an overall view of the Mexican economy from 1940 to 1970. During López Portillo's administration, the same trends prevailed in regard to *government finances.* Thus, although the ratio of public-sector income to gross domestic product reached 30 percent, the ratio in terms of expenditures increased to as much as 37 percent in 1980.[42] In 1980, subsidies continued to account for a large share of the public deficit, although some interesting changes in the tax system were introduced. While income taxes were reduced for lower income groups, a new value added tax (VAT) was put into effect, with the objective of preventing tax evasion and improving the government's tax collection rate. VAT might have some positive effects on the general state of public finances in the near future.[43] The government also tried to add to its revenues through the sale of gold and silver coins and of oil bonds.

The *current account* situation deteriorated even further under López Portillo (see Table 5.4). The deficit had been cut down from US$3 billion in 1976 to US$1.6 billion in 1977, but then it increased to the all-time record of US$6.6 billion in 1980 and then to US$11 billion in 1981. The dramatic rise in oil's share of exports of goods is implied in Table 5.5. In 1980, oil accounted for practically all of the 68 percent share of extractive industries in exports of goods, and for about 75 percent in 1981. At the same time, imports of capital goods, food, and the service of the foreign public debt continued to account for most of that deficit. Were it not for huge revenues from increasing oil exports (US$10 billion in 1980 and US$14.5 billion in 1981), such a deficit in current account could have become an insurmountable constraint on economic growth, a bad omen as an impending world oil glut would soon wreak havoc on Mexico's oil revenues.

The *foreign public debt* grew at an even faster pace than during the Echeverría administration. The figures below suggest that the change in traditional oil policy allowed López Portillo's government to continue relying on deficit financing, at least to some extent. In 1979, the debt amounted to more than US$29 billion (up from US$19 billion in 1976), and the debt service/export ratio was a staggering 62.1 percent! These figures mean, among other things, that two out of every three dollars received from export revenues had to be used to service the debt in that year. This fact, however, can be explained by the government's efforts to change the structure of payments on its debt. In 1978 and 1979, the government made advance payments on its short-term debt, which is due within one year and carries with it higher interest payments. Today, most of the debt is contracted on a longer-term basis and at lower interest rates. Thus, in 1980 the foreign public debt had increased to US$34 billion, but the debt service/export ratio of 30 percent was substantially lower than the ratio of 62 percent of the previous year (see Table 5.3). There is still no detailed information on various aspects of the huge increase in the foreign debt to US$51 billion by the end of 1981, soaring still much higher in 1982.

In the *social* sphere, available figures add to the long list of records that the López Portillo administration, unfortunately, holds. Table 5.2 shows that government social investments averaged less than 10 percent during the period. Additionally, as already mentioned, real wages fell significantly. The working classes were particularly hard-hit by annual rates of inflation of 20 to 30 percent, which were not compensated for by corresponding wage increases.

Thus, there was ample evidence for a bleak interpretation of the Mexican economy. Other indicators, however, suggested a reinvigoration from 1978 to 1981. One of the most significant improvements came in the area of employment: The number of jobs grew faster than the population due to the great increase in public works and in private-sector investments. Another positive feature was that income per capita, after decreasing again in 1977, rose in the three subsequent years. The economy grew by 6 percent in 1978, and by almost 8 percent from 1979 to 1981, compared to a rate of population growth of about 3.1 percent.[44] Table 5.1 also indicates that the ratio of gross fixed capital formation to gross domestic product increased in real terms. In 1980, the ratio was 25.6 percent, the highest ever recorded. The public sector's share of the total (44 percent) was also unprecedented. Ironically, although public involvement in the economy was greater than ever, the attitude of the business community was a far cry from its confrontational tone of the mid-1970s. To be sure, there were remaining disagreements, but the private sector seemed generally satisfied with the policies that restored high rates of economic growth. The cooperation of the business community, we have argued, is essential for securing political stability through steady economic growth. This cooperation was obviously shaken when López Portillo surprised everyone, in September 1982, by expropriating all domestic private banks; these banks, he charged, had encouraged a dangerous flight of capital from Mexico. Until that point, however, regime-business relations during López Portillo's tenure had been quite good, contrasting sharply with the years of confrontation that had characterized those relations during Echeverría's tenure. Analysis of two specific official policies, toward the agricultural and industrial sectors, can help to illustrate the pattern of interactions between the regime and the business community since Echeverría left office.

In the agricultural sector, a central goal of the López Portillo administration was to attain self-sufficiency in the production of basic foodstuffs. Although Mexico is a large agricultural producer, imports of products that are part of the basic diet of the population have been increasing at an alarming pace. For example, more than 10 million tons of maize, beans, wheat, and other basic foodstuffs, valued at US$1.5 billion, were imported in 1980 alone.[45] The administration implemented two main policies aimed at reducing food imports. First, the president announced in early 1980 the establishment of the Mexican Food System (SAM). A government study has been completed that includes detailed information pertaining to production of foodstuffs by region, as well as projections of output and consumption levels for the near future.[46] On this basis, SAM aimed *to establish a formula for sharing risks between the government and the peasantry* in order to reach certain production goals for maize, beans, and other products. The government committed itself to providing the peasant with fertilizers, seeds, and other inputs at very low prices; it promised to see that products would be bought at established prices; and it guaranteed a minimum income in the event that the crop is lost because of a natural disaster. The peasant, for his part, committed himself to devote his efforts, his land, and his labor to attaining official production goals. In this sense, a rather atypical relationship emerged between the state (as employer) and the peasant (as wage earner).

In addition to SAM, the highly controversial Agricultural Development Law was approved by Congress in 1981.[47] Before passage of this law, peasants were not allowed to lease their land, but Article 32 legalized what had been an unlawful and yet a very common practice. Thus, peasants would be allowed to integrate their lands with those of large landowners, ostensibly to increase productivity. In this manner, large agricultural enterprises are given a more secure environment to plan their long-term investments, which the government hopes will be helpful in reaching its own objectives. Large landowners were thus reassured that no more lands would be expropriated. In addition, they did not need to worry about extending their territories at the expense of peasant lands. Now they could negotiate openly and directly with peasants to use their lands in exchange for a wage and an as-yet-indeterminate share in total profits. These enterprises, therefore, would control even if they would not own the land. And the peasant, as in the case of SAM and the state, would become a wage earner dependent on his employer. These new policies were of special significance at a time when the government decided to abandon one of the key commitments (land distribution) on which it has based its legitimacy. Of course, we argued in Chapter 4 that *policy change* has been an important feature of Mexican politics; that is, a future administration may decide to emphasize once again its rhetorical commitment to a fundamental land reform—especially if López Portillo's policies fall short of attaining

their goals. However, the government undertook these risky new measures hoping that closer cooperation with the peasantry and large
landowners would help alleviate the crisis in the agricultural sector.

In industry, significant changes are also required, changes that are
sometimes difficult both to understand and to implement. This situation
is often complicated by the fact that many issues are debated in an
environment characterized by a high degree of ideological prejudices.
To illustrate this point, consider the debate that ensued over López
Portillo's proposal to become a member of GATT. GATT is an agreement
signed in 1947, mainly by the industrialized nations. Its chief objective
has been to "liberalize trade," that is, gradually to reduce all types of
existing barriers to the free flow of goods across the borders of the
negotiating parties. As of 1980, there were eighty-three member countries,
which together accounted for 85 percent of the world's trade. Members
who grant concessions to any nation are obliged to extend them to all
members on a nondiscriminatory basis. There have been seven major
multinational meetings, the more celebrated of which are known as the
Kennedy and Tokyo rounds. In each session, the list of products exempted
from trade restrictions has been expanded, although there are also some
escape clauses to continue protecting certain domestic producers. It is
assumed that greater trade leads to attainment of other goals, such as
greater investment and employment, ultimately contributing to a better
standard of living all around.

Analysts generally agree that GATT has been very beneficial for
the industrialized countries, but opinions vary about how appropriate
it is for industrializing countries to become members. For example, the
bulk of exports of the latter countries are often products that are still
subject to protectionist policies in the industrialized nations (e.g., agricultural exports). Believing that the benefits of membership in GATT
would be mostly one-sided, several developing nations supported the
establishment of the United Nations Conference on Trade and Development (UNCTAD) in 1964. To many, however, UNCTAD has over
the years produced only good studies and resolutions, having little
impact in the real world. Moreover, practically no one denies that
Mexico needs to take some measures to increase the competitiveness
of its products, not only to increase its exports, but because of the
positive domestic side effects of lower prices and better-quality products.
It was against this background that representatives of the Ministry of
Commerce of Mexico met with a team of GATT experts to discuss the
prospective Mexican membership. After several months of negotiations,
a broad agreement was reached opening the way for Mexico's formal
application for membership. But because the government was aware
that much was at stake in this crucial decision, it called upon business,

professional, and other organizations to debate the issue.[48] Such calls for participation have generally been viewed, in studies of Mexican politics, as legitimizing covers for government policies that have already been decided.[49] Here, however, the issue was really still unresolved, the process vibrant indeed.

The proponents of GATT at the Ministry of Commerce soon found themselves isolated. Business organizations, however stereotypically identified with conservatism or imperialism, generally opposed the move, largely because they would have to bear most of the costs. In some quarters GATT proponents were simply accused of favoring U.S. interests, while its opponents were hailed for their firm stand in defense of "national interests." Professional organizations and some university professors, although agreeing that it is necessary to put an end to excessive protectionism, pointed out that foreign actors have greater resources and experience and would therefore find it easy to push local producers out of the way. But was the only choice between GATT and the end of protectionism with high costs, and the perpetuation of excessive protectionism? In fact, GATT is a multilateral negotiating forum in which small countries such as Mexico could find it very difficult to influence policy. Moreover, as most of Mexico's trade takes place with the United States, Mexico could opt instead to continue negotiating for trade concessions at the bilateral level. Mexico, some would argue, has greater leverage today because of its oil exports to the United States. It might be a better strategy to link an increase in exports to progress made in other areas of bilateral concern.[50] Still others would point out that Mexico can take measures unilaterally to reduce excessive protectionism: The government could grant financial and other supports to smooth the transition toward a more open economy without having to overcommit itself by entering GATT or by abandoning the option of bilateral negotiations with the United States.[51] Therefore, there are alternative courses of action to correct overprotection, one of the central policies associated with the traditional growth model; these alternatives need more careful evaluation. This is one of the critical issues confronting the de la Madrid administration.

CONCLUSIONS

The 1970s was a decade of transition. Several policies aimed at providing a sound basis for self-sustained economic growth. Echeverría's emphasis on the expansion of the public sector and on the improvement of income distribution failed partly because he alienated the business community, a central actor whose organizational strength and economic power cannot be ignored. Under López Portillo, public involvement in the economy continued rising, but his emphasis on investments, efficiency, and growth led to a basically cooperative attitude on the part of the business community, at least until the departing president took over the private banks; it is too early to assess the long-term effects of this action on regime-business relations.

As we enter the 1980s, several long-term development plans have been formulated. These plans, particularly the Global Development Plan and the Industrial Development Plan, are commendable efforts at spelling out a general framework within which economic growth should proceed.[52] Certain aspects of the last stage of the import substitution strategy are being emphasized (e.g., the development of a domestic capital goods industry), while certain elements closely linked to the pursuit of an export-led growth strategy are also the focus of government attention (e.g., modernization of ports and of agriculture as the basis of a major export drive). But overall these plans are indicative, rather than compulsory. It is not yet fully clear to what extent the private sector will cooperate with the government to attain the government's stated goals. The regime, for its part, has taken a positive step: The appointment of Miguel de la Madrid, former minister of programming and budget and the mastermind of the Global Plan, to succeed López Portillo, may indicate that the basic assumptions and objectives of these plans will stick at least through the six years of de la Madrid's administration. Because it is still too early to evaluate their outcomes, these plans are discussed in a broader framework in the final chapter of the book, which provides a look into the future. First, however, realizing that Mexico's domestic political and economic systems do not exist in a vacuum, we turn our attention to Mexico's position in the international system.[53]

NOTES

1. Raymond Vernon, *The Dilemma of Mexico's Development: The Roles of the Private and Public Sectors* (Cambridge, Mass.: Harvard University Press, 1963); Roger D. Hansen, *The Politics of Mexican Development* (Baltimore: Johns Hopkins University Press, 1971); Leopoldo Solís, *La realidad económica mexicana: Retrovisión y perspectivas*, 10th ed. (Mexico City: Siglo XXI, 1980).

2. Nacional Financiera, *Statistics on the Mexican Economy* (Mexico City, 1977), pp. 5, 13–15.

3. Stanford A. Mosk conducted a study showing that the Alemán administration went out of its way to support young and ambitious entrepreneurs, many of whom became leading figures in the industrialization effort. While President Alemán's sympathy for the business community is no secret, it is

also true that the public sector remained an important economic actor during his tenure. See Mosk's *Industrial Revolution in Mexico* (Berkeley: University of California Press, 1954). For a pathbreaking work assessing Mexican government policy through its expenditures, see James W. Wilkie, *The Mexican Revolution: Federal Expenditures and Social Change Since 1910* (Berkeley: University of California Press, 1967).

4. E.V.K. Fitzgerald's comprehensive study on this topic arrives at conclusions similar to the analysis that follows. However, his data and ours are not strictly comparable because they are arranged differently in terms of time-series. See Fitzgerald's *Patterns of Public Sector Income and Expenditures in Mexico* (Austin: University of Texas, Institute of Latin American Studies, 1978).

5. Roberto Anguiano E., *Las finanzas del sector público en México* (Mexico City: UNAM, 1968); Banco de México, *Informe Anual*, various issues.

6. Robert E. Looney, *Mexico's Economy: A Policy Analysis with Forecasts to 1990* (Boulder, Colo.: Westview Press, 1978), p. 49. Fitzgerald reported an even lower ratio of taxes to gross domestic product during the 1960s and a 9.1 percent ratio for 1975 (*Patterns*, p. 8).

7. See the analysis by Mexican tax expert Luis Bravo, "La política impositiva," in *Opciones de política económica en México: Después de la devaluación*, ed. Gerardo Bueno (Mexico City: Tecnós, 1977), pp. 161–198.

8. An unusual discussion of this subject can be found in President López Portillo's fourth annual State of the Union Address. México, Secretaría de Programación y Presupuesto, *Cuarto Informe de Gobierno* (Mexico City, September 1980), pp. 25–26.

9. Fitzgerald, *Patterns*, p. 16.

10. A thorough analysis of debt-related issues is presented by Rosario Green, *El endeudamiento público de México, 1940–1973* (Mexico City: El Colegio de México, 1976); see also her article "Endeudamiento externo y debilidad estatal," in *Foro Internacional* 20, no. 1 (1979):73–117.

11. Inter-American Development Bank, *Economic and Social Progress in Latin America* (Washington, D.C., 1980), p. 101; World Bank, *World Development Report* (Washington, D.C., 1980), pp. 134–135.

12. Peter Vander Spek, "Mexico's Booming Border Zone: A Magnet for Labour-Intensive American Plants," in *Inter-American Economic Affairs*, 29, no. 1 (1975):33–48.

13. L. Antonio Aspra, "Import Substitution in Mexico: Past and Present," *World Development*, 5, no. 1/2 (1977):111–124; René Villarreal, "The Policy of Import-Substituting Industrialization, 1929–1975," in *Authoritarianism in Mexico*, ed. José Luis Reyna and Richard Weinert (Philadelphia: Institute for the Study of Human Issues, 1977), pp. 67–108.

14. World Bank, *Mexico, Manufacturing Sector: Situation, Prospects and Policies* (Washington, D.C.: World Bank, March 1979), p. 56. For a more general discussion about the role of the public sector in encouraging domestic production of capital goods in developing countries, see the study by the World Bank, *The Capital Goods Sector in LDCs: A Case Study for State Intervention?* Staff Working Paper 343 (Washington, D.C.: World Bank, July 1979).

15. Villarreal, "Policy". Another study that questions the wisdom of a capital goods import substitution policy in developing nations is by the World Bank, *Fostering the Capital Goods Sector in LDCs: A Survy of Evidence and Requirements*, Staff Working Paper 376 (Washington, D.C.: World Bank, March 1980).

16. Bela Balassa, *The Newly Industrializing Countries in the World Economy* (New York: Pergamon Press, 1981).

17. Solís, *La realidad económica mexicana*, p. 111.

18. Shlomo Eckstein and Reyes Osorio, "Desarrollo polarizado de la agricultura mexicana," in *La sociedad mexicana: Presente y futuro*, ed. Miguel Wionczek (Mexico City: Fondo de Cultura Económica, 1973), pp. 30–31.

19. Vania Almeida and Kristen de Appendini, *Agricultura capitalista y agricultura campesina en México*, 2d ed. (Mexico City: El Colegio de México, 1977).

20. CONASUPO is a state monopoly supplying poor people with some basic products, primarily food, at substantially subsidized prices.

21. México, Secretaría de Programación y Presupuesto, *Informe sobre las relaciones económicas de México con el exterior* (Mexico City, 1979), p. 62.

22. Inter-American Development Bank, *Economic and Social Progress*, p. 309.

23. México, Secretaría de Programación y Presupuesto, *La población de México, su ocupación y sus niveles de bienestar* (Mexico City, 1979). In its first evaluation of the Global Development Plan, the government acknowledged that there are 18 million people who do not receive any modern medical care. See México, Secretaría de Programación y Presupuesto, *Plan global de desarrollo: Primer informe de avance, 1980–1982* (Mexico City, 1981), p. 18.

24. México, Secretaría del Trabajo y Previsión Social, *Proyecto. Plan nacional de empleo, 1980–1982* (Mexico City, November 1979); and Secretaría de Programación y Presupuesto, *La población* (1979).

25. Saúl Trejo Reyes, "La política laboral," in Bueno, *Opciones*, p. 150. Regarding women in the work force, it is worth noting that a few have recently ascended to very prominent positions; Mexico has only recently had its first female governor and its first female minister.

26. Banco de México, *Informe Anual*, various issues; United Nations Economic Commission for Latin America, *México. Notas para el estudio económico de América Latina* (Washington, D.C., 1979).

27. World Bank, *World Development Report*, 1980, pp. 156–157.

28. The analysis of higher education policy comes from a book manuscript in progress: Daniel Levy, "The State and Higher Education in Latin America: Private-Public Patterns." For a brief analysis of Mexico's social-welfare policy, see Rose Spalding, "Welfare Policymaking: Theoretical Implications of a Mexican Case Study," *Comparative Politics* 12, no. 4 (1980):419–438.

29. David Ibarra, "Mercados, desarrollo y política económica: Perspectivas de la economía mexicana," in *El perfil de Mexico en 1980*, by the editors of Siglo XXI (Mexico City: Siglo XXI, 1970), Vol. 1, pp. 186–187.

30. México, Secretaría de Programación y Presupuesto, *Segundo Informe de Gobierno, Anexo I* (Mexico City, September 1978), pp. 295–300.

31. Banco de México, *Informe Anual*, various issues.

32. México, Secretaría de Programación y Presupuesto, *Informe*, p. 58.

33. México, Secretaría de Patrimonio Nacional, *Law to Promote Mexican Investment and to Regulate Foreign Investment* (Mexico City, 1973).

34. John M. Connor and Willard Mueller, *Market Power and Profitability of Multinational Corporations in Brazil and Mexico* (Washington, D.C.: Government Printing Office, Report to the Subcommittee on Foreign Economic Policy of the Committee on Foreign Relations, US Senate, April 1977), pp. 5–12.

35. Mauricio de María, "Política y resultados en materia de inversiones extranjeras," in *Comercio Exterior* (special issue, July 1976), p. 32; Banco de México, *Informe Anual*, various issues.

36. Banco de México, *The Mexican Economy in 1977* (Mexico City, 1978).

37. Nacional Financiera, *Statistics*, p. 370.

38. Douglas Bennett and Kenneth Sharpe, "El estado como banquero y empresario: El carácter de última instancia de la intervención económica del estado mexicano, 1917–1970," in *Foro Internacional* 20, no. 1 (1979):72.

39. Roger D. Hansen, "The Evolution of U.S.-Mexican Relations: A Socio-Political Perspective," in *United States Relations with Mexico: Context and Content*, ed. Richard D. Erb and Stanley R. Ross (Washington, D.C.: American Enterprise Institute, 1981), pp. 39–48; E.V.K. Fitzgerald, "The State and Capital Accumulation in Mexico," *Journal of Latin American Studies* 10, no. 2 (1978):263–282.

40. Lawrence Whitehead, "La política económica del sexenio de Echeverría: ¿Qué salió mal y por qué?" *Foro Internacional* 20, no. 3 (1980):484–513; and Sidney Weintraub, "Case Study of Economic Stabilization: Mexico," in *Economic Stabilization in Developing Countries*, ed. William R. Cline and Sidney Weintraub (Washington, D.C.: Brookings Institution, 1981), pp. 271–296.

41. For an analysis of the relationship between oil policy and broader economic policy objectives, and the implications for Mexico's domestic and foreign policies, see Gabriel Székely, "The 1976 Oil Export Decision: Effects of the Oil Boom on Mexico's Political Economy," Ph.D. dissertation, George Washington University, 1983.

42. Banco de México, *Informe Anual*, various issues.

43. It is difficult to assess the impact of the elimination of income taxes for the poorest groups, because inflation has been so high, because many people do not receive the minimum wage, and because of the introduction of indirect taxes (VAT) that are paid by everyone.

44. Banco de México, *Informe Anual*, various issues.

45. Ibid., 1980, p. 84. All tons are metric.

46. Oficina de Asesores del C. Presidente de la República, "Sistema Alimentario Mexicano," Mexico City, 1980, unpublished draft. This study includes twenty projects, of which only fourteen are available to the public.

47. México, Secretaría de Gobernación, "Ley de Fomento Agropecuario," in *Diario Oficial* (Mexico City, January 2, 1981), pp. 9–25.

48. For the debate, see "Opiniones sobre el ingreso de México al GATT," *Comercio Exterior* 30, no. 2 (special issue, February 1980); and "México ante el GATT," *El Economista Mexicano* (special issue, January-February 1980). For a

good analysis see Dale Story, "Trade Politics in Mexico: GATT and the Song of the Sirens," paper presented at the annual meeting of the Southwest Political Science Association, Dallas, Texas, 1981.

49. Susan Kaufman Purcell, *The Mexican Profit-Sharing Decision: Politics in an Authoritarian Regime* (Berkeley: University of California Press, 1975).

50. The linkage of oil to negotiations on other bilateral issues has been expounded, notably, by Foreign Minister Jorge Castañeda, "En búsqueda de una posición frente a Estados Unidos," *Foro Internacional* 19, no. 2 (1978):292–302; in the United States, see the supporting statement of Undersecretary of State for Economic Affairs Myer Rashish at New York's Center for Inter-American Relations, "North-American Economic Relations," September 22, 1981.

51. See the position paper of the National Association of Economists of Mexico, *Excélsior*, May 26, 1979.

52. México, Secretaría de Programación y Presupuesto, *Plan global de desarrollo, 1980–1982* (Mexico City, 1980); and México, Secretaría de Patrimonio y Fomento Industrial, *Plan nacional de desarrollo industrial, 1979–1982* (Mexico City, 1979).

53. For further reading, see Clark Reynolds, *The Mexican Economy: Twentieth Century Structure and Growth* (New Haven, Conn.: Yale University Press, 1970); and Jorge Domínguez, ed., *The Political Economy of Mexico: Challenges at Home and Abroad* (Beverly Hills, Calif.: Sage Publications, 1982).

Photo Section

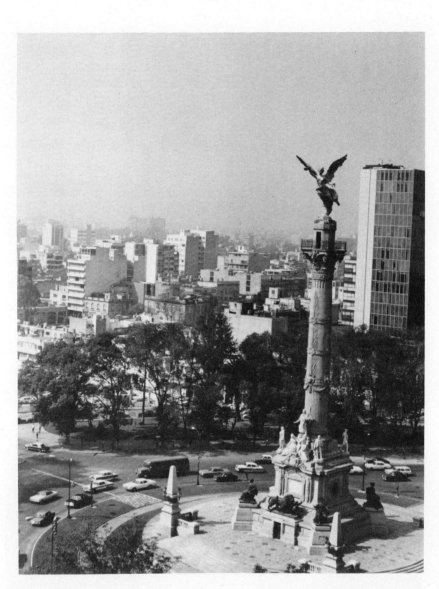

View of El Angel (The Angel) monument and modern areas of Mexico City.
(Photo courtesy of the Mexican National Tourist Council)

Mexico City's famous Plaza de las Tres Culturas (Plaza of the Three Cultures) at Tlatelolco. (Photo courtesy of the Mexican National Tourist Council)

View of Mexico City at night. (Photo courtesy of the Mexican National Tourist Council)

Sunday entertainment, reflecting Mexico's heterogeneity, at Chapultepec, Mexico City's largest park.

The western city of Morelia. The building is adorned with one of the regime's ubiquitous political slogans ("We Are All The Solution").

Rural scene near Cuautla, close to Mexico City.

Outdoor cantina in the southern state of Chiapas.

Peasant house in southern Mexico. (Photo courtesy of James P. Brochin)

Agricultural activity in the central state of Hidalgo. (Photo courtesy of James P. Brochin)

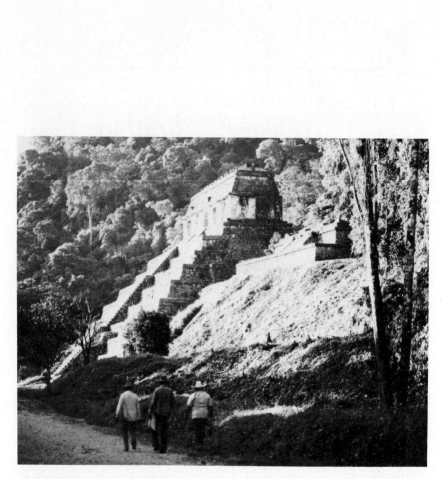

Mayan ruins in southern Mexico. (Photo courtesy of James P. Brochin)

6

Foreign Policy: In the Giant's Shadow

Poor Mexico: So far from God and so close to the United States.
—attributed to Porfirio Díaz

The first element of Mexican foreign policy is . . . its relations with the United States. . . . This is, I repeat, an irrefutable reality, not a political option. It cannot be denied by past problems or historical experiences; it is simply a fact of life.
—Jorge Castañeda, June 1980[1]

Our two quotations, from two distinct eras, suggest a profound continuity in Mexican foreign policy—the central importance of the United States. Surely, as discussed in Chapter 1, Mexico is also becoming increasingly important to the United States. But Mexico is one among many important nations for U.S. foreign policy, while the United States is probably more important than all other nations combined for Mexican foreign policy. When, for example, a recent U.S. ambassador apologized for bothering Mexico's foreign minister with a trivial matter, the minister reassuringly dismissed the apology, explaining that 85 percent of his time was devoted to relations with the United States.[2] A different indicator, to be explored shortly, is that Mexico has relied on the United States for roughly two-thirds of its import and export trade.

Mexico has made significant efforts, especially since 1970, to become more assertive, to build a foreign policy less covered by the giant's shadow. Although some success has been achieved, the shadow remains large indeed. This chapter first summarizes the evolution of Mexico–United States ties. It then analyzes the increased breadth and assertiveness of contemporary Mexican foreign policy beyond the United States, recog-

171

nizing that Mexico–United States relations are affected by this change. Finally, the chapter returns to major, specific issues in contemporary Mexico–United States relations.

EVOLUTION OF MEXICO-UNITED STATES RELATIONS

Annexation

Products of very different colonial heritages, Mexico and the United States had little contact until the nineteenth century. Before long, however, contact was intense and conflictual.

When Mexico achieved independence it was not yet clear that it would be much the weaker neighbor. Within two decades, however, the United States had established its superior strength. Although still relatively equal to the United States in land size, Mexico had fallen far behind in population.[3] Importantly, the United States had avoided the brutal cycle of economic crisis and political instability that had characterized Mexico. Thus, when the two nations went to war in 1846, the United States proved itself far stronger than Mexico.

The issue was Texas. After Mexico complained that the first U.S. ambassador meddled in Mexico's domestic politics, the United States appointed a successor who meddled even more, actively plotting against Mexico's interests in Texas. U.S. settlers had been immigrating into Texas. Fearing revolutionary consequences, Mexico limited the legal flow in 1830. This should be remembered, in one of history's ironies, as the year that Mexico slammed the border shut on the United States—or attempted to do so. The measure proved impossible to enforce, just as contemporary U.S. laws fail to keep Mexicans out, and the first wave of "illegal aliens" crossed the border. In 1836, Texans declared their independence from Mexico and soon defeated General Santa Anna's Mexican troops. Although President Andrew Jackson happily recognized Texan independence in 1837, the United States initially rejected Texan requests for annexation and statehood. Abolitionists opposed the addition of another slave state, and there was some concern that Mexico not be provoked any further. But pressures built, and President Polk was a powerful proponent of U.S. expansion.

In 1845, the United States annexed Texas, and one of the more lopsided wars in U.S. history ensued. From Mexico's point of view the war's cause was clear: U.S. aggression. Not only did the United States annex Texas, but it claimed boundaries for Texas that Mexico simply could not accept. The United States resorted to more complex rationalizations, ones that could not even unite U.S. opinion. Polk did get his war resolution through the Senate with only two dissensions—the same number that would defy President Lyndon Johnson's Gulf of Tonkin resolution for military action in Vietnam more than a century later. As with the Vietnam War, however, considerable dissent quickly developed. Some leaders in the Old South feared that the United States was going too far against Mexico, while many northeasterners unambiguously decried "Mr. Polk's War"; the Massachusetts legislature condemned the U.S. role. Prominent dissenters ranged from literary figures such as Henry David Thoreau and Ralph Waldo Emerson to political figures such as young Abraham Lincoln. Unlike the Vietnam War, however, the war with Mexico represented the ascent of the United States as an active—or overactive—international power and ended in striking military success. Indeed the war itself was short. General Winfield Scott captured the key port of Veracruz and marched on to take Mexico City. Mexico's most treasured war memory lies in the heroism of six young cadets who jumped to their death rather than surrender themselves at Chapultepec Castle. Today there are prominent monuments to the *Niños Héroes* throughout Mexico, from the castle itself, to a subway station, to streets in many major cities, to significant attention in public school textbooks.

However militarily undramatic the war was, the settlement reached with the Treaty of Guadalupe Hidalgo was quite dramatic—and unjust. Mexico lost about one-half of its territory, including all or parts of what are now Arizona, California, Colorado, Nevada, New Mexico, and Utah. As a postscript, the United States swallowed still more Mexican territory with the Gadsden Purchase of 1853, when Mexico—desperately in need of money—sold off a chunk of its land. That chunk would eventually include copper mines and create an unnatural border, actually splitting cities in half. Moreover, the war obviously hurt Mexican efforts to build unity, stability, and prosperity in the new nation.

It would be difficult indeed to understand contemporary Mexican attitudes toward the United States without reference to the enormous land grab of the mid-nineteenth century. Not that most Mexicans feel an active anger about the war or advocate "taking back the land." Rather, sentiment remains like a dormant volcano in the historical consciousness. There is a sense of resentment based on the unhappy role Mexico played in U.S. expansionism. The war may not be an explicit political issue, but it is a vital historical referent and symbol. Consequent "wounded nationalism" perhaps serves today as a useful foreign policy bargaining chip: Mexican policymakers can tell their U.S. counterparts that, restrained by sensitive public opinion, they must negotiate tenaciously.

From Accommodation to Revolutionary Conflict to Accommodation

As Mexico next came to suffer at the hands of a different foreigner, France, relations improved with the United States. President Abraham Lincoln continued to recognize the regime of President Benito Juárez throughout the period of French intervention. Outstanding claims between Mexico and the United States were settled in 1868. Mexico–United States relations deepened when the porfiriato replaced the reform and created just the sort of domestic environment that pleased U.S. economic interests. Unaffectionately dubbed "father of foreigners and stepfather of Mexicans," Porfirio Díaz extended further the already attractive invitations to foreign investors. He eased requirements for acquiring land in border regions and on use of subsoil resources and generally encouraged increased foreign economic activity in Mexico. Most important, Díaz secured the political stability that foreign investors demanded. Mexico's doors flew open not just for its northern neighbor but for West Europeans as well; nonetheless, the United States took greatest advantage of the opportunities and established its predominance among foreigners in Mexico's economy. There was even increased foreign penetration of the priesthood, to the natural dismay of many Mexican clergy.

As the Mexican Revolution replaced political stability and friendliness to foreign investment with instability and nationalism, Mexico–United States relations predictably worsened. And, unfortunately for Mexico, the United States was in an imposing muscle-flexing period. Its easy 1898 victory in the Spanish-American War and its construction of the Panama Canal reflected the emergence of the United States as a true world power, including a heightened predominance in the New World. If subsequent events are viewed within this political-economic context—Mexico torn by revolutionary instability, the United States prepared to impose its will—then the machinations of individual political actors may count for little. Still, individual behavior not only helped shape events but left scarring symbols in Mexico's memory. U.S. Ambassador Henry Lane Wilson, for example, is perhaps a stereotypic villain. In complicity with Mexico's counterrevolutionary leaders, he is widely believed to have participated in the sinister assassination of President Madero, the elected and conspicuously nonrevolutionary democrat. The ambassador hoped to return Mexico to his own conception of peace, progress, and prosperity.

President Wilson, by contrast, emerged as perhaps the higher-minded villain. Whereas the preceding president, William Howard Taft (1909–1913), had clearly based his actions on U.S. self-interest, without trying to "improve" Mexico's own system, Wilson was a human rights activist, a zealous democrat, albeit a paternalistic one. This is not to say that he would subordinate U.S. material interests to moral concerns, but that he identified them with a type of political regime that Mexico did not have. Whatever justifications he saw, Wilson was an interventionist, to the point of using military force and the threat of further military force. He managed to antagonize not only those he opposed but also those he favored. He helped to topple the Huerta government (which the United States itself had helped install) by denying diplomatic recognition, cutting off Huerta's European arms supply, authorizing arms sales to Huerta's opponents, and seizing on a very limited provocation for the capture of Veracruz (by now a favorite U.S. pressure point).

There are differences of opinion over the extent to which the United States shaped Mexican domestic politics in the early revolutionary years. Suffice it to say that the United States did not create all the strife but did intervene forcefully to influence the outcome. At various points, the United States supported Madero, Huerta, and Villa, before settling on Carranza as the most likely figure to win the military battle, establish stability, and deal with U.S. economic interests in an acceptable manner.[4] As with Indian disunity and Cortés's conquest, or nineteenth-century disunity and the U.S. and then French actions, so again in the early years of the revolution, Mexican independence was undermined by domestic disunity and instability as well as by blatant foreign intervention.

Angered over U.S. intervention on behalf of Carranza, Villa undertook vengeful raids across the border. U.S. general John Pershing unsuccessfully pursued him through northern Mexico, thus inadvertently contributing to Villa's immortalization. Even today, Villa remains the hero of numerous popular ballads. Although tensions mounted still further, additional Mexico–United States hostilities were ultimately averted. Mexican politics stabilized somewhat, and Wilson and Pershing were soon preoccupied overseas with U.S. participation in World War I. Nonetheless, bilateral bitterness lingered. Mexico did not support the United States and its allies in the world war. It did, however, reject the tantalizing Zimmerman note in which Germany opportunistically solicited Mexican support in exchange for a promise that a victorious Germany would return to Mexico the lands previously taken by the United States.

The main source of conflict now became compensation for U.S. properties nationalized as a result of Mexico's revolution. As general and then president, Carranza proved to be more of a nationalist than the United States had hoped. Diplomatic recognition of Carranza's successor (Obregón) was delayed three years, until Mexico in 1923 signed the Bucareli Agreements, promising not to apply certain legislation retroactively. Only a mini-era of good feeling would follow the Bucareli Agreements. By 1925, Mexico's new president, Plutarco Elías Calles, had toughened national policies on oil and land; one provision declared that disputes would be handled by Mexican adjudication, not U.S. citizens' recourse to their own government's actions. Both oil and land proved to be tough issues, major problems for Mexico–United States relations.[5] The new U.S. ambassador undiplomatically proclaimed Mexico on trial. Additionally, Calles unleashed a brutal attack on Mexico's church, provoking many conservative Catholics, both in Mexico and in the United States, to solicit U.S. intervention.[6]

The crisis abated, partly through the efforts of the new U.S. ambassador, Dwight Morrow, a Yankee Wall Streeter who demonstrated respect for Mexican political independence and enthusiasm for Mexican culture. Deeper roots for Morrow's success lay in Mexico's inclination to temper further reforms. When Lázaro Cárdenas assumed the presidency in 1934, Mexico's economy, save agriculture, was possibly more controlled by foreign interests, certainly by U.S. interests, than in 1910, after the porfiriato's noted coziness with foreigners.[7] Mexico's most renowned revolutionary president then began to alter the ownership balance, nationalizing the railroads and—most important—petroleum (see Chapter 7). Now another deep root for improved Mexico–United States relations developed. Despite the challenge to U.S. business interests, a historical pattern was broken: Mexico–United States relations did not sharply deteriorate as Mexico asserted its independence. Franklin Roosevelt's Good Neighbor Policy set a new tone of acceptance, prevailing over considerable domestic pressure for retaliation. The change was symbolized by the friendly ambassadorship of Josephus Daniels, himself formerly the secretary of the navy that had occupied Veracruz; his assistant had been F.D.R. As with the Mexican revolution and World War I, so with Mexican nationalization and World War II: A "soft" U.S. policy toward Mexico was motivated largely by widening U.S. foreign policy concerns.

With World War II came increased Mexico–United States cooperation. Mexico declared war on the Axis powers in 1942 and made a strong contribution to the war effort. Mexican soldiers did not participate significantly in active combat, but they did add to the manpower reserve. Most important, the Mexican economy accelerated its production of raw materials, and Mexico and the United States entered into the "*bracero*" program that brought Mexican workers to the labor-drained United States; in fact, these two contributions would further integrate the Mexican economy into the U.S. economy, thus shaping future Mexican foreign policy.

As we reach the era in which Mexico's regime institutionalizes and stabilizes itself, no longer subject to repeated fundamental policy reorientations, we shift from a chronologically to conceptually oriented account. Grand historical disputes over territory, property rights, debts, diplomatic recognition, and active intervention gave way to lesser problems, mostly economic, over water rights, fishing, tariffs, migrant workers, and drugs. In time, some of these would become very serious, but during the 1940s, 1950s, and 1960s, Mexico–United States relations were comparatively smooth. If the Cárdenas-Roosevelt era represented a transitional stage away from continually tense conflict, the new equilibrium would generally hold for the ensuing three decades. Mexico's domestic development clearly favored a stable industrialization that encouraged secure, profitable U.S. investment. The Mexican Revolution, by all serious accounts, was over. Naturally, the United States was eager to foster this sort of (nonrevolutionary) relationship. In 1947, President Truman paid the first U.S. presidential visit to Mexico City since the revolution, and President Eisenhower met with Mexico's president on several occasions. John Kennedy's trip to Mexico evoked an enthusiastic response by millions to his Alliance for Progress concerns, his youth and glamor, his religious affiliation (as the United States's first Catholic president), and the promise of a better future through bilateral cooperation. Johnson's early contacts were soon overshadowed by his preoccupation with the Vietnam War and by both his and President Díaz Ordaz's domestic troubles, and the Nixon and Ford administrations paid only intermittent attention to Mexico–United States relations. Oil has headed those bilateral issues that have made Mexico a major concern for Presidents Carter and Reagan alike.

REACHING BEYOND THE UNITED STATES

Mexican foreign policy is not determined wholly by Mexico–United States relations. The tug between the efforts to achieve greater independent breadth and the constraints encountered therein form one of the themes of Mexican foreign policy. For decades, "universalism" and "leftism" have suggested a respectable degree of independence. These concepts will be defined and then examined most closely in Mexican-Cuban relations. Additionally, since 1970, Mexican foreign policy has entered an era of increased assertiveness. The respective efforts and constraints involved in this change will be examined in terms of Mexican policy toward Central America and the Caribbean and toward the rest of the Americas. Finally, the Iranian crisis of 1979 will be reviewed as an example of Mexico's independent orientation in foreign affairs *beyond* the Americas.

Universalism, Leftism, and Cuba

A foreign policy obedient to U.S. leadership would befriend U.S. allies and reject U.S. foes. Mexico has generally repudiated such criteria in favor of more universal diplomatic ties. The universalistic approach is poignantly proclaimed in the Estrada Doctrine, issued in 1930: Mexico grants diplomatic recognition to any government. Mexico does not judge others as the United States continually judged Mexico or still judges others. Instead, Mexico champions a host of platitudinous principles, widely popular at least in rhetoric: national sovereignty and self-determination, equality among nations, nonintervention, peaceful settlement of disputes. Thus, it opposed veto power for Security Council members at the United Nations, favoring greater weight for the General Assembly, in which all members have equal representation. Mexico is one of the nations to honor most the Latin American tradition of providing asylum for political refugees. "Friend of all" is the way official Mexican propaganda sometimes likes to characterize it, although noted exceptions have qualified that approach to the point where Mexico has sometimes disavowed not only friendship but even diplomatic recognition. In fact, the breadth and vagueness of such platitudinous principles leaves great flexibility for Mexico's president. He can justify almost any foreign policy with consecrated principle. Universalism provided a sure rationale for ignoring the U.S.-led boycott of the 1980 Moscow Olympics in the aftermath of the Soviet invasion of Afghanistan, but had López Portillo wished to boycott he could have claimed to be defending Afghanistan's national sovereignty. Universalism has been one major component of Mexican foreign policy, but it is not automatically applied.

Mexico is a participant and supporter of international organizations, including the Organization of American States (OAS), Inter-American Development Bank, and Association for Latin American Integration (formerly the Latin American Free Trade Association), and beyond the Americas, the United Nations, International Monetary Fund, and World Bank. But Mexico tries to balance participation with independence. It is wary of U.S. domination in the inter-American organizations. It has joined neither GATT on the one hand nor OPEC or the movement of non-aligned nations on the other. It has, however, entered the 1980s by assuming a seat on the UN's Security Council for the first time since 1946. Mexico is striving to increase its participation in international fora when, and only when, such participation would not jeopardize its independence.

Beyond its universalistic, rather than pro-U.S., posture, Mexico sometimes seems to relish the "leftism" of its foreign policy. By "leftism," we mean Mexico's sympathy for leftist movements outside Mexico. Why, paradoxically, does a regime that is conservative at home propagandize a leftist foreign policy? One reason is genuine conviction, genuine support for nationalist or popular movements. To dismiss this factor is to indulge in over-cynicism and to impute too much surreptitious calculation to every decision. Another reason is to maintain, and trumpet, some independence from the United States. Another, however, is to divert attention from unprogressive domestic policies.[8] A populist foreign policy, "easy leftism," comes at relatively little cost to Mexico's rulers; a populist domestic policy would involve far greater sacrifices. After the 1968 demonstrations against Mexico's lack of democracy, the two biggest Mexico City demonstrations in the 1960s and 1970s were against the Vietnam War and the 1973 coup in Chile, demonstrations that not only cost the government nothing, but even provided it opportunities for popular rhetoric. Another recent example: President López Portillo pointedly refused to attend the 1977 Washington, D.C., signing of the Panama Canal treaty, protesting that it did not go far enough for national sovereignty and that the event was marred by the presence of certain South American military dictators. A cartoon in the satirical comic book *Los Agachados* (March 17, 1976) captures the domestic policy–foreign policy paradox: A Mexican leader pontificates that Mexico will resume diplomatic relations with Spain (then under Franco) only after the dictatorship is overthrown and democracy established, to which the Spanish general replies: "In Mexico." And, in fact, the Spanish political system did shortly become more democratic than Mexico's.

Relations with Cuba offer a revealing case of the domestic politics component of Mexico's foreign policy. Mexico was the only Latin American nation that did not break diplomatic or commercial relations with communist Cuba, despite strong U.S. and OAS pressure. It has opposed the U.S. embargo against Cuba. One motivation has been to defend (Cuba's) national sovereignty in the face of (U.S.) intervention. At the same time, Mexico has asserted its independence of the United States and gained a degree of revolutionary legitimacy. President López Mateos used recognition of Cuba and criticism of the 1961 U.S.-backed Bay of Pigs invasion to support his claim to be "within the constitution, of the extreme left." President Echeverría repeatedly tried to reap revolutionary credibility via the Cuban connection. Even President López Portillo, conservative at home, strengthened the connection by receiving Castro in Mexico in 1980. Later, López Portillo announced a future reciprocal trip, giving Castro a tremendous boost at precisely the moment that he suffered what many considered the international humiliation of seeing thousands of disenchanted Cubans grab a sudden opportunity to flee their island. Indeed, Mexico has been trying, in recent years, to reintegrate Cuba into Latin American organizations.

The Mexican government's domestic exploitation of Cuba's revolution goes beyond seizing leftist legitimacy. It has even included skillful manipulation of the Mexican left![9] By not joining in U.S. pressures against Cuba, the Mexican government denied its left an exclusive claim to favorable Mexican public opinion on Cuba. Moreover, the government carefully monitored its left. It did not oppose the strong anti-Cuba campaign launched by Mexico's church, press, and conservatives in general. In fact, at that time facing economic troubles, the government was looking for support from the foreign and domestic business community. It is also plausible that the government welcomed the prospect of winning part of the new U.S. sugar market opened by the U.S. embargo on Cuba. In any case, when leftist pro-Cuba demonstrations seemed to pose the danger of formidable domestic mobilization, the government clamped down. It was made clear that the Cuban revolution was relevant to Mexican domestic policy only insofar as the regime could shore up its own revolutionary credentials through a leftist foreign policy. In return for its friendly foreign policy, the Mexican government expects Cuba to stay out of Mexican domestic politics.[10]

Increasing Assertiveness

Mexico's universalism and leftism have represented a degree of foreign policy independence. Yet Mexico's foreign policy until 1970 has also been described as essentially defensive and limited in geographical scope.[11] Mexico's international relationships have generally been more ceremonial than important, even in inter-American affairs. The point should not be overstated. Mexico has probably asserted its independence in foreign policy more than have most Latin American nations. For example, it has played a prominent role in negotiations concerning disarmament and the law of the sea.

Whatever the balance between defensiveness and assertiveness prior to 1970, assertiveness has increased markedly since then. There are several explanations for this new assertiveness. One concerns the decline of bipolar international dominance, especially the diminished U.S. ability to have its way in international affairs. The Mexican government itself has spoken hopefully of the "activism of middle-range powers." Certainly, Mexico could not pretend to undo its strong ties to the United States, but it has tried to break the fatalistic acceptance of the idea that nothing important could be done about it; Mexico has tried to increase its *degree* of independence. Additionally, Echeverría's administration acknowledged fundamental problems with Mexico's development model, problems that required not just domestic but foreign policy change. Disenchantment with Mexico–United States economic relations was deepened by new U.S. protectionist trade policies. Finally, inheriting a crisis of political legitimacy, the Echeverría administration could enhance its popular image by emphasizing its independence of the United States.[12]

Leftism, that mixture of true independence and guile, has become more pronounced. Mexico has sought leadership in the Third World. In 1975 alone, Mexico established diplomatic relations with thirty-three developing nations. It also pushed the "Charter of Economic Rights and Duties of States," championing Third World positions, although in reality the developed world's objections to widespread redistribution seemed to leave Mexico with only a symbolic diplomatic success. Similarly, Echeverría's attempt to broaden diplomatic and trade relations with communist nations has had only mixed results, although Mexico has markedly strengthened ties with Western Europe and Japan. If presidents since the 1940s have traveled widely to demonstrate their independence of the United States, Echeverría outdid them all. He was dubbed the "around the world in eighty days president." Wherever he went, Echeverría damned superpower politics, multinational corporations, and indiscriminate foreign investment. He accepted, perhaps even pridefully, the wrath of U.S. political and economic elites.

Mexico under Echeverría provided many examples of using foreign policy as a showcase for leftist expression, but also instances of truly asserting, successfully or not, a more active, independent foreign policy. Within Latin America, Echeverría improved relations with Cuba. More dramatic was his almost ostentatious support of Chile's Marxist president, Salvador Allende. Echeverría did not simply stand by the traditional Mexican position of nonintervention, serving notice that Mexico would once again criticize U.S. moves to topple a Latin American experiment in socialism. He repeatedly proclaimed Mexico's enthusiasm for Chile's experiment, much to the chagrin of Mexico's right but with the approval of much of Mexican public opinion and, predictably, of the officially organized political groups. He and Allende exchanged solidarity visits. Allende praised Echeverría's progressivism in standing up to Uncle Sam. And when Allende was toppled, Mexico did not restrict its criticism to U.S. interventionism but extended it forcefully to Chile's ensuing military regime, labeling it a pariah and breaking diplomatic relations (which were not restored under López Portillo). Mexico welcomed a tremendous influx of Chilean refugees. Here was an important case of moving beyond universalism to a more assertive posture of identifying with friends and actively opposing enemies. Previously, Mexico's opposition to Franco's Spain, a special case involving the mother country and the political regime hated by the many prominent Spanish refugees who had settled in Mexico, was an unusual example of such active negativism (including nonrecognition) in Mexican foreign policy.

Beyond Latin America, Echeverría's bid for Third World leadership often involved both leftism and independence of the United States. One notorious failure was Echeverría's ignominious support, which set Mexico apart from most of Latin America's major nations, for a 1975 UN resolution equating Zionism with racism. Mexico soon tried to disavow the vote, but not before provoking a strong outcry and a tourist boycott. Even economic expediency could not have explained Echeverría's blunder, for Mexico is one nation invulnerable to the Arab oil weapon. The episode contributed to an image of Echeverría's impulsiveness, symbolic leftism, and ultimate ineffectiveness.

Under Echeverría, Mexico had moved further away from defensive, U.S.-oriented foreign policy toward greater activism in favor of friends and even challenges to foes. Paradoxically, however, Mexico's initial period of jarring assertiveness may have led to "much more dependence on the exterior,"[13] perhaps illustrating the limits to independence, or at least to overzealous expressions of it.

President López Portillo's main challenge (now de la Madrid's) was to sustain Mexico's increased assertiveness while restoring confidence in the underlying pragmatism of Mexican foreign policy. Activism associated with any one leader, however bold, might have appeared transient, even irresponsible. Sustained activism might be seen as fundamental to Mexican foreign policy, institutionalized, and highly responsible. Definite parallels emerge with domestic policy and the desire to depart from the pre-1970 development model in a pragmatic way that would effectively sustain, even revitalize, other aspects of the model. And substantial success has been achieved in restoring credibility. President López Portillo was greatly helped by his foreign minister, Jorge Castañeda. Mexico's increased activism has now clearly proven itself to be based on strengthened national resolve with solid political-economic underpinnings. For example, Mexican relations with Israel have returned to normalcy and cordiality, involving cultural and technological interchanges as well as Israel's need for oil.

Some observers question whether Mexico has continued its assertiveness as well as it has restored its credibility. Perhaps post-Echeverría Mexico is returning to its traditional defensiveness, caution, and restraint in international affairs, to a clear priority on relations with the United States rather than the Third World; just as López Mateos's activism was curtailed by Díaz Ordaz, so Echeverría's may have been curtailed by López Portillo.[14] To go further, one might regard much of López Portillo's apparent assertiveness as a cover for a return to past foreign policy. While such an interpretation merits consideration, there is considerable evidence that a "new" (post-1970) assertiveness is now fundamental to Mexican foreign policy. Just as we must not mistake rhetorical leftism for substantive leftism, so we must not let López Portillo's more "businesslike" and diplomatic approaches obscure the reality of increased assertiveness. For example, Mexico assumed a leadership role in the 1981 North-South conference (see Chapter 7).

In relations with the United States, Mexico's return to pragmatism did not undermine its firm diplomatic posture. Indeed, López Portillo enthusiastically symbolized Mexico's foreign policy assertiveness in direct meetings between heads of state. After López Portillo had become President Carter's first official foreign visitor, Carter returned the visit—and his host wrote a new chapter on standing up to Uncle Sam. The Mexican president immediately delivered a symbolic statement at the airport by making Carter walk over to greet him. It was to be at best a calculatedly cool visit. Some will remember February 14, 1979, as a Valentine's Day massacre. Cruel jokes circulated contrasting Carter's presence to the proximate ones by truly welcome superstars like Brigitte Bardot and Sophia Loren, not to mention the pope and, for a fairer comparison, the president of France. A low point came when Carter's undiplomatic attempt at a humorous comment about Moctezuma's revenge met with stony silence. López Portillo's visible independence earned him high marks— and provided some revolutionary legitimacy with which to blunt criticism of conservative domestic policies.

The Mexican government shrewdly affected surprise over the negative U.S. reaction to Mexican treatment of a beleaguered President Carter. After all, Mexico had simply spoken frankly, as a confident equal, not a scrappy troublemaker. Carter, Mexico argued, had been reasonable, not weak. To his credit, Carter spoke some in Spanish, always an appreciated gesture. To the Mexicans, the fact that his statements acknowledging Mexico's rightful interests should cause a stir in the United States only reflected U.S. "media hype" and the persistence of colonial "gringo" mentalities. There is a fear in Mexico that these mentalities may have once again taken over the White House with the Reagan presidency. Although early meetings were generally cordial, bilateral tensions increased by 1982.

Mexico has reason to fear, moreover, that the United States still treats it as a junior partner, not a nation with an independent foreign policy meriting first-class recognition. Despite the elevation of Mexico within U.S. foreign policy concerns, the choices of recent U.S. ambassadors to Mexico have been seen as slights. President Carter selected Patrick Lucey, ex-governor of Wisconsin, hardly a diplomat steeped in knowledge of Mexico. Lucey spoke no Spanish. When he subsequently resigned to return to domestic U.S. politics, Carter left the position vacant for an unusually long time. He finally appointed Julian Nava, the first Mexican-American to serve in the post, who was regarded as hostile by many of Mexico's foreign policymakers. President Reagan then appointed John Gavin. Like the president an ex-actor, Gavin was known in Mexico mostly as the rich, erudite gentleman in a prominent Bacardi rum commercial. The appointment was greeted by many Mexicans with dismay and ridicule. On the other hand, Gavin's mother was Mexican, and Gavin, fluent in Spanish, held a degree in Latin American studies and had some experience associated with the OAS. He could be seen as more professionally prepared than Lucey, more sympathetic than Nava. But the new ambassador had been primarily an actor and really had no record on Mexico, except perhaps for one speech in which he advocated, of all things not likely to win Mexican confidence, a North American common market. The appointment was especially disturbing after rumors had circulated that former Senator Jacob Javits would be selected. With his extraordinary experience and prestige in foreign affairs, Javits might have been a symbol of U.S. acceptance of Mexico's claims to increased foreign policy significance. Mexican dissatisfaction with Gavin intensified in 1982, when the ambassador rather undiplomatically, if indirectly, raised questions about Mexican political stability and also suggested that Mexico join GATT.

Relations With Central America and the Caribbean

No region outside the United States has recently been more important to Mexican foreign policy than Central America and the Caribbean. Geography obviously accounts for that. Mexican policy toward the region has expressed many of the key tenets of Mexican foreign policy in general. One has been the principle of nonintervention. Mexico opposed the U.S. ventures into Guatemala in 1954, Cuba in 1961, and the Dominican Republic in 1965, all to thwart leftist victories. Mexico saw each U.S. action as a blow to the sovereignty of small nations. Furthermore, since the late 1970s, it has made clear that it strongly opposes potential U.S. intervention in Nicaragua or El Salvador. It also opposed Guatemalan moves to assert its territorial claims over tiny Belize, formerly controlled by Great Britain and independent only since November 1981. Mexico itself had territorial claims in Belize, to the point that hostilities with Guatemala seemed possible in the mid-1970s, but Mexico then renounced its claims as inconsistent with nonintervention and self-determination.

Nonintervention has been relaxed to allow for growing assertiveness. Mexico gave strong public support, in the late 1970s, to the Sandinista insurgency against Somoza's government in Nicaragua. The Estrada Doctrine notwithstanding, Mexico broke diplomatic relations with the besieged dictatorship. It also supported the insurgent left in El Salvador, although it pushed more for a political accommodation when the guerrilla's 1981 offensive failed to topple the regime. With France, Mexico publicly urged recognition of the guerrillas as a "representative political force" with which the government should negotiate. The initiative was rejected not just by El Salvador and the United States, but also by most of Latin America's powerful nations. Yet Mexico did not react by diminishing its activism. On the contrary, in 1981–1982, it offered itself as a "communicator" to help reach wide-ranging compromises between the United

States and each of its Central American adversaries: the Salvadoran guerrillas, the Nicaraguan government, and even Cuba. It urged greater restraint by all parties, including a "truce of silence" to reduce tensions. In return for leftist moderation, especially in terms of not exporting revolution, the United States was urged to renounce the use, support, or threat of force. The Reagan administration responded with interest in elements of Mexico's proposals but also with resentment against what it perceived as Mexico's indiscreet diplomacy and excessive tolerance for leftist political forces, and it soon became clear that the United States had implicitly rejected the Mexican initiative. Nonetheless, López Portillo's general arguments were endorsed by candidate de la Madrid, who emphasized an independent Mexican foreign policy and the need for United States–Cuban negotiations.

Perhaps Mexico is playing the independent leftist, foreign policy game. Perhaps it is genuinely pursuing its concerns for social reform. Probably most important, however, is Mexico's concern for its *own* political stability. Few nations feel secure when instability grows in neighboring nations. Just as the United States wants a stable Mexico, Mexico wants a stable Central America. Mexico's view is that regional stability is best served, in the long run, by replacing narrowly based dictatorships with more popular regimes dedicated to reform.[15] Fear of communism is not a major driving force in Mexican foreign policy.

Contemporary Mexico, therefore, does not simply work with whoever is in power; it takes sides. In doing so, it has repeatedly found itself at odds with the United States. Tensions mounted as the new Reagan administration seemed to emphasize the external (Cuban-Soviet) roots of instability (whereas Mexico emphasizes the indigenous roots) and therefore emphasized military support for anticommunist dictatorships, de-emphasizing human rights. When, for example, Reagan suggested a "get tough" policy on Cuban interference in El Salvador, López Portillo responded indirectly but clearly by praising Cuba, even at one point calling Cuba the country "most dear" to Mexico's heart.

Mexico's increased activism is not merely verbal. With Venezuela, Mexico has developed pioneering policies, based on low-interest credit, to supply oil to Central America and the Caribbean (see Chapter 7). These policies are aimed at helping small nations in need and thus promoting regional stability. They represent a creative response to the sad observation that the oil boom for a few privileged Third World nations has spelled economic disaster for many others. Given that many Caribbean nations (such as Jamaica) are democracies, the policies take on added political implications. They demonstrate a Mexican commitment not to leftism only, but to political stability based on popular legitimacy; leftist popular legitimacy, however, does not scare off Mexico as it scares off the United States. And so, beyond the program with Venezuela, Mexico also helps Cuba to explore for needed oil. This action has predictably drawn negative reaction from the United States, even though it may help Cuba diminish its overwhelming dependency on the Soviet Union. Similarly, Mexico has offered a mixed reaction to the United States's own plan to help small nations in the area, President Reagan's Caribbean Basin Initiative. Mexico generally praises the search for political solutions through economic assistance but also regards the plan as both piecemeal and too tied to armaments policy.

Mexico's assertive regional policy is sometimes leftist, sometimes not, but it brushes aside what it regards as ultimately self-defeating U.S. paranoia about Cuban interventionism. In effect, however, Mexico is contesting not just the United States but Cuba for leadership in the region. Mexico in the 1960s denounced and even restrained Cuban and U.S. efforts to influence the region, but it did not yet actively compete with them. A good illustration of Mexico's recently increased assertiveness came in an April 1981 meeting between López Portillo and the president of Venezuela. The two leaders extended their oil program from nine to eleven nations. But the meeting's main purpose was to demonstrate determination to check foreign influence in the region. While Venezuela pointed its finger principally at Cuba, Mexico pointed its finger principally at the United States. López Portillo denounced "paternalistic" pretexts for foreign intervention based on the alleged prior intervention of others (Cuba and the Soviet Union) as an "insult to intelligence." Instability, he reminded everyone, is rooted not in communist infiltration but in social injustice. He joined the Venezuelan president in calling for aid to Nicaragua's revolutionary regime, just a week after the United States had cut off its economic aid because of alleged Nicaraguan support of the insurgent left in El Salvador. Similarly, later in 1981, Mexico pledged to aid leftist Grenada, despite U.S. antipathy to that island's "Cuban tendencies." In both the Caribbean and Central America, Mexico's specific policies have clearly had the common purpose of asserting influence. "Our voices in unison," López Portillo declared, "are raised loud and strong in our region."

Relations with South America

If a look to Mexico's immediate south shows some of the opportunities for assertiveness and independence in Mexico foreign policy, a look further south points up some of the more profound obstacles. There are inherent affinities between Mexico and South America based on common language, heritage, culture, traditions, and have-not status compared to the United States. Yet South America remains marginally important, compared to the United States, in Mexican foreign policy. In fact, Mexico has purposely limited its role in inter-American organizations—largely because it has recognized U.S. dominance within them. Thus, it has favored the UN over the OAS. The United States is much less dominant in the UN; for example, U.S. efforts to isolate Cuba were backed in the OAS but not in the world body. Mexico has consistently opposed U.S. attempts, especially forceful in the early 1960s, to create an inter-American military force.[16]

Mexico's posture has made it a maverick more than a leader in inter-American affairs. At a 1954 Caracas conference, Mexico proposed an amendment barring action against fellow OAS members to a U.S. proposition on international communism; the amendment was soundly defeated. When Mexico voted against the 1962 OAS resolution to expel Cuba, it found itself together with Cuba in a group of two. OAS nations are more likely to look to Argentina or Brazil for leadership. Mexico may be respected for its independence, but that very independence often sets it apart. Even Mexico's role in the world's North-South relations, where it is a champion of redistribution toward the South, ironically has made Mexico a leader more to some African and Asian than South American nations. Economically, as we will see shortly, Mexico has very little trade with most South American nations. In 1982 President López Portillo and President-designate de la Madrid sided with almost all of Latin America by supporting Argentina in its violent South Atlantic confrontation with Great Britain, but Mexico certainly did not assume a leadership role.

Relations with Canada

Similar constraints on establishing significant, independent policies emerge when we look northward, beyond the United States to Canada. If political desire were more powerful than economic realities, then Mexico would probably balance its involvement with its two northern neighbors. Mexico has much in common with Canada in terms of foreign policy objectives and the search for independence in the giant's shadow. These are the only two nations bordering the world's richest nation. There are parallel difficulties in Canada–United States and Mexico–United States relations. There is concern over fishing rights, cross-border pollution, cultural penetration, and especially economic penetration, even control. Both Mexico and Canada fear U.S. inclinations toward some sort of North American common market. Both already receive heavy U.S. investment, and while Mexico is the United States's third major trading partner, Canada is *the* major partner; while Mexico was the second foreign nation President Reagan visited, Canada was the first. Many Canadian workers depend on U.S. business, and tourism is a major industry. Canada's hope of strengthening its economic position through "Canadianization" of the

U.S.-dominated petroleum industry echoes the Mexicanization of oil in 1938. The United States has become increasingly concerned with Canada's stability (which seems threatened by regionalism). A *U.S. News and World Report* (March 9, 1981) cover story sensationalized heightened U.S. interest in its neighbors: "Our Troubled Neighbors—Dangers for the U.S." The United States disapproves of Canadian friendship toward Cuba and permissiveness toward leftist movements in Central America; Canada, for its part, fears U.S. intervention in that region. On all these points there is substantial overlap of interests between Canada and Mexico. Illustratively, the 1981 North-South meeting in Mexico was cohosted by the chief executives of Mexico and Canada, both critical of what they saw as Reagan's unhelpful posture toward the South.

The hard reality for both U.S. neighbors, however, is that they must deal with the giant between them as a giant. Although Canada shares many development characteristics with the United States, it does not afford Mexico an important counterweight to U.S. power. There have been steps to increase Mexican-Canadian trade and diplomacy, but these are infinitesimal compared to the relationship of each with the United States. Canada absorbs roughly 1 percent of Mexico's exports and provides 2 percent of its imports.[17] For all their common interests, Mexico and Canada cannot jointly minimize their dependency on the United States. As a Canadian diplomat was quoted (in the March 9, 1981, *U.S. News and World Report*): "The Canada-U.S. relationship often is described as that of a mouse sleeping with an elephant. If Mexico climbs into the same bed, it merely means that two mice will be sleeping with the elephant."

Mexican Policy Outside the Americas: The Iranian Case

Mexico's relations with nations beyond the Americas, despite their increasing prominence, are still rather marginal in Mexican foreign policy. It is nonetheless worth noting that Mexico does pursue an *independent* line in those relations. The Iranian crisis of 1979 provides a vivid example. Mexico pointedly rejected what the United States saw as Mexico's proper role. Instead, Mexico saw its own broad foreign interests in conflict with U.S. interests and made no apologies for asserting an independent position. We analyze this episode not in terms of its complex details, but in terms of the conflicting viewpoints held by many in the United States and Mexico respectively. Not all these viewpoints were held equally strongly, and certainly not all were equally based on facts. Indeed some may be frivolous, others grossly inaccurate. We are less interested here in what was factually accurate than in perceptions.

In November 1979, militant Iranian students took over the U.S.

embassy in Tehran. For the return of the more than fifty hostages, their principal demand was the return to Iran of the (ex-) shah. The shah was temporarily in the United States for medical treatment that he claimed he could not get in Mexico, where he had been living. The United States refused to extradite the shah and expected him to return to Mexico. Very much to the United States's chagrin, Mexico refused to have him back.

Seen from the U.S. side, Mexico's refusal to readmit the shah was a blatant betrayal, not just of the shah himself, but of the United States. Mexico is the United States's friend and neighbor. It boasts a proud tradition of extending asylum to political exiles, regardless of ideological stripe. The shah had lived in Mexico from June 10 to October 22, and nearly everyone expected him to return after receiving U.S. medical attention. Mexico's foreign minister confirmed the expected return just weeks before the shocking reversal. The official U.S. version did not go beyond this. But the White House left the clear impression that it supported angry statements by Senator Lloyd Bentsen of Texas accusing Mexico of selfishness and cowardice; Mexico had let the United States down when the United States was most vulnerable. Furthermore, this episode followed hard on the heels of other Mexican affronts to the United States, including refusal to pay compensation for damage caused by a runaway offshore oil well and the holding in Mexico City of an international conference advocating Puerto Rican independence from the United States. Adding insult to serious injury, Mexico subsequently criticized U.S. economic sanctions against Iran as "aggressive and precipitous."

Why then, according to the United States, did Mexico refuse the shah? There were a few possibilities. The widely circulated reason of not provoking Iranians into sabotaging Mexican interests around the world was most significant. This was understandable, but the United States saw in it capitulation to a terrorism that threatens all civilized nations. Moreover, Mexico was also out to prove its independence of the United States, to look progressive in foreign policy, and to placate its own left, especially by declaring gratuitously that the shah himself bore considerable responsibility for the militants' actions. Whatever the motivation, the suddenness of Mexico's announcement, allegedly without prior notification to a neighbor now to be plunged into still deeper trouble, was seen as a horrible blow. Some in the United States would believe that López Portillo's own admonition, only recently thrust at the United States over a different issue, seemed to fit: "Between permanent rather than casual neighbors surprise moves and sudden deceit and abuse are poisonous fruits that sooner or later will have an adverse effect."

Seen from the Mexican side, national interest was the key factor. Mexico's foreign policy must be independent. It must be based on Mexican, not U.S., interests. There is more to Mexico's place in the world than just its relations with the United States. The United States, arrogant yet hurting, still thought of Mexican foreign policy as but an extension of Mexico–United States relations. Such a vision was, at best, outdated. Hostile U.S. reactions simply reflected the frustrations of a shrinking imperial giant, one that has fully realized neither that it no longer has the power always to have its way nor that its still considerable might does not give it right. Just as the United States would not accept Mexico's revolutionary assertion of sovereignty decades ago, so it still resisted it. The "Colossus of the North" would not accept that Mexican foreign policy must reflect Mexican interests. Images of U.S. imperialism could only be aggravated by the prominent involvement in the case of David Rockefeller and Henry Kissinger, symbols par excellence of U.S. international influence.

Why, López Portillo asked aloud, should Mexico become embroiled in "a conflict which is not ours"? He vehemently denied that there were any Mexican "commitments." He specifically blasted a *Los Angeles Times* report (December 20, 1979) that (1) he had assured the shah in writing and in person that the shah could return and that (2) the White House knew of and counted on this. He acknowledged only that he had visited the shah before the shah went to the United States and that he had told the shah that he was welcome to come back while his visa was good (six months from issuance). The *Los Angeles Times* report, and Senator Bentsen's charges, were dismissed as part of a vicious anti-Mexico campaign. Therefore, Mexico's reaction was predictably animated, to say the least. Mexican newspapers cranked out combative articles under colorful titles: "Here Come the Gringos!" "Gratuitous Hostility," "No One Manipulates Us," "The U.S.: Unleashing Passions." The Mexican Congress quickly jumped into line. The leader of the Chamber of Deputies pointed out that if Bentsen (head of the U.S. delegation to the United States–Mexico intercongressional committee) was a friend, Mexico hardly needed enemies. Labor provided revolutionary legitimacy. Its official leader, Fidel Velásquez, said of Bentsen: "This gentleman does not know that this is a sovereign country that rejects pressures of any kind." A more leftist labor leader denounced Bentsen as a mere voice of "imperialist exploiters" who feel that Latin Americans "should be on their knees."[18]

To understand this clash more fully it would be necessary to analyze the viewpoints of different groups within the United States and Mexico. Still, the general lines of a government-versus-government confrontation, each supported relatively broadly by its society, are clear. Although misunderstandings played a part, basically conficting interests were at stake. Mexico's perceived interests obviously undermined the United States's perceived interests. And Mexico asserted itself forcefully.

The Iranian crisis was only a passing issue in Mexico–United States relations, but it reflected ongoing differences. Mexico feels that it must and will pursue its own broad foreign policy objectives—whether the United States approves them or not. On issues such as Iran, Cuba, Chile, Central America, and North-South relations, it indeed asserts its foreign policy independence of the United States. Yet, inescapably, most of Mexico's major foreign policy issues remain fundamentally bilateral ones with the United States. Ultimately, this is where independence meets its most critical test.

PRINCIPAL BILATERAL ISSUES

The Asymmetry of Economic Interdependency

Specific bilateral issues must be seen against the background of the vital U.S. role in the Mexican economy. Political assertiveness is one thing, economic sovereignty another. Nationhood is one thing, independence another. Economically, Mexico is profoundly dependent on the United States—despite growing U.S. dependency on Mexico. As with cultural interdependency, Mexico–United States economic interdependency is asymmetrical.

Although Mexico now ranks behind only Canada and Japan as a leading trading partner for the United States, U.S. trade is spread widely across many nations. By contrast, Mexico relies overwhelmingly on the United States as its principal trading partner. The 1980 figures show Mexico taking in only 5.4 percent of total U.S. exports and sending off what would amount to 3.7 percent of total U.S. imports. By contrast, Mexico sent 61.8 percent of its exports to the United States and took in 62.3 percent of its imports from there. And even these figures represent a recent decline in Mexico–United States trade asymmetry; that is, Mexico had previously accounted for even less of U.S. trade and the U.S. had accounted for even more of Mexican trade. Moreover, Mexico exported less to the United States (US$12.5 billion) than it imported from the United States (US$15.1 billion).[19] Oil itself helps to redress the imbalance, but it also leads to increased Mexican demands for U.S. goods. Perhaps more important than moderate changes in Mexico–United States imbalances is that the volume of trade—this basically asymmetrical trade—is increasing enormously. The volume dwarfs Mexican trade with other countries, including the rest of Latin America. Mexico sends roughly 2 percent of its exports to Central America and the Caribbean and only 4 percent to the rest of Latin America. Furthermore, universalism and leftism notwithstanding, the entire communist world accounts for only about 1 percent of Mexico's exports and imports.[20]

U.S. investment in Mexico is also increasing enormously, again deepening an asymmetrical economic relationship. The United States provides 69 percent of the roughly US$7.5 billion in direct foreign investment received by Mexico, while Mexican investment is but a small part of foreign investment in the United States.[21] The United States invests more in Mexico than in all but a few nations anywhere. Moreover, U.S. capital is concentrated in critical areas, including many of the fastest growing and most profitable. Whereas foreigners historically invested in mining, increased investment in the last few decades has focused on services (including tourism) and especially on industrial manufacturing (automobiles, chemicals, pharmaceuticals, cosmetics, processed foods, and drinks). Trying to relieve the underdevelopment syndrome of exporting agricultural for manufactured goods, Mexico has developed some new exports in recent decades. Agriculture (sugar, coffee, beef, tomatoes) is still important to Mexico, although extraordinary problems came to the fore in the late 1970s (see Chapters 1 and 5), and oil is now becoming more important.

Certainly Mexico has tried to diminish its economic dependency on the United States, e.g., by broadening trade with other areas, including South America, Europe, and Japan. Also, as we saw in the previous chapter, attempts to toughen rules for foreign investment and technology transfers have yielded some success. But powerful factors, even beyond the obvious geographical ones, maintain the U.S. role. The Mexican private sector is in many ways tied to U.S. economic interests, and there are binational organizations promoting favorable policies. The Mexican middle class demands U.S. exports. U.S. lobbies, governmental and private, press for close economic ties. Nor is official Mexican policy clearly opposed to foreign economic penetration, even though there is unease about the huge U.S. share. On the one hand, the regime upholds protectionist policies, defending domestic producers; on the other hand, it encourages foreign investment and trade and maintains the low wages, political stability, and general economic industrialization model that foreign economic interests want. Whatever the ideological preferences of Mexican policymakers, a terrible constraint is simply the recent failure of the domestic economy. Herein looms the threat of the "food for crude" crisis alluded to in Chapter 1. If Mexican agriculture cannot feed Mexico, then Mexico is forced to rely on the United States.

Whether or not most Mexicans support the bilateral economic status quo, the point is that the interests of many powerful groups, indeed the central domestic development policies themselves, basically encourage it. Basic encouragement, however, hardly means full or conflict-free acceptance. From the U.S. side, some isolated protestations about imperialism and dependency excepted, the common perception is that U.S. economic activity in Mexico is a result of natural and beneficial economic forces. Again, however, this attitude hardly precludes heated debates over specific policies.

Each of the following specific issues is too complex for detailed analysis and evaluation here. Certainly, we make no pretense at offering solutions. Instead, we again concentrate on contrasting Mexican and U.S. perceptions of the key factors. Again, we are neither endorsing any of these perceptions nor asserting that all have factual validity, much less equal moral validity. While we emphasize government perceptions, we acknowledge intragovernmental disagreements and dissent by some non-governmental actors. Thus, bilateral cooperation and conflict involve more than intergovernmental agreement or disagreement.

Trade: Tariffs and Quotas

The issue of trade is obviously central to economic policy and therefore was largely treated in the last chapter. Of particular relevance here are the discussions of the recent GATT decision, border economics, and, especially, the role of trade in Mexico's economic growth model. Thus, rather than reformulating those discussions here, this brief section focuses on conflicting Mexican and U.S. perceptions of proper tariff and quota policies.

Mexico–United States disputes over tariffs and quotas are so repetitive that they become fairly predictable as different products capture the headlines. In the early 1980s, there were few signs of diminishing tensions. Mexico's viewpoint is usually clear. Mexico wants to sell its products competitively in the United States. Does not international capitalism mean that laws of free trade and comparative advantage should hold? If Mexico can produce shoes, textiles, and agricultural products cheaply because its labor costs are low, U.S. consumers should buy from Mexican rather than more expensive U.S. producers. Only with such revenue can Mexico afford to buy the more sophisticated, capital-intensive goods that the United States is better suited to produce. Only with such sales can Mexico employ its population. To deny Mexico its market for labor-intensive goods is to increase Mexican unemployment and force job-seekers across the border. To deny Mexico its rightful market is to block Mexican progress and encourage disorder. If the United States wants good relations with Mexico, it must offer Mexico a fair chance. In fact, Mexico has gone beyond this and asked for a "special relationship" in which its goods would be given privileged treatment in the United States. That would be seen as a genuine and important measure to bolster Mexican economic development and political stability. Yet the United States insists that it cannot now give special treatment to Mexico without undercutting its own relationships with other countries. Instead, Mexican products are either slapped with tariffs that destroy their competitive edge in the U.S. market or denied access altogether by restrictive quotas or tough sanitary requirements.

Why is U.S. policy not more accommodating? A major factor is that powerful U.S. domestic interests conflict with Mexico's desires. Labor fears a loss of jobs if consumers reject U.S. products for less expensive foreign ones. Small businesses in particular see trouble for their own precarious situation. Besides, they ask, how open is Mexico, with its own protectionist policies, to foreign competition? Mexico obviously musters greater policy agreement for free exporting of its own products than for free importing of foreign products. It has declared its right to select specific trade policies that serve Mexico's interests rather than to adhere doctrinally to free-trade principles. Rightly or wrongly, some in the United States believe that Mexico has unduly thwarted free competition by subsidizing some of its own exports, by claiming extensive sea and fishing rights off Mexico, by unilaterally terminating a fishing agreement with the United States, by its zeal for "revolutionary" nationalizations, and by its recently toughened restrictions on foreign investment and technology transfers. The culminating point came in 1980 when Mexico declined to enter GATT. Moreover, the issue of Mexican reluctance to move toward free trade (although López Portillo liberalized the protectionist system somewhat) could surface contentiously if the United States presses for some sort of common market (although even President Reagan had apparently lost his enthusiasm for that concept by 1982). There are many intermediate possibilities, however. One is a common energy market based on Mexican raw materials and U.S. capital. Another is an extended free-trade zone, running perhaps 200 miles (320 kilometers) into each nation; goods produced within the zone would pass duty-free between the countries. Economically important border transactions may already represent embryonic arrangements of this kind. Perhaps some U.S. notion of a common market will mesh with some Mexican yearnings for a special relationship.

There is no U.S. consensus on these matters, even within the government. Some U.S. groups support the Mexican case. Consumers want inexpensive products. What emerges is a classic domestic political struggle between smaller, organized groups and larger, unorganized groups. U.S. pluralist democracy generally makes the organized groups stronger than numbers alone would suggest. And because domestic U.S. politics obviously affects foreign policy, it is hard to overstate the importance to Mexico of understanding the complex U.S. maze. In 1976, to take an example of conflict over quotas, the U.S. government came under tremendous pressure from shoe producers demanding a limit on the import of Mexican shoes. Congress supported the call. So did the International Trade Commission and the Treasury Department, but the Department of Commerce opposed the move, fearing trade retaliation by Mexico and other affected nations. The State Department and National Security Council also opposed the quotas, not wishing to jeopardize good relations or to cause unrest abroad.[22] Mexico obviously wanted to export its shoes as freely as possible.

A specific example of Mexico–United States tariff tensions concerns the 1979 "Great Tomato War." Florida growers and truckers complained that nearly one-half of the winter greens eaten in the United States came from Mexico. Furthermore, Mexicans allegedly "dumped" tons of tomatoes, squash, peppers, cucumbers, and eggplant cheaply on the U.S. market in order to drive Florida producers out of business. The producers therefore asked the Treasury Department to impose tariffs. Otherwise, U.S. interests would not be able to compete with Mexico's cheap labor and laxer laws against insecticides. Mexico, in turn, argued that tariffs would be unfair, drive up prices to U.S. consumers, drive up U.S. inflation, put Mexicans out of work and onto the road northward, and adversely affect bilateral relations. What a terrible irony: Mexicans are forced north where they help produce food in the United States that Mexico is forced to import! How could the United States put the clamps on one of Mexico's few major exports while Mexico consumes so much from the United States? Finally, Mexicans have argued, tariffs on vegetables and fruits would force more Mexican farmers into a more lucrative quasi-agricultural activity—production of drugs.

Drugs

By the mid-1970s there were perhaps one-half million heroin addicts and at least 15 million marijuana users (or many more, depending on the definition of "user") in the United States; Mexico is their principal supplier. Mexico's importance as an exporter of drugs accelerated when World War II interrupted heroin supplies from the Middle and Far East. A second wave was inaugurated in the 1970s by Turkey's crackdown on poppy growing, the severing of the "French connection," and the communist takeover in Vietnam. Mexico now supplies the United States perhaps 10 million pounds (45,000 kg) per year of marijuana, or 70 percent of U.S. consumption, plus 70–80 percent of U.S. heroin and some cocaine. Drugs are grown in poor states such as Guerrero and Oaxaca and in richer ones such as Sinaloa. Sinaloa's drug income may exceed its income from legitimate agriculture, even though Sinaloa has more irrigated land than any other state in Mexico![23]

Leaving aside U.S. drug users, who not unlike consumers of other agricultural products might like to see their goods flow across the border even more freely, *the U.S. tends to blame the drug traffic on Mexico.* According to the United States, Mexico (1) fails to encourage legitimate agricultural alternatives, (2) tacitly encourages the drug enterprise, which now brings many jobs and fabulous income into Mexico, some into the hands of corrupt government officials, (3) has sometimes run inadequate, corrupt antidrug campaigns, (4) lacks the will to confront local caciques or guerrillas on their home turf, and (5) fails to cooperate adequately with the United States, exacerbating tensions by mistreating U.S. citizens imprisoned on drug charges. Even when the United States acknowledges that the drug traffic has its perpetrators in both nations, it sometimes implies that only one government has been resolved to confront the problem. Tensions hit a low point in 1969 when President Nixon embarked on the sort of unilateral action dictated by this hard-line U.S. view of the drug problem. Under Operation Intercept very careful border searches were launched. The operation angered Mexicans and hurt them economically, for its significantly slowed tourism and frontier trade. Within days, Operation Cooperation followed as a less offensive substitute.

The Mexican side of the story is quite different. *Prime responsibility is placed on the United States.* One must look at the *demand* side of the equation; without U.S. demand Mexicans would not grow the supply. Free-market economics, the United States should understand, is hard to suppress. U.S. consumers are in fact all too eager to pay well for their habits and illicit pleasures. Moreover, U.S. drug pushers benefit from the trade.

What has been at the heart of the bilateral drug controversy, therefore, is not fundamental misunderstanding or bad faith but conflicting legal and economic interests; in each country, some groups want to solve the problem while others do not. According to one close observer, only when the Mexican government came to see its own interests threatened did greater cooperation emerge.[24] Some Mexican leftists argue that their government has merely seized upon drugs as a cover under which to attack peasants and dissidents in drug-producing regions, while not seriously harassing Mexico's organized crime. In any case, by the mid-1970s, the bilateral Operation Condor was under way, bringing Mexico's military and judicial forces into action. Mexican manpower combined with U.S. money and reconnaissance technology. Mexico–United States cooperation had indeed materialized. In 1976, an unprecedented prisoner exchange symbolized this new cooperation. Even if we were to assume that both governments are fully committed to fighting the drug problem, however, there would be no society-wide Mexico–United States consensus as long as many people rely on drugs to provide their jobs, to provide their illicit incomes, or to satisfy their habits.

Tourism

Tourism is usually one of the least conflictual issues associated with Mexico's international economic relations. It shows instead the strong mutual interests between Mexico and the United States. During the 1970s, the number of U.S. citizens visiting Mexico increased from slightly more than 2 million annually to nearly 3.5 million annually. Moreover, tourism is a reciprocal Mexico–United States industry. There is a good deal of advertising in Mexico for U.S. attractions such as Disney World, Las Vegas, and New York City. Roughly 2.5 million Mexicans visited the United States in 1979.

As in all major Mexico–United States economic relations, however, there is a strong degree of asymmetry. While 13 percent of U.S. foreign travel reaches Mexico, 95 percent of Mexican foreign travel reaches the United States. While Mexicans are one foreign group among many visiting the United States, U.S. citizens make up the vast majority (although the percentage fell from 93 percent to 83 percent during the 1970s) of tourists in Mexico, and the vast majority (though down from 88 percent to 75 percent during the 1970s) of Mexico's roughly US$1.5 billion annual tourist income.[25]

Various Mexican regions have grown primarily because of tourism. Acapulco, a small town before World War I, has become one of the world's best-known vacation spots. Puerto Vallarta, Mazatlán, and Cancún are other favorite coastal resorts. Mexico's attractiveness for tourists is easy to understand. Hotels, food, entertainment, and handicrafts are still inexpensive by U.S. vacation standards. Most of all, Mexican proximity to the United States makes for low-cost round-trip transportation, especially from populous areas such as southern California and Texas. If the following sounds like a tourist promotion, it also indicates how Mexico can sustain a profitable industry. Mexico is blessed with beautiful, extensive, and warm beaches. Tourists can choose from modern entertainment and fine tourist accommodations, "quaint" folklore, or archeological treasures. A visit to Mexico City offers not only the sights of a huge metropolis, but short side-trips to a great number of tourist attractions: pyramids, hot springs, Taxco ("the silver city"), Cuernavaca (the "city of eternal spring"), Querétaro (a charming colonial city), and Puebla (a historic metropolis with Spanish influence). Acapulco and Veracruz are fewer than eight hours by car or two by plane from the capital.

Although foreign interests own much of the tourist industry, Mexican businesses also profit. And tourism creates jobs. According to

Mexico's Ministry of Tourism (as reported in *Lloyd's Economic Report* of April 1980), tourism brought 220,000 new jobs to Mexico from 1977 to 1979. So the Mexican government treats the industry carefully, building necessary infrastructure and maintaining strong tourist bureaus to prevent mistreatment of tourists. It advertises avidly and skillfully, catering especially well to what U.S. tourists want to hear.[26]

There are many problems, however. Tourists are walking symbols of the development gap between Mexico and the United States. Such symbols are especially resented when they play the "ugly American" role of patronizing local society. Even short of this, many tourists naturally do not acquit themselves well in Mexican eyes. For instance, "the majority of the tourists are more interested in admiring the countryside and the famous monuments than in feeling a live culture. They react only to their own expectations. . . . They do not visit a country but the image of a country."[27] In fairness, one can respond that not every tourist need be an amateur archeologist or sociologist. Yet, unlike most of their South American counterparts, Mexicans see so many U.S. tourists that they may well tire of them. Despite conventional assumptions, tourism does not necessarily lead to greater understanding among peoples.

Many Mexicans, especially on the left, see their country catering too much to tourist desires. Their government often moves quickly, and brutally if necessary, to suppress local disturbances that could frighten away tourists. Development projects are chosen largely to make Mexico attractive to foreigners rather than to Mexico's masses. The tourism ministry, for example, is known to push against ejido ownership because small communal landholdings are harder to seize and turn into tourist sites. Coastal regions are being "denationalized," many charge. Foreign investment and control is found in much of the tourist industry. Finally, Mexico cannot assert itself with the United States too much on other issues because it must fear repercussions in its vital tourist industry. According to this negative view, the Mexican government zealously pursues its tourist policies because they fit so well into the regime's development model—rewarding those the regime caters to, regardless of the consequences for others.

Since the 1970s, the tourist industry has faced a new threat—inflation. As prices soar, Mexico loses its competitive advantage over the other tourist spots, and most Mexicans themselves are attracted to vacation outside their country.[28] Ironically, domestic hard times may promote Mexico's tourist industry. For example, the massive peso devaluations of 1982, with all the pain they represented for Mexicans, instantly made prices once again very attractive for U.S. tourists. Whatever the future, Mexico's tourism has traditionally benefited not only from the country's geography and natural beauty, but from a development model that has held inflation and prices low, encouraged foreign trade, and preserved political stability.

Migration

If tourism is the most important factor motivating U.S. citizens to cross the border, the most important factor for Mexicans is work. Mexico's most important exports to the United States are not foodstuffs and drugs, but oil and people. "Green-card" holders work legally in the United States; the problem focuses on the millions who cross the border without legal documentation from the United States.

So thorny is this bilateral problem that the Mexican and U.S. governments cannot even agree on what to call the migrants. Mexico regards the label "illegal alien" as pejorative, even implying that the migrants are not quite human. It refers instead to "undocumented workers." The United States generally regards this label as too benign: Most Mexican migrants are in violation of U.S. law, and not all are workers. We therefore refer here simply to "migrants," a label that addresses neither the legality nor the desirability of the influx.

There is a developing consensus that the migration problem is very difficult, that there are not easy answers. At least each side should better understand the other.

First, Mexico argues, *the United States rather hysterically exaggerates the problem.* William Colby, former director of the Central Intelligence Agency, has hyperbolically called the migrants, not the Soviet or Chinese communists, the greatest menace to U.S. security. Others talk of a "silent invasion." Estimates of the total number of migrants in question range from 3 to 12 million; Mexicans tend to accept the lower figure, allowing that well over half are Mexicans. Furthermore, many are in the United States only temporarily or seasonally. Most pay U.S. taxes but do not claim the full benefits of U.S. welfare, health, education, or food stamp programs, for fear of exposure.

Second, Mexico argues, *migration is a natural or even inevitable phenomenon* wherever wealth and poverty are in close proximity. There are more jobs in the United States. More important, these jobs offer perhaps three or four or even seven times as much salary for comparable work.[29] Just as Switzerland pulls in Italians, Venezuela pulls in neighboring South Americans, and Mexico itself pulls in Central Americans, the United States pulls in Mexicans. Contemporary migration in Western Europe seems to offer a parallel better than even historical Mexico–United States immigration to contemporary Mexico–United States immigration. Beyond legal guest-worker programs, many emigrate from nearby less developed nations to work in Europe's more developed nations. Migrants today seek work in capital-intensive societies in which the demand is less for labor than for cheap labor, in societies with elaborate and costly social services that would have to be made available to native workers or to legally admitted immigrants. Thus, although illegal, mass Mexican migration serves the U.S. economy. In effect, it takes two to migrate. That is, there must be demand on the receiving end. Someone in the United States wants the migrants, just as someone wants the drugs. Mexico feels that the United States overemphasizes the factors that "push" people out of Mexico, ignoring the factors in the United States that "pull" in people. In Mexico's view, U.S. quotas, for migrants as well as for agricultural goods, block free trade. Yet laws forbidding migration are like laws against prostitution, gambling, or alcohol: They are hard to enforce because they run counter to strong impulses and interests.

Mexicans go on to argue that if they must suffer all the natural disadvantages of proximity to a colossus, at least they should also be allowed the natural benefits. They note that many U.S. citizens enjoy more luxurious lives in Mexico than they possibly could in the United States. *Los Agachados* (March 9, 1976) has satirized U.S. concern about Mexican migrants by affecting reverse hysteria: The gringos are out to do what they did to Texas—move in, cause trouble, and annex! "Unfortunately, YES, the news is correct: More gringos live in Mexico than Mexicans in the U.S. . . . The only Mexicans that you still see on the *Reforma* [one of Mexico City's major streets] are the traffic cops."

A third Mexican argument is that *U.S. policy exacerbates rather than relieves* the flow. The United States could relax barriers to the entry of Mexican goods, thereby promoting employment opportunities in Mexico. It could raise the *legal* quota for immigration and grant more seasonal work permits. Instead, the United States has historically pursued narrowly self-serving policies. Until the late 1920s it allowed unrestricted immigration—to fill its need for cheap labor. The Great Depression brought Operation Deportation—to remove competition for scarce jobs. World War II then brought the bracero program—to attract needed workers for a shorthanded nation at war. Although Mexicans were legally admitted to harvest crops until 1964, the United States predictably cut back the program almost immediately after the war, in 1947. In 1954, Operation Wetback entrusted to a military general the task of efficiently deporting more than 1 million Mexicans, now excess workers. No wonder this has been called the flower-petal policy: "I need you, I need you not, I need you. . . ." In the 1960s and 1970s, quotas on Western Hemisphere nations, including Mexico, became more rather than less restrictive. Mexicans feared that a continued U.S. recession in the 1980s, with increased domestic unemployment, could mean harsher crackdowns. Some of these fears were soon realized with "Operation Jobs," a spring

1982 roundup and forced departure of thousands of Mexican migrants, just when Mexico found itself mired in its own economic crisis and when Mexico once again felt victimized by tariff policy.

Fourth, Mexico argues, *U.S. attitudes about migrants lead to violations of human rights.* The violations include unlawful arrests, forced confessions, beatings, and emotional abuse. Several incidents at the border itself have recently embarrassed the beleaguered and understaffed U.S. Immigration and Naturalization Service. The whole migration issue presents a difficult moral issue. Says López Portillo: "The fact that men can buy men is the most serious matter of our time. This is what happens to our people who go to the U.S." A recent *Los Angeles Times* poll (reported July 15, 1979) indicates that perhaps 90 percent of the population of Mexico City feel that Mexicans working illegally in the United States are being abused. In 1974, Mexico successfully urged the UN to approve a resolution that nations should accord foreign workers, regardless of their legal status, the same human rights as citizens. No nation voted against the resolution, but the United States, aware of the finger-pointing, was one of four abstaining.

While not disagreeing with all the tenets of Mexico's position on migration, the United States has tended to emphasize different factors. First, the United States argues that *the migration problem is both serious and fundamentally rooted in Mexico itself.* Whether because of irresponsible population growth coupled with ineffectual economic policies, or because of the uncontrollable problems of underdevelopment, Mexico produces an excess work force. The worsening of Mexico's economic crisis in 1982 offered a ready example. As the peso was severely devalued, and employment opportunities looked grim, there was an immediate surge in the number of Mexicans attempting to emigrate. In fact, the United States had already put the number of Mexican migrants in the millions, arguing that even the "temporary" ones spend more time in the United States than in Mexico. Plainly the number continues to increase.

Second, the United States argues, *Mexico benefits from the migration.* The welfare burden on the U.S. government represents a relief for the Mexican government. Thus a crucial "safety valve" allows Mexico to export its social burdens. Moreover, Mexican migrants remit perhaps US$3 billion a year, more than Mexico's tourist income;[30] this remittance is, in effect, money taken out of the U.S. economy. The Mexican political system also benefits because of the "safety-valve" effect. Mexico need not address fundamental problems in population, agriculture, employment, and so forth as long as it can release many of those it cannot satisfy. Another reason that the Mexican regime may not want to stem emigration is that Mexicans migrate not just to the United States but, within Mexico, to the more populated areas. Mexicans migrating to the United States no longer come predominantly from rural areas, and if fewer migrants went to the United States more would remain in already overcrowded Mexican cities. Could Mexico address all these added burdens at a time when stability may depend on satisfying some degree of oil-inspired rising expectations?

A third argument made in the United States is that *Mexico proposes no viable alternative* but instead merely complains about U.S. policy, calls for further study, and hopes that oil and industrialization will create more jobs in Mexico. This argument follows from the first two, which hold that Mexico has the responsibility but not the incentive to tackle the problem. Although the Mexican regime has become more concerned about its employment problems, it is unlikely to address them with labor-intensive policies that could slow economic growth. Indeed, even López Portillo has acknowledged that Mexico could not provide sufficient employment for all its workers during this century.[31] Although migrants may represent a loss of useful human capital, the loss would pale before the benefits Mexico presently reaps from its policy of benign neglect.[32]

Although there is virtual consensus in the United States that Mexico benefits from the migration, there is in fact no U.S. consensus on what adverse consequences the United States suffers. The strongest opposition to Mexican migration comes from the labor unions. The AFL-CIO opposes plans to legitimize or increase the flow of migrants, legal or illegal. Thus a fourth argument heard in the United States is that *U.S. unemployment is aggravated,* especially among the poor, in the agricultural, service, and manufacturing sectors where many Mexicans find work. If Mexicans cannot be prevented from coming, then many U.S. opponents advocate stiff penalties to discourage potential employers from hiring them.[33] But so far, legal initiatives along these lines have failed. Labor maintains that the migrants are robbing U.S. citizens of jobs and increasingly usurping better jobs; no longer are migrants confined to jobs unwanted by domestic workers. Moreover, foreign workers indirectly deflate the wages of domestic workers by expanding the available labor pool. They have been used, historically, to prevent or weaken union-ization. Such effects are felt today mostly where low-income domestic labor is involved. Along with some Chicano leaders, representing U.S. citizens of Mexican descent, Black leaders have been wary of the Mexican influx, just as they were wary of the 1980 Cuban influx. Some have argued that talk of the United States's ability to absorb immigrants is based on the history of an era, a bygone era, in which the United States was an expanding society seeking more laborers.

Although U.S. public opinion probably tends to agree with labor that Mexican migrants basically constitute a problem, U.S. scholarly opinion tends to be more sympathetic to Mexico's arguments. And many

U.S. conservatives see the migrants in positive economic terms; the United States may increasingly experience labor shortages because of its stagnant population growth and aging work force. More specifically, big agriculture and many small businesses are delighted with the large and *cheap* pool of eager laborers, either satisfied with the wages offered or afraid to complain. In fact, many conservatives advocate diminishing international constraints on the free flow of capital and labor. Cheap Mexican labor allows U.S. business to produce goods (such as fruits, vegetables, wine, and clothes) that are priced more competitively on the international market and more inexpensively for domestic consumers. Remove cheap Mexican labor and many U.S. businesses would close, raise prices to uncompetitive levels, or relocate outside the United States in places where cheap labor *is* available. Besides, the United States gets an instant work force, one it does not have to train expensively through its public-school system. Furthermore, some detect a paradox: If the U.S. pressures Mexico to slow migration, it must be prepared for domestic Mexican policies that put job creation ahead of capital-intensive growth— that is, for policies alien to the Mexican growth model that U.S. private business so enthusiastically supports. Ronald Reagan's presidency brought the possibility of a U.S. tilt toward a position more favorable to migration. Candidate Reagan talked about opening the border and allowing Mexicans to stay long as they like. President Reagan restated the benefits of increased migration in moral terms, in economic terms, and—most emphatically—in political terms: "It is to our government's interest also that the safety valve is not shut off," because the United States wants to insure against any "breaking of the stability south of the border." But, in fact, the president soon backed away from this sympathetic stand on migration.

U.S. domestic political forces tend to line up something like this: On the antimigration side, labor and the Treasury Department hope that public opinion and labor pressures will keep Congress inclined toward their position. On the other side, the Department of Agriculture responds to agricultural interest groups in the Southwest, and the Departments of State and Justice add that harsh proposals to "seal the border" would hurt relations with Mexico.[34]

U.S. opinion is also fragmented on whether migrants should be counted in the census. To do so is to grant them legitimacy and to reward localities (with government funds based on population) for attracting them. Not to do so is to deprive localities of revenues that they desperately need to support services used by migrants and to have "taxation without representation" insofar as migrants do pay taxes. It is ironic that some who claim that migrants do not really drain welfare resources also claim that their localities need more such resources because migrants do use them! Similarly, there is great debate, especially in border states, over whether children without legal residency status should be allowed in the public-school system. Those in favor argue that the children are innocent victims of circumstances and that to deny them access to education is unconstitutional and unjust and sows the seeds of civil disorder. Opponents maintain that U.S. taxpayers should not have to finance the education of persons here illegally and that to do so can only encourage more to come. But opponents lost an important 1982 court case concerning migrant children living in Texas.

U.S. authority on migration policy has been fragmented among the Departments of Labor, Education, Health and Human Services, Justice, and State, the Immigration Service and frontier patrol, Congress, and interest groups ranging from unions and businesses to Chicanos and police. It is more difficult for the United States than for Mexico to form one coherent official position.[35]

We have focused more on the conflicting viewpoints on both sides of the border than on the hard facts in the case. This is because our main purpose is to understand how the parties themselves see things, because there are only so many unambiguous, provable facts, and because limited space precludes the attempt to deal with empirical details. Suffice it to reiterate these probabilities: that most Mexicans come to the United States either to find employment that they cannot find in Mexico or higher salaried employment than they can find at home; that most do return home, although many come back periodically; that most (although not all) take unwanted jobs; that they may adversely affect unskilled labor's interests; that they lower costs for U.S. employers and probably consumers; that they send important revenue back to Mexico; that they give some relief from Mexico's terrible employment problem; and that many are improperly treated in the United States.[36]

At least until recently, the debate has only rarely gotten beyond the level of unproductive charges and countercharges, and when it has, it has become painfully clear that there is no satisfactory solution. It is not even clear to all that a solution should be found, for while some suffer, others benefit from the migration. The Mexican government makes little pretense at having the answer, arguing nonetheless that more enlightened U.S. policy could ameliorate the situation. On the other hand, de la Madrid has shown considerable interest in border problems and in promoting better studies of them. Both the Carter and Reagan administrations have advocated policies to legitimize the status of those in the United States while cracking down on continued migration. Reagan's plan would put many Mexicans living in the United States on a ten-year track toward legalization but would make it more difficult and dangerous for employers to hire migrants. A major sticking point is the identification card. Without it, the government would find it difficult to compel employer compliance. With it would come a bureaucratic nightmare and perceived threats to human rights. Reagan's policy has thus far shunned the identification card. Reagan has also proposed doubling the size of the guest-worker program for a two-year experimental period, while at other times proposing harsh policies involving emergency powers. Midway through his presidential term, Reagan still had not settled on a policy and various congressional initiatives remained under discussion. While some Mexicans would favor any expansion in permitted migration, with appropriate safeguards, others feel that such an expansion would mostly help U.S. employers, would favor semiskilled and skilled workers who are needed by Mexico, and would falsely raise the expectations of many Mexicans concerning their employment possibilities. In sum, official U.S. migration policy remains very much unsettled, and the Mexican government has done still less, at least publicly, toward presenting major policy proposals. In a sense, migrants and their employers, not the two governments, have been making migration policy.

Unfortunately, the only measures that might seem adequate to address the roots of the problem also seem impossible to implement. Mexico could change its development model so as to create more and better employment. It could control its population growth. The United States could lend massive assistance to Mexico's development efforts, especially in labor-intensive agriculture. But such measures would run counter to the general development model pursued by Mexico and supported by the United States. This model includes neither the degree of coercion necessary for a decisive assault on the population problem nor sufficient emphasis on employment. Similarly, the United States has not seriously considered legalizing an unimpeded flow, regulated only by U.S. economic demands. Nor, in the early 1980s, is the economically troubled United States in a mood to grant massive foreign assistance. Moreover, all these root proposals concentrate on solutions within Mexico, on the "push" factors. Short of an unimaginable narrowing of the Mexico–United States development gap, however, the United States would continue to "pull" Mexicans across the border. Even if Mexico drastically cut its unemployment, for example, Mexicans could still be attracted northward by higher wages. The only other road that might weaken the "pull" further might be a severe U.S. recession or a radical program of border and employment vigilance and probably repression, beyond anything yet seriously contemplated.

The improbability of the root solutions makes it imperative to consider the more limited alternatives. In fact, these too engender little easy agreement. There is some opposition to increased legal or guest-worker flows, to the legalization of many migrants already living in the United States, to stiffer legal vigilance, to freer U.S. importing of Mexican goods, and to plans to create much more employment in Mexico's countryside. Whatever help better understanding of the specific causes and consequences of Mexican migration to the United States may provide, officials would still face an entanglement of conflicting cross-national economic, social, individual, moral, and political interests.

CONCLUSIONS

Surprising as it may seem from reading the news, contemporary Mexico–United States relations are comparatively good.[37] There are, of course, very important qualifications to this positive view, including increased tensions since 1970. But one has only to compare the last fifty years to the hundred preceding them to appreciate the great improvement. No longer is there warfare, or the threat of it. No longer do U.S. warships blatantly bully Mexican politicians by seizing Veracruz. No longer is diplomatic recognition problematic. A sense of history puts contemporary problems into perspective.

The key explanation for good contemporary relations is that both sides are benefiting. Mexican development has been tied to imports of U.S. goods, capital, and technology and to U.S. imports of Mexican products and workers. In return, the United States sees in Mexico an unusually close, secure, and profitable land for investment, a large market for U.S. exports, a needed supplier of energy and even workers, and a stable, noncommunist southern neighbor. Domestic politics and foreign policy are vitally intertwined, and for roughly fifty years Mexican domestic politics has served U.S. interests well.

A quick historical overview supports the proposition that bilateral relations have been harmonious when Mexico's domestic politics have promoted political stability, economic growth, and investment opportunities, more than when they have prompted instability or reform. The best example would be the good relations existing during the porfiriato. Conversely, relations were bellicose during the 1840s when Mexico's internal problems made it especially vulnerable to U.S. aggression. Relations were also strained during the early decades of the revolution, when U.S. economic interests were threatened. Thus, the end of U.S. gunboat diplomacy is really as much a reflection as a cause of improved relations. The United States can penetrate the Mexican economy without recourse to blatant political intervention. On balance, contemporary Mexican policies have promoted good relations with the United States, despite important strains since 1970. Mexico's universalism has rarely been sustained by diminishing economic relations with the United States, and leftist foreign policy has not produced leftist or radical domestic policies—which could be far more dangerous to U.S. economic interests.

Nonetheless, Mexico's foreign policy is strikingly independent for a nation that is so much weaker than its superpower neighbor. Mexico is no Finland, bound to support the foreign policy of the superpower on its border. Mexico's positions on foreign policy often clash with those of the United States, and Mexico is a tough negotiator with the superpower on bilateral issues. In short, Mexican foreign policy is no mere appendage of U.S. policy. The U.S. accepts this because of the strength of the Mexican position, its own increased dependency on Mexico, and the restoration of confidence in the stability of the Mexican economy and the stability of the Mexican political system. If Mexico's independent foreign policy provides some cover for conservative domestic policy, it is also true that successful domestic policy—in terms of stability and growth—has allowed Mexico to strike an independent foreign policy. By the same token, Mexico's 1982 economic crisis, and the desperate need for U.S. support, threatened to undermine Mexican independence. Surely, U.S. policy toward Mexico is influenced by Mexican foreign policy, but it is probably influenced more by Mexican domestic policy.

Good relations do not depend on Mexico's serving U.S. interests alone. Significant Mexican interests are also being served. This chapter has repeatedly shown that bilateral problems are rooted in conflicting interests, not just misunderstandings; similarly, the fundamentally harmonious aspects of Mexico–United States relations are rooted in overlapping interests. "Poor Mexico" is still poor partly because it is so close to the United States, but significant benefits also stem from that proximity. There can be legitimate debate over whether such proximity is, on balance, good for Mexico, but less doubt concerning whether it serves Mexico's present political economy. Of course, to write of "Mexico" is to oversimplify. Some Mexicans benefit, others suffer. A key factor is that *powerful* groups in both nations tend to benefit and therefore to promote the present bilateral pattern. Those (particularly in Mexico) who do not have much influence over foreign policy may well be suffering from that pattern, just as they suffer from the domestic policy with which the foreign policy is consistent.

In sum, if Mexican foreign policy is too "dependent," the causes lie not only in foreign influence, but in Mexico's development model and in Mexico's geography. Given its domestic development model and its geographic position in the giant's shadow, contemporary Mexico has forged a remarkably independent foreign policy.

NOTES

1. The "Poor Mexico" phrase is generally attributed to Díaz, but it may in fact have been coined by someone else. We hope that readers already familiar with Mexico will forgive yet another citation of this quotation; we use it here in juxtaposition to the quotation of Castañeda, Mexico's foreign minister in 1980 (at the forty-second annual Council on Foreign Relations meeting, June 6, 1980).

2. Robert McBride, "U.S.-Mexican Relations," *Princeton Alumni Weekly*, March 13, 1978, reporting on a 1969 incident.

3. Karl M. Schmitt, *Mexico and the United States 1821–1973: Conflict and Coexistence* (New York: John Wiley, 1974), pp. 44–50. Also on Mexico's potential strength see: Daniel Cosío Villegas, *American Extremes*, trans. Américo Paredes (Austin: University of Texas Press, 1964), p. 35; and Jesús Silva Herzog, *Trayectoria ideológica de la revolución mexicana* (Mexico City: S.E.P., 1973), p. 188.

4. On Wilson's changing preferences, see Schmitt, *Mexico and the United States*, pp. 126–149.

5. On the central importance of revolutionary nationalism in Mexico–United States conflicts, see Lorenzo Meyer, *Mexico and the United States in the Oil Controversy 1917–1942* (Austin: University of Texas Press, 1977).

6. There is a traditional anti-U.S. strain in the Mexican Catholic Church. This orientation stems from a rejection of U.S. Protestantism, liberalism, individualism, and materialism. Changes occurred in the twentieth century, however; a foreign policy factor was the Catholic Church's kinship to the anticommunist crusade led by the United States.

7. Wayne A. Cornelius, "Nation-Building, Participation, and Distribution: The Politics of Social Reform Under Cárdenas," in *Crisis, Choice and Change: Historical Studies of Political Development*, ed. Gabriel Almond, Scott Flanagan, and Robert J. Mundt (Boston: Little, Brown and Co., 1973), p. 399.

8. These three reasons are not mutually exclusive, and given foreign policies may be based on mixed motivations. For example, the regime may support a leftist cause partly to express genuine sympathy, partly to oppose U.S. intervention, and partly to strengthen its support among many intellectuals, bureaucrats, and other nationalists. Such policies may even make it easier for some intellectuals to accept public office. None of this means that the domestically most conservative presidents pursue the most leftist foreign policies. Díaz Ordaz, for example, was not as leftist in foreign policy as his predecessor (López Mateos) or his successor (Echeverría).

9. The best account of Mexico's Cuban policy, an account sensitive to nuance, is Olga Pellicer de Brody's *México y la revolución cubana* (Mexico City: El Colegio de México, 1972). Our summary draws especially on pp. 22–29, 95–103.

10. Wolf Grabendorff, "Mexico's Foreign Policy—Indeed a Foreign Policy?" *Journal of Interamerican Studies and World Affairs* 20, no. 1 (1978):87–88. There is also an interesting interplay between domestic policy and foreign policy with the Soviet Union. Mexico shores up its leftist and independent credentials while

the Soviet Union praises the regime's independence, even if that means undercutting Mexico's Communist party. On the eve of the 1976 elections, for example, the Soviet ambassador publicly brought Echeverría the "friendly greetings" of the Soviet Communist party.

11. For a brief overview of the defensive component of Mexican foreign policy, see Rosario Green's "México: La política exterior del nuevo régimen," *Foro Internacional* 18, no. 1 (1977):1–9. Notwithstanding the tensions, a number of significant agreements were concluded between Mexico and the United States on air quality, air transport, water rights, flood and other natural disaster control, wildlife, sanitation, and extradition procedures. Compared to such issues as trade and migration, these are the "easy" issues.

12. For a basic account of these motivations, see Olga Pellicer de Brody, "Cambios recientes en la política exterior mexicana," *Foro Internacional* 13, no. 2 (1972):139–154.

13. Mario Ojeda, "México ante los Estados Unidos en la coyuntura actual," *Foro Internacional* 18, no. 1 (1977):33.

14. See Olga Pellicer de Brody, "Veinte años de política exterior mexicana: 1960–1980," *Foro Internacional* 21, no. 2 (1980):152–159. Such a view of the last four administrations may evoke the image of a pendulum swing in foreign affairs, paralleling pendulum swings in left-right sexenio politics domestically.

15. The U.S. government did not want its position stereotyped as the opposite of Mexico's. President Carter and, despite more skepticism, President Reagan called for political solutions based on what they regarded as reformist centers, opposed not only to leftist but to rightist extremes.

16. Mario Ojeda, *Alcances y límites de la política exterior de México* (Mexico City: El Colegio de México, 1976), pp. 58–61. One astonishing indicator of Mexico's independence from the United States is that it received only 0.2 percent of U.S. military assistance to Latin America from 1950 to 1967.

17. Departamento de Planeación, "Sumario estadístico" *Comercio Exterior* 31, no. 2 (1981):243 (based on figures for January–November 1980).

18. Statement of the secretary of the Sindicato de Obreros Libres (Free Workers Union), quoted in "La política," *Ocho Columnas* (Guadalajara), December 19, 1979. Interestingly, Mexico's conservatives remained relatively quiet during the crisis, but many did rebuke Mexico's foreign minister for allegedly misleading everyone just shortly before the decision to readmit the shah. Responsibility for such inconsistencies logically falls on the president, but conservatives did not violate the unwritten code against public criticism of the chief executive.

19. On Mexico's number three ranking, see U.S. House of Representatives, *U.S.–Mexico Relations: An Update*, Hearings before the Subcommittee on Inter-American Relations of the Committee on Foreign Affairs, June 10, 1981 (Washington, D.C., June 1981). On the percentages of U.S. trade and Mexican trade, respectively, see U.S. Council Economic Advisors, *Economic Report of the President*, January 1981, p. 350; and Departamento de Planeación, "Intercambio comercial México-Estados Unidos," *Comercio Exterior* 31, no. 4 (1981):469. On the volume of Mexican-U.S. trade, see José López Portillo, *Quinto Informe de Gobierno* (Mexico City: Secretaría de Programación y Presupuesto, September 1981).

20. Departamento de Planeación, "Sumario estadístico," *Comercio Exterior* 31, no. 2 (1981):243–244 (using figures for January–November 1980).

21. Additionally, Mexico relies on the United States for most of its credit. The United States provides about 80 percent of all private bank loans to Mexico. On direct foreign investment (1980), see López Portillo, *Quinto Informe*; on private foreign investment and the comparisons to Mexican investment in the United States, see "Los ilegales mexicanos, legado de la historia y presión de la economía," *Comercio Exterior* 28, no. 7 (1978):804.

22. Tomás Peñaloza, "La formulación de la política exterior en los Estados Unidos de América y su impacto sobre México," *Foro Internacional* 18, no. 1 (1977):26. Ultimately, President Ford decided against imposing quotas.

23. We use the word "drug" loosely, not in a medical sense, to include marijuana. Among the sources we consulted are the U.S. State Department's Bureau of Public Affairs, *Gist*, December 1978, and "Mexico: The Connection," *Latin American Political Reports*, March 17, 1978, pp. 85–86. Mostly, however, we draw on the social science/detective work of Richard Craig; see his two articles in the *Journal of Interamerican Studies and World Affairs*, "La Campaña Permanente: Mexico's Antidrug Campaign," 20, no. 2 (1978):107–132, and "Operation Condor," 22, no. 3 (1980):345–364.

24. Craig, "Operation Condor," pp. 359–361. Craig argued that the drug issue had become an international embarrassment, that drug use was growing among middle- and upper-class young people, and that tremendous drug revenues threatened to create excessive power outside the central government.

25. Our data on tourism came from Departamento de Planeación, "Intercambio," p. 479. The US$1.5 billion figure is for 1980.

26. Tourists may find a handsome bilingual publication, *A Giant Awakens* (Mexico City: Ministry of Tourism, 1979), in their hotel rooms!

27. Jacques Bugnicourt, "La otra cara del turismo: Sus efectos culturales," *Comercio Exterior* 28, no. 5 (1978):593.

28. Alan Riding, "Mexico's Economic Imbalances," *New York Times*, April 6, 1981.

29. Wayne Cornelius, "La migración ilegal mexicana a los Estados Unidos: Conclusiones de investigaciones recientes, implicaciones políticas y prioridades de investigación," *Foro Internacional* 18, no. 3 (1978):402; Kenneth Johnson, *Mexican Democracy: A Critical View* (New York: Praeger Publishers, 1978), p. 198. Most studies of the migration problem have been based on field research in the United States. A pioneering attempt to gather data and insights from within Mexico itself is headed by Jorge A. Bustamente. "Nuevos hallazgos," *Uno Más Uno*, December 10, 1979, and "El estudio de la zona fronteriza México–Estados Unidos," *Foro Internacional* 19, no. 3 (1979):471–516.

30. "Los ilegales," p. 804.

31. U.S. House of Representatives, Committee on Science and Technology, *U.S.-Mexico Relations and Potentials Regarding Energy, Immigration, Scientific Cooperation and Technology Transfer* (Washington, D.C.: Government Printing Office, 1979), p. 18.

32. See Barry W. Poulson, "The Brain Drain from Mexico to the United

States," in U.S.-Mexico Economic Relations, ed. Barry W. Poulson and Noel Osborn (Boulder, Colo.: Westview Press, 1979), pp. 245–260.

33. Such, for example, was the strongly voiced opinion of Carter's secretary of labor, F. Ray Marshall, "Economic Factors Influencing the International Migration of Workers," in Views Across the Border: The United States and Mexico ed. Richard W. Weatherhead and Stanley R. Ross (Albuquerque: University of New Mexico Press, 1978), pp. 178–179.

34. Peñaloza, "La formulación," pp. 26–27.

35. Within their respective domestic political contexts, the Mexican president has a freer hand than his U.S. counterpart in making foreign policy. There is less division, at least less public and intragovernmental division, than in the United States; similar points could be made about certain other bilateral issues. Mexican foreign policy consensus should not be exaggerated, however. For example, some Mexicans favor a new guest-worker program, while others strongly oppose it. One way to approach the plurality of views in both nations is through "linkage," considering bilateral issues integrally instead of separately. The United States has generally been more wary of linkage than Mexico has, but both sides have recently rethought their positions. On linkage, see Richard E. Feinberg, "Bureaucratic Organization and U.S. Policy Toward Mexico," in Mexico-United States Relations, ed. Susan Kaufman Purcell (New York: Academy of Political Science, 1981), pp. 32–42. An alternative is to conclude that not all bilateral problems are solvable by government (government may even aggravate some problems) and to encourage conflict resolution through private and incremental procedures.

36. Additional sources on migration include the entire issue of Foro Internacional 18, no. 3 (1978); Antonio Ríos-Bustamente, ed., Mexican Immigrant Workers in the U.S. (Los Angeles: UCLA, 1981); and Wayne Cornelius, Leo R. Chávez and Jorge Castro, "Mexican Immigrants and Southern California: A Summary of Current Knowledge," Working paper no. 36, Center for U.S.-Mexican Studies, University of California at San Diego, March 1982. Some policy suggestions are offered in Jorge A. Bustamante, "Migración indocumentada," Foro Internacional 19, no. 2 (1978):317–325.

37. Schmitt, Mexico and the United States (p. 193), described the 1945–1970 period as more "harmonious and carefree" than any previous period in Mexico–United States history, with the possible exception of the porfiriato. Schmitt's book is perhaps the best English-language overview of Mexico–United States history. Among the most recent works that provide overviews of contemporary Mexican foreign policy, especially concerning the United States, see Jorge Castañeda, México y el orden internacional (Mexico City: El Colegio de México, 1981); Richard D. Erb and Stanley R. Ross, eds., United States Relations with Mexico: Context and Content (Washington, D.C.: American Enterprise Institute, 1981); Lorenzo Meyer et al., Lecturas de política exterior mexicana (Mexico City: El Colegio de México, 1979); Poulson and Osborn, U.S.-Mexico Economic Relations; Purcell, Mexico-United States Relations; Carlos Vásquez and Manual García y Griego, eds., Mexican-U.S. Relations: Conflict or Convergence? (Los Angeles: UCLA,

1981). *Foro Internacional* is the journal that deals most fully with Mexican foreign policy. Additionally, the Center for U.S.-Mexican Studies at the University of California, San Diego, is producing a formidable series of working papers, especially on migration. Similarly, the Overseas Development Council in Washington, D.C., has developed a U.S.-Mexico project.

7

Oil Policy: A Case Study of Mexican Development

In 1973, Mexico produced less than 1 million barrels per day of crude oil and gas equivalent, a production insufficient to meet even its own demand. By late 1981, output had increased fourfold. *Oil had become Mexico's principal export.*

Estimates of potential Mexican oil and gas production and exports for the 1980s found in various studies conducted by U.S. government agencies have proven hopelessly conservative when judged by Mexico's actual performance. Crude oil output peaked in mid-1981 at 2.75 million barrels per day (mbd), of which about 1.5 mbd, or 55 percent, was being exported. Gas output was more than 4 billion cubic feet per day (bcfd), which is equivalent to an additional 800,000 barrels of oil per day. Because only 2.7 bcfd of total gas production was being consumed domestically and only 0.3 bcfd was being exported to the United States, gas flaring (gas burned into the atmosphere) amounted to between 0.6 and 1.0 bcfd. In late 1981, crude oil production and exports fell due to the glut in the world oil market, but by mid-1982 production and exports rose once again, following Mexico's agreement to increase oil sales destined for the U.S. strategic petroleum reserve. Mexico's proven hydrocarbon reserves rose from 5.4 billion to more than 72 billion barrels of crude oil and gas equivalent during the 1973–1981 period.[1]

Thus, Mexico is today among the world's top four nations in terms of three crucial factors: crude oil reserves, production, and exports. A very large gap still separates Mexico from the largest oil powers; in terms of production, for example, the Soviet Union, Saudi Arabia, and the United States each produces more than twice what Mexico produces. Nevertheless, as anyone who follows the news knows, there are strong indications that Mexico is itself becoming a leading oil producer. Less well known is that Mexico was a leading oil producer in the early 1920s.

213

At that time the Middle East and Venezuelan oil fields had not been developed, and Mexico accounted for one-fourth of the world's oil production. As a result of Mexico's oil revival, many politicians, private entrepreneurs, and scholars in oil-importing and oil-exporting nations have developed a special and sudden interest in Mexico. Some have expressed concern over the potentially disruptive effects of rapid oil development on domestic political and socioeconomic relations. They have cautioned that in order to avoid the Iranian syndrome (rapid change leading to instability) or even the Venezuelan syndrome (consumption outstripping infrastructure), the Mexican oil development program should proceed at a moderate pace. Others speculate about the potential effects of increasing Mexican oil production and exports on world oil supply and price levels. Rising oil prices, and the continual fear of another Arab oil embargo, have put additional pressure on already tense world economic and political relations. Thus, Mexico's future decisions regarding its oil production and exports are linked to other nations' economic, political, and even military interests.

The focus of this chapter, however, is more restricted than the possibilities for research offered by this topic might suggest. Here, after briefly reviewing the significance of oil in historical perspective, we analyze the various reactions of key domestic actors to Mexico's official oil policy as set forth in 1976. Thus, this chapter offers the reader an opportunity to apply some of the concepts about Mexican politics developed in earlier chapters. Oil is, after all, the most important new factor affecting Mexican politics, affecting the development model. We argued that in 1976 the economy was a shambles, the political environment tense. The new oil export policy helped to restore confidence in the development model, at least until 1982. We conclude this chapter by discussing some of the links between the new oil policy and Mexico's economic and foreign relations.

BRIEF BACKGROUND ON
THE MEXICAN OIL INDUSTRY

The history of Mexican oil can be divided into five phases.[2] In each of these phases there have been important changes in regard to *resource ownership* and *the primary goal or destination of production.*

The first phase extended from precolonial times to 1884. During that period, the state owned the resource, but no commercial production took place. Oil was known to the Mayas and Aztecs, who used the term *chapopote* to refer to the large oil seepages found primarily in southern regions, but their use of this natural resource was only marginal. So it would also be under the Spanish crown. Yet Spanish law, which influenced independent Mexico, provided for public ownership of underground natural resources.

The second phase began when a new law allowed the government to grant property titles to foreign companies—an important illustration of Porfirio Díaz's general tendency to encourage foreign entrepreneurs' participation in Mexico's first major drive for industrialization.[3] Exploratory efforts were started in 1886 in southern Mexico. By 1901, commercial production of oil began. Ironically, the first shipment of oil exports left Mexico in 1911, just when Porfirio Díaz himself boarded the *Ipiraña* on his way to exile in France. Mexican society had exploded in revolution.

The third phase opened with the provision in Article 27 of the new 1917 Constitution, establishing that underground natural resources were considered once again the exclusive property of the Mexican state. Understandably, this law set the stage for an eventual confrontation between the government and the foreign companies operating on the basis of the 1884 law. Their differing positions over resource ownership rights gradually evolved into an actual conflict that did not end until the 1940s. Interestingly, revolution and turmoil had not stymied oil development. In fact, output picked up, and by 1921, Mexico accounted for 25 percent of the world's total production. Mexico was the world's single largest oil exporter! During this period, most production coming from Mexico's famous golden belt (*faja de oro*) was exported to the United States, which was slowly increasing its use of oil and gas to fulfill its growing energy needs.

Our analysis in Chapter 2 of the effects of Mexico's revolutionary assertion of its economic sovereignty on Mexico–United States relations deliberately left details of the oil controversy for our discussion here. Washington withheld diplomatic recognition of the revolutionary regime for some time, in part because of the 1917 Constitution's provisions regarding private property and social policy issues, which were perceived by the United States as too radical in their material effects on U.S. interests. Normalization of diplomatic relations followed Obregón's ascendency to power in 1920, but only after the signing of the Bucareli Agreements (1923) on oil and other matters.[4] In particular, the government of Mexico committed itself not to implement retroactively the provisions of Article 27. The U.S. government accepted, for its part, that the companies' property titles be referred to from then on simply as "concessions." Because concessions are usually granted for a limited time only, the U.S. position left open the possibility of an eventual end to the presence of foreign oil firms on Mexican soil.

Bilateral relations became strained once again following the decree of a new Petroleum Law in 1925 by President Plutarco Elías Calles. The decree demanded that companies register their titles before local authorities, and it limited concessions to a maximum of fifty years. The companies, already disturbed by the Bucareli Agreements, found these provisions unacceptable and lobbied heavily in the United States in favor of their case. In an attempt to strengthen their domestic base of support, some went so far as to advocate the use of military force to settle once and for all the list of outstanding issues with Mexico. In 1927, Calles dramatized the situation by ordering General Lázaro Cárdenas, then commander-in-chief of the oil provinces, to set the fields afire if the United States conducted any kind of military action against Mexico. But several events combined to prevent that scenario from unfolding. For one thing, Calles did not push the companies to comply immediately with the law; more important, the new U.S. ambassador, Dwight Morrow, played a conciliatory role that led to an eventual revision of the law, to the satisfaction of some of the oil firms. In any event, the uncertainty generated by the controversy over resource ownership was among several factors that caused the major oil companies to concentrate their efforts in other lands. Large oil fields were found in Venezuela in the 1920s and in the Middle East in the 1930s; production costs were lower in these areas than in Mexico. Cost was a very important consideration, because oil was competing with cheap and abundant coal, the major source of energy in the industrial world.[5] Thus, the center of world oil production eventually shifted from Mexico and the United States to the Persian Gulf and Venezuela. Note also that in the 1920s—quite unlike the 1980s—Mexico was a leading producer of a resource that was *not* the world's principal energy source.

The fourth phase in Mexico's oil history began in 1938 with the nationalization of the oil industry by President Cárdenas. Mexico was no longer a major oil exporter, partly as a result of the declining production that accompanied the prolonged struggle between the foreign companies and the government. At the same time, domestic demand for hydrocarbons increased steadily as Mexico engaged in a new drive for industrialization after 1938. The decision to nationalize the industry followed the challenge to Mexico's judicial authorities by foreign oil firms. The courts had ruled in favor of union demands to improve workers' living standards. Unions were particularly strong because President Cárdenas had supported the establishment of the Confederation of Mexican Workers in 1936. This case is a good example of how the political dynamic that followed the revolution affected oil development. The state could resort to a strong and well-organized actor (labor) to face the challenge of the foreign companies. After long and hard bargaining, the companies refused to comply with the recommendations of the courts. President Cárdenas believed that this questioning of the legitimacy and the authority of the regime was intolerable, and he proceeded accordingly. In his own words:

It is clear that the problem presented to the national executive power by the disobedience of the Supreme Court's verdict is not simply a problem of implementing the verdict, but a situation that must be resolved at once. . . . It is the nation's sovereignty itself that could be exposed to maneuvering by foreign capital, which has forgotten its previous commitment to respect national laws, and is now seeking to avoid fulfillment of its duties as dictated by the country's authorities.

It is a clear-cut case, and it leaves the government no choice other than to apply the current Law of Expropriation.[6]

Although there was talk again of imminent U.S. military intervention in Mexico, overall U.S. foreign policy objectives at the time rendered such an event highly unlikely (see Chapter 2). Roosevelt's Good Neighbor Policy was intended to keep the nations of the Western Hemisphere together when the outbreak of world conflict was most feared. Partly for this reason, the U.S. government opted instead for pressuring Cárdenas to compensate the firms as they requested. It was only the amount of compensation, then, that was at issue, because the Mexican government had already expressed its intention of following the Constitution, which included compensation rights for those affected by this kind of government action. But the companies wanted to go much further and to teach rebellious Mexico a lesson, hoping that in the future other host countries would refrain from effecting nationalizations—especially after Bolivia's attempts to nationalize its oil industry in 1937. They pressured the U.S. government to cut down imports of Mexican silver, Mexico's main source of foreign exchange. In fact, a complete boycott of Mexican oil products and of other exports ensued. But because a growing share of Mexican oil was diverted to the Axis powers, U.S. government policy soon shifted. This time, the U.S. government put pressure on the companies to come to an agreement with Mexico, on the grounds of national security interests. It was thought that Mexican oil production could be increased on short notice should an emergency situation require it. In that sense, it was important to maintain good relations with Mexico. A final settlement came in 1942, when a bilateral governmental team worked out an agreement whose terms were accepted by the U.S. companies. Total compensation amounted to only a fraction of the $400 million once demanded by U.S. Secretary of State Cordell Hull.[7]

Today, there is a constitutional ban on the involvement of foreign firms in most aspects of the oil industry, primarily due to their intolerable behavior in the past. However, the government has not hesitated to ask for foreign assistance when the country's capacity to fulfill certain needs (e.g., domestic consumption needs) has been in jeopardy. That is, economic independence is a recurrent theme in Mexican politics, but it can be compromised in order to attain a different or even a higher priority, such as economic growth. Thus, for example, President Miguel Alemán allowed PEMEX to sign several contracts, in 1949 and 1951, with U.S. firms to conduct exploration works in the Gulf of Mexico. The companies, if successful, would be paid partly with a share of 15 to 18 percent of the value of production. Although these contracts were honored until their respective expiration dates twenty years later, Article 27 of the Constitution was amended in 1958 with the specific purpose of preventing any similar kind of contracts in the future.[8]

Since the 1938 nationalization, a top priority of governmental policy has been to supply sufficient oil and gas, which together have accounted for about 90 percent of total domestic energy needs during the rapid industrialization since the 1940s. Because domestic consumption was rising rapidly while hydrocarbon reserves had increased more modestly, from 1.2 billion barrels in 1938 to 5.2 billion in 1964, the search for oil and gas went on during the 1960s. President Díaz Ordaz supported greater exploration efforts in the Gulf of Mexico. In 1967, according to the *Wall Street Journal*, PEMEX officials estimated total reserves from that area at about 10 billion barrels of crude oil and gas equivalent.[9] Those estimates were not then confirmed, but it did not take many years before press speculation regarding potential huge deposits of oil and gas in Mexico started anew.

On March 18, 1973, during the annual commemoration of the oil nationalization, the director general of PEMEX referred publicly for the first time to the oil and gas findings. A few months later, President Luis Echeverría himself spoke about the "oil discoveries" in southern Mexico, during his State of the Union address.[10] In some quarters, these declarations were not taken seriously at first. After all, Mexico had stopped exporting crude oil in 1969, and the country had been a net importer of oil in recent years. Nonetheless, others became increasingly interested in what was going on in Mexico's oil and financial circles. The issue was discussed by President Echeverría and President Gerald Ford during their meeting in October 1974.[11] In the eyes of the U.S. president, the issue probably looked uncomplicated. Mexican authorities began to talk publicly about the new oil fields before the energy crisis of late 1973 and early 1974. That was an indication that Mexico had an independent interest in selling oil. Now that the United States could be subjected to an Arab oil embargo, and now that oil prices were rising quickly, friendly Mexico would presumably find it even more appealing to increase its oil output and exports. And the United States, for geographical reasons, is in purely economic terms the natural market for Mexican oil exports. But things looked more complex to President Echeverría. He was aware that there would be some domestic resistance to any sharp break from the oil-for-domestic-consumption-only policy of the last decades. In addition, his self-image as a "leader of the Third World" could be damaged if the effectiveness of an Arab oil embargo was undercut by Mexican oil exports to the United States.

Despite these considerations, and even though Echeverría did not dramatically depart from traditional oil policy, he provided the rationale and laid the foundations so that a new administration could pursue a fundamentally new oil policy if it wished. The rationale, as discussed in Chapter 5, was provided by the state of economic disarray when Echeverría left power. López Portillo could make a strong case when he argued that the constraints on growth imposed by the disequilibria in the external sector of the economy (e.g., lack of foreign exchange and the growing foreign debt service) could be overcome much sooner with greatly expanded oil production than without it. But at least as important were the foundations already established by governmental efforts during the Echeverría years to develop the oil industry. The figures show that there is a greater degree of continuity in oil policy between administrations than is usually assumed. The oil sector accounted for 17 percent of total public investment during Echeverría's tenure, and PEMEX received several foreign loans, totaling about $4 billion, to fund its expansion. The results were satisfactory by most standards. Output rose from 0.8 mbd of oil and gas equivalent in 1970 to 1.3 mbd in 1976. More than half of total output in 1976 came from the new fields. Similarly, the nominal production capacity of the national network of refineries increased by 55 percent. During the period, Mexico's status changed from that of a net oil importer to that of a net oil exporter. The 1975 figure of nearly 100,000 barrels per day (which was soon to be surpassed) was the highest crude oil export level since 1928.[12] In short, when López Portillo came to power he did not have to start from scratch to implement a new oil policy. Rather, the efforts of the previous administration made it easier for him to move swiftly in that direction. The 1973–1976 period may be considered a transitional stage between the fourth and fifth phases in the history of Mexican oil policy.

The fifth phase, the present phase, started in late 1976. Resource ownership was no longer an issue, as the decisive 1938 nationalization initiated in the fourth phase had also been implemented during that phase. But now domestic production was once again more than sufficient to satisfy national energy needs, and for the first time in decades, Mexico would begin exporting oil and gas in substantial amounts. López Portillo in fact went much further than his predecessor in expanding the oil industry. Today, PEMEX is a giant enterprise. Its budget in 1980 amounted to US$15 billion (about one-quarter of the total budget of the public sector), and it has been ranked thirty-fourth in *Fortune*'s list of the 500 largest enterprises in the world.[13]

What were the original objectives of López Portillo's oil policy? Three weeks after the inauguration of the new government, PEMEX Director General Díaz Serrano announced that the figure for proven reserves had been increased from 6.3 billion to 11.1 billion barrels of oil and gas equivalent. PEMEX invited a prestigious U.S. firm, De Golyer and McNaughton, to certify the authenticity of these figures. But why are reserve figures important in any case? At a minimum, reserve figures indicate the capacity of any country to export oil for some period of time. In Mexico, at current rates of production and consumption, 11 billion barrels would be expected to last twenty-three years. Because experts agree that a well-balanced reserve-to-production ratio should be equivalent to at least fifteen years, it was safe and justifiable that Mexico engage in an oil export program. How long beyond twenty-three years Mexico could remain an exporter would depend on the success of its exploration in adding to current reserves. A closely related factor was that PEMEX needed to secure foreign loans to finance its ambitious development program. There could hardly have been anything more valued than oil to convince foreign banks and international financial institutions that, despite the general economic chaos prevailing in Mexico, lending money to PEMEX was still a wise financial policy. Further, it was expected that oil might help to put the economy back in good shape and thus improve the prospects for continued political stability. Mexico could put its finances in order with the assistance of oil export revenues. It turned out that when the specifics of PEMEX's expansion plans became publicly known, not only bankers but also many industrialists, and even some governments, became very enthusiastic. Many hoped to do business with PEMEX or simply saw Mexico as a more secure source of oil imports than OPEC countries.

PEMEX's budget for 1977–1982 was estimated at US$40 billion, with investments alone accounting for about one-third of the total. By 1982, Mexico's crude oil output was expected to have increased to 2.25 mbd; output of natural gas was expected to be some 4 bcfd. Originally, it was planned that half of total crude oil output would be available for export, but no mention was made of gas exports. Other major goals included doubling the nominal refining capacity to 1.7 mbd, as well as a threefold increase of production capacity of basic petrochemicals to 18 million tons per year by 1982. How have PEMEX's expansion plans evolved and how have they been implemented? And how have domestic political actors reacted to the new oil policy?

THE DOMESTIC DEBATE
OVER THE NEW OIL POLICY

It took several months before the first dissenting voice was raised. Moreover, for some time it seemed as if there were only two participants in the debate. One of them, predictably, was the PEMEX director general. He represented and defended the government's position. Less predictably, the other participant was Heberto Castillo, a university professor and founder of the small Mexican Workers party. In fact, he has the distinction of having initiated the debate that eventually drew the attention of intellectuals and other actors previously inactive in this respect. Castillo advocated a return to the old oil policy on grounds that hydrocarbons are a nonrenewable natural resource, a natural resource on which Mexico depends heavily to satisfy its own energy needs. He further argued that because alternative energy sources have not been fully developed as yet, and the technology required will be largely beyond Mexico's control, it would make sense to stretch the lifetime of hydrocarbon reserves as long as possible. He also contended that the main value of hydrocarbons is not as a fuel but as a raw material for production of other goods, such as plastics and fertilizers. Fertilizers presumably would help to increase output of food that would help feed Mexico's needy, ensure national economic independence, and improve the peasants' lot.[14]

Castillo made a strong case, but he had little chance of success. The government perceived oil as the best means to overcome quickly the economic crisis. And Castillo did not command enough political resources to press his view. Still, his criticisms became the focus of the debate because, for some months, he systematically embarrassed the government by presenting evidence of the incoherence and lack of consistency of the information presented by PEMEX in support of its development program. For example, Díaz Serrano went before Congress in October 1977 to explain a new project—PEMEX wanted to invest an additional US$1 billion to build a gas pipeline (*gasoducto*) that would reduce gas flaring. (As oil is extracted, gas also emerges; and because Mexico has not found adequate outlets for the gas, it must destroy it.) The gas surplus, Díaz Serrano argued, could be sent to the United States through the gasoducto, with exports reaching more than 2 bcfd by 1982. But many of PEMEX's statistics, such as the official record of how much gas was being flared, were inconsistent. Furthermore, the financial calculations to justify the gas project were not totally accurate.[15] Thus, Castillo found in the gasoducto affair an additional focus for his criticism of government policy. He appealed to nationalist feelings, warning that Mexico would become more linked than ever to U.S. national security.

Mexico could even become a target of Soviet missiles during a superpower confrontation. He suggested that Mexico instead use the surplus gas domestically or liquefy it and send it overseas, despite greater financial costs.[16]

The Castillo-PEMEX controversy did not directly influence actual policy. In fact, PEMEX's plan fell through temporarily because the U.S. government did not approve the gas export contract signed by PEMEX and six U.S. gas firms in the summer of 1977. The pricing system for natural gas in the U.S. was being hotly debated in Congress, and the terms of the gas deal with PEMEX (US$2.60 per 1,000 cubic feet of gas) went beyond what was acceptable to the U.S. Congress at the time.[17] An embarrassed Mexican government ended up conducting a program to substitute gas for oil as a fuel in many of the nation's industries. And when an agreement was reached two years later to export 300 million cubic feet per day of gas to the United States, it was of a far more modest nature than was originally planned. Nonetheless, the Castillo-PEMEX controversy is interesting as an indication of the changing political environment in Mexico. Ten years earlier, in 1968, Castillo had been put in jail for criticizing the government during the university confrontation with the regime. Now, granting that the nature of the challenge was different, he could express his opinion through a largely independent magazine and even elicit a civil public response from government officials.

A return to an oil policy without exports is highly unlikely. If the government decided to eliminate oil exports, public finances would deteriorate dramatically, and the country's capacity to import would be severely restricted. There is no reason to believe that the government would make a decision that would most certainly aggravate Mexico's ongoing foreign exchange shortage. At present, at the risk of oversimplifying, one can identify two main positions regarding the preferred course of Mexican oil policy. One can be termed the *moderate oil development program*, the other the *all-out production and export program*. In what follows, the central arguments in support of each position will be discussed. Actors publicly advocating one or the other of these positions will be identified. A note of caution, however, is that these alternative policies have not been presented with the degree of coherence that is implied here. Nor are the actors on one side or the other necessarily working together to further their views. Mexican politics simply do not characteristically lend themselves to such coherent public debate, unrestricted participation in policymaking, mobilization, or organizationally based coalition building. Yet, this discussion is particularly relevant as Mexico is once again experiencing severe economic problems. Like his predecessor, President de la Madrid may well face important debates concerning how much to rely on oil as an economic remedy.

The Moderate Oil Development Program

López Portillo's decision to develop oil resources rapidly took many by surprise. Furthermore, it was soon realized that the issue was no longer whether to return to the old oil policy without exports, but rather how much and at what pace oil and gas would be produced and exported. Those who feared that excessive reliance on oil would exacerbate rather than solve Mexico's socioeconomic and political tensions gradually rallied in support of the *original* oil development program discussed earlier. They have presented several arguments in support of their efforts to establish a fixed ceiling to oil and gas production and exports.

From the point of view of *resources*, the moderates argue that PEMEX should be careful not to rush, in its quest to fulfill its production targets, to a point that could risk depletion of resources. At the same time, the country should be allowed sufficient time to invest in developing alternative energy sources. Initial investments have in fact been made in nuclear and geothermal energy projects, with the hope that Mexico will gradually reduce its excessive dependence on hydrocarbons. But this process requires time, and only hydrocarbons can guarantee that time by insuring that Mexico will not have to face energy shortages at the turn of the century.

A concern with the varied effects of oil development on the *rest of the economy* is also central to the moderate position. Oil might be instrumental in solving some of Mexico's short-term economic problems, but it is not a substitute for implementing necessary reforms in the tax system, income distribution, and other areas. Beyond this, a new strategy for increased agricultural production and industrialization must be developed, in which oil is but one of many factors to be considered. In addition, there should be enough time available to work out solutions to insufficient storage facilities and transportation systems (bottlenecks) and to control inflation. Finally, oil development should be expected to have positive side effects on the economy only if domestic entrepreneurs are granted sufficient time to produce locally many goods that otherwise would have to be imported. In short, moderates see fundamental problems in the development model that rapid oil expansion will only temporarily cover, not solve. In fact, covering over may diminish the chances for realistic long-run policy.

To a greater or to a lesser extent, several actors have identified themselves with this position. Within the government itself, as we saw in Chapter 3, different ministries hold different ideological and policy orientations. The minister of national resources and industrial development under López Portillo was the strongest advocate of a moderate oil development program. He is, by law, the chairman of PEMEX's Board of Directors; but in fact PEMEX's director general has exercised much greater power, as he has been a closer associate of the president. Nevertheless, under the leadership of José Andrés de Oteyza, the Ministry of National Resources provided two very important documents: the National Industrial Development Plan and the National Energy Plan.[18]

The Industrial Development Plan proposes annual rates of economic growth of up to 10 percent, starting in 1979 and continuing through 1990. Industry is expected to grow at an annual average rate of 12 percent, petrochemicals and capital goods at 20 percent. The plan discusses the instruments and incentives the public sector will have to provide to private investors. It is designed to decentralize Mexican industry geographically by encouraging it to move outside Mexico City. For example, for those investing outside Mexico City, it grants substantially subsidized prices for oil, gas, and petrochemical products (up to 30 percent below already low domestic prices). There is a more specific link between the Industrial Plan and oil policy. The plan was based on the assumptions that crude oil output would have stabilized at 2.25 mbd at the end of 1980 and that any subsequent rise in output would only compensate for the growth of domestic demand. Revenues from exports of 1.1 mbd of crude oil would be instrumental to achieving the objectives of the plan. Gas exports were not considered at all, probably because the negotiations with the United States were at a standstill. As has been shown, the production and export targets of the *original* oil development program (which were included in the Industrial Plan) have been revised substantially. PEMEX's crude oil production of 2.25 mbd was reached two years ahead of schedule, gas has been exported since January 1980, and the *new ceiling for oil production alone*—which implies a higher output of oil plus gas associated with oil—has been increased to 2.75 mbd.

Still, the importance of the Industrial Plan is that it provided, for some time, a rallying point for all those groups and individuals who disagreed with PEMEX's policy of rapidly expanding oil production and exports. Furthermore, by giving great publicity to the government's commitment to a certain oil output ceiling, Oteyza may have earned some added leverage with the president regarding decisions to change that ceiling. An indication of this situation is that Oteyza got the president's approval for his National Energy Plan in November 1980. On the other hand, the president's approval probably reflects his own receptivity to the plan's major tenets, for no ministry pushes the president against his will.

In presenting the National Energy Plan, Oteyza stressed that "any expansion in energy production should be a function of the nation's global development needs only. It should not be a function of the volumes of reserves *per se*, nor of greater demand by foreign economies."[19] Specifically, departing from the oil production ceiling of 2.75 mbd set earlier by López Portillo, the plan establishes an export ceiling of 1.5 mbd of crude oil and 300 million cubic feet per day of gas (the level of gas exports to the United States in 1980). In addition to this new attempt to freeze oil and gas production and export levels, the plan establishes that oil exports are to be diversified. That is, no more than 50 percent of Mexican oil should end up in the same country, and no country should come to depend on Mexico to fulfill more than 20 percent of its oil import needs. What is the meaning of these export rules? From 1974 to 1979, before those rules existed, more than four-fifths of Mexican oil exports went to the United States. By 1981, that proportion had fallen sharply, to about 50 percent. Thus, Mexico fulfilled its goal, at least temporarily, of not sending too much of its oil to the United States.[20] Many fear that, even if this proves to be a temporary phenomenon, due to decreasing oil production and exports by Nigeria and other suppliers and even if the U.S. government has so far not tried to influence explicitly Mexico's oil policy, excessive U.S. reliance on Mexican oil imports might tempt the U.S. toward such intervention. The apparent intention of the export rules is to forestall that kind of situation. But such fears were naturally heightened by the 1982 economic crisis and Mexico's agreement to sell the United States increased quantities, at preferential cost.

The minister of national resources under López Portillo had some "allies" within the administration, as well as some influential sympathizers elsewhere. In official circles, for example, economic-policy-making authorities consistently expressed their concern with the effects of oil development on rising inflation. Further, as we argued in Chapter 5, the National Development Bank has a special interest in promoting the development of a domestic capital goods industry that, in time, could supply a share of the needs of PEMEX and other industries. And the Ministry of Finance and the Central Bank would like to exert greater influence on decisions regarding where and how oil revenues should be invested.

The governors of oil-producing states, particularly of Chiapas and Tabasco in the south, can also be counted among those who would rather support a moderate oil development program. Not only do state governments see a very small share of the oil money but, at the same time, they have to deal with rising tensions, such as those resulting from expropriated peasant lands and delays in paying compensation. They also have to deal with pollution in lakes, the ocean, and farms. In fact, there are reports, many published in Mexico's generally cautious press, of protests by peasants and fishermen affected by PEMEX's activities. In addition, complaints in oil-producing states are growing because inflationary rates are even higher there than in Mexico City, urban areas are overcrowded, crime is on the rise, and so forth.[21] In other words, some of the threats to stability discussed in Chapter 1 are manifested particularly in the oil-producing states.

Although they are mostly of secondary importance due to the distribution of political power in Mexico, other potential proponents of the moderate policy include some private investors who need time to reap the full benefits of increasing aggregate demand; opposition political parties concerned with rising government corruption and waste of public funds; and university professors concerned with the hazardous environmental, social, and political effects already brought about by PEMEX expansion.

How far can PEMEX go? There are important actors who have expressed their support for the development of the oil industry at a pace much faster than has been the case so far. They would like to see PEMEX producing and exporting higher levels of oil and gas on the basis of its huge reserves. Their position was somewhat weakened, at least temporarily, by the events of the summer of 1981: The existence of a glut in the international oil market became clear, leading some other nations to lower their output in order to avoid a further fall in oil prices. Nonetheless, conditions in the world oil market are changing constantly and unpredictably. As pointed out earlier, Mexico managed to increase its mid-1982 production back to 2.75 mbd, in spite of the glut. Some political actors have consistently hoped that Mexico would develop its oil industry much more rapidly.

The All-Out Production and Export Program

Several arguments have been put forward in support of a more ambitious development of the oil industry. Some overlap with those discussed in support of a more moderate development program.

Mexico is confronted today, so the argument goes, with a unique opportunity brought about by the combination of fortuitous conditions. The world's demand for oil is high and on the rise, even though it may have slowed temporarily due to the world economic recession of the early 1980s. Furthermore, Mexico already has great hydrocarbon reserves, which may increase even further, as only one-tenth of its potential oil-bearing territory has been thoroughly explored. And oil prices have increased more than tenfold, from about US$3 to US$34 a barrel, since Mexico discovered the southern fields before 1973. (Because of the world oil glut, the export price of Mexico's best-quality crude slipped to US$32.50 per barrel in mid-1982.) At the same time, Mexico lacks sufficient capital to solve its unemployment and other critical social problems. With added capital from oil revenues, the opportunities for enhanced economic growth would multiply, with expanded benefits for all social sectors. The Mexican economy need not be distorted by the great infusion of oil funds. In contrast to most OPEC nations, Mexico has a sophisticated industrial base, human resources, and managerial skills in both its private and public sectors. It also has a broad natural resource base that includes resources other than oil (e.g., silver, steel, copper, uranium). Moreover, oil revenues can finance projects to develop the alternative energy sources on which the country will have to rely at some point in the future in any event. In a broader sense, oil can be an agent of modernization in terms of fueling greater interaction with the industrial countries, particularly in the areas of trade and technology. In sum, the proponents of this position argue that not many countries have been blessed with such a golden historical opportunity as that offered to Mexico by its wealth in a resource in such high international demand. Mexico would be well advised to reap the full benefits of such an opportunity. Of course, Mexico's economic troubles in 1982—attributed by many to rapid oil development—have somewhat weakened this position.

Among those officials who have identified themselves publicly with this position, the former PEMEX director general, Jorge Díaz Serrano, stands out. Although he resigned in 1981 following an intragovernmental controversy over the pricing of oil exports, the following discussion is still relevant as an illustration of support from influential figures for the more radical oil development position. Díaz Serrano's political and managerial talents stunned many in Mexico and abroad. He gradually led PEMEX to where it stands today. Recognizing the central policymaking role of the president, Díaz Serrano's first success was to convince his friend and then presidential "candidate," López Portillo, to commit himself to a new oil policy. Recognizing the important role of the United States in Mexico's political economy, Díaz Serrano also tried to convince U.S. oil and financial circles that Mexico's oil findings were notable indeed and that they should support PEMEX's expansion plans. Under attack by some of his opponents, he turned his attention back home and added two more to his list of achievements. First, despite domestic opposition from many groups and the initial failure of the gas export deal with the United States, he carried on with the gasoducto project. Construction of the gasoducto was completed in late 1979. Second, during a hearing before the Mexican Congress, he outsmarted the opposition. There were claims that his links to one of PEMEX's major private contracting firms created a typical Mexican situation of conflict of interest with his current public responsibilities. Díaz Serrano presented legal documents showing that he no longer had an interest in the firm (Gulf's Offshore Perforations), through which he had gained much of his experience about the oil industry and had developed contacts in the United States. Those contacts included George Bush, himself linked to oil interests in Texas at the time, who later became U.S. vice-president.[22]

More relevant for our purposes is that as soon as it became clear that PEMEX would, in 1980, reach its 1982 production target, the debate within the government focused on what limits to establish to increasing oil and gas production capacity. Here lies the importance of the concept of an *oil production ceiling* discussed earlier. Díaz Serrano had repeatedly emphasized that such a ceiling might be subject to change. For example, he told former French president Giscard d'Estaing during a visit to Mexico City that it was conceivable that Mexico might be producing 4 mbd of crude oil in 1982.[23] That was not official policy, but Mexico's proven reserves had increased, justifying greater production (at least on technical grounds alone). In any event, Díaz Serrano succeeded in raising the official oil production ceiling from the original 2.25 mbd to 2.75 mbd.

There is another important factor to be considered. Mexico's port facilities are being expanded to accommodate oil supertankers and greatly increase export capabilities. The mastermind of this project is Rodolfo Moctezuma Cid, who had been one of López Portillo's chief economic advisers and his first minister of finance. Following an unusual public dispute over official economic policy with Carlos Tello (López Portillo's first minister of programming and budget), López Portillo fired both Moctezuma and Tello in 1977. But he eventually went on to appoint Moctezuma to succeed Díaz Serrano as director general of PEMEX, thus working closely with Moctezuma to implement Mexico's all-important oil policies. Previously, however, the president had appointed Moctezuma to head a very important presidential commission, the Special Development Projects. The central task of this commission is building four major industrial ports on the Gulf of Mexico and the Pacific. Many firms will set up their facilities near these ports in order to cut transportation costs. It is hoped this will also help to alleviate the already overburdened national railway network; that is, the ports are expected to help solve one of the major development bottlenecks discussed in Chapter 5. But more important, these ports, together with the ports of Pajaritos and Dos Bocas built by PEMEX, will establish a total oil export capacity of 5 mbd by 1985![24] It may well be that Mexico's new, impressive sea-based oil export capacity will remain idle—especially in face of unfavorable world oil market conditions. However, insufficient facilities will not stand in the way of a future government decision to increase oil exports substantially, under favorable international conditions.

One of the most obvious proponents of the all-out policy is PEMEX's labor union itself. The PEMEX union, with about 125,000 members, is the strongest of the national industrial unions discussed in Chapter 3. The salaries and fringe benefits enjoyed by most oil workers are such that there have been abundant reports regarding corrupt union leaders who sell jobs for several thousand pesos. The more PEMEX expands, the greater the number of positions available for sale. And enhanced economic power is usually accompanied by more political power. Another, more disturbing source of corruption is encouraged by concessions given the union by PEMEX's management. Because Mexico did not have the technology needed to conduct oil-well perforations offshore, it had to rely on U.S. firms such as Brown and Root. PEMEX has given the contracts to two Mexican firms, Gulf's Offshore Perforations and Proyectos Marinos, which in turn have subcontracted Brown and Root and others. Previously, however, PEMEX had to negotiate with the union that enjoys exclusive rights over perforation works. It has been reported that an agreement was reached whereby the union keeps control over 40 percent of contracts given to third parties for these perforation works. Much money is involved in that operation, inviting even further corruption.[25]

All those private firms that have been able to keep pace with the increase in aggregate demand caused largely by PEMEX's expansion are potential backers of this position. And, as we argued in Chapter 4, business is Mexico's most powerful political actor, other than the government itself. The all-out position may also have the backing of a much less important but now partially reemerging political actor: the military. The military is in charge of security and protection of all oil installations. Its public assertiveness, which already increased during the stage of the moderate oil development program, would be further increased. The military may hope to parlay its legitimacy, based on its role as guardian of Mexico's economic lifeline, into expanded political power.

Here we outline two conclusions to be drawn from this section. First, there is a more open political system in Mexico today, but by and large, key strategic decisions are still a result of intra-elite discussions only marginally influenced by most societal actors and public opinion. The heads of PEMEX and of the Ministry of National Resources tried at some point to rally the support of other key (rather than marginal) actors in order to influence the future course of Mexico's oil policy. Second, the particular case of oil policy shows that, contrary to much rhetoric in Mexico and to misperceptions in the United States, the strength of the opposition and the role of vaguely defined concepts such as "nationalism" in influencing public policy have been exaggerated. For example, despite the opposition from the left to the gasoducto project and despite Mexican "strident nationalism," the gas export deal with the United States went ahead, and foreign firms are assisting PEMEX in its expansion plans. It seems that whatever oil policy López

Portillo, de la Madrid, or their successors decide to follow, it will originate in their evaluation of the broader economic policy objectives to be attained with the assistance of oil. As we argued earlier, those economic objectives are rooted, in turn, in the need to preserve the traditional relationship between sustained economic growth and overall political stability.

OIL POLICY AND THE ECONOMY

The analysis of the Mexican economy since 1976 (Chapter 5) shows that there are some pressures that could tip the balance in favor of an oil policy of the *all-out* rather than of the *moderate* development type. Basically, these pressures are rooted in Mexico's economic difficulties. Despite the successful achievement of oil production and export targets in both the government's original and revised plans, many of the problems associated with the 1976 economic crisis—indeed with the underlying development model—remain largely unsolved. In particular, a key strategic objective of the López Portillo government was to reduce the unusually high level of inflation that prevailed during the Echeverría years before actively pursuing high rates of economic growth. López Portillo wanted to avoid repetition of a painful episode in recent Mexican history. Following the economic boom brought about by huge agricultural exports to the United States during World War II, Mexico experienced a decade of economic growth combined with high rates of inflation. This led eventually to a devaluation of the peso in 1954. The regime then opted for relying on foreign funds to help maintain price stability at home and to support the value of the Mexican peso. That policy worked well for about twenty years, followed in the 1970s by a short period of no growth, combined with high inflation.

The late 1970s saw the return of high economic growth rates combined with high inflation. The Mexican economy grew by an annual average of 7.5 percent from 1978 to 1981, while inflation ranged from 20 to 30 percent. In addition, the record shows a continuing deficit in public finances, a deficit in the current account of the balance of payments (US$11 billion in 1981, in spite of oil export revenues that amounted to more than US$14.5 billion), an ever-increasing foreign public debt (US$51 billion in 1981, up from US$19 billion in 1976), declining exports of manufactures, increasing imports of foodstuffs, and so forth. Moreover, the government needed more revenues to fund the ongoing expansion of port facilities, railroads, capital goods, and petrochemical plants—all necessary to the oil and other industries—and to support its new agricultural production programs. In short, all this meant that the government needed extra revenues to finance its various projects and to revitalize the development model. And given traditional trends characteristic of Mexican economic policy, changes in tax and subsidy policies were expected to have only a marginal effect in supplying total governmental revenue needs. *It followed that greater oil exports were the most likely source of additional government revenues.*

Just as in the case of many oil-rich economies, Mexico has found it very difficult to avoid excessive reliance on oil to keep the economy growing. And, as happened in 1976, a desire to attain various economic objectives is likely to be a major factor legitimizing government decisions to produce and export more oil. It thus seems that such decisions on oil policy are strongly influenced by the needs of the development model *and* by the deep, still unresolved problems in that model. In turn, such policy decisions reinforce that model, strengthening it in many important ways (e.g., reattracting foreign capital) but not solving many of the problems (e.g., inflation and income maldistribution) that have accompanied that model. By 1981 and 1982, Mexico's severe economic setbacks had shown that oil was not fulfilling the promise many had expected. The Mexican regime has understood that oil is an enormous political as well as economic resource, but it remains to be seen how wisely that political capital is spent in the future.

OIL AND FOREIGN POLICY

We close this chapter with an analysis of how oil has affected foreign relations, particularly how it has reinforced trends, analyzed in Chapter 6, toward a diversification—however constrained—of Mexico's foreign policy away from its traditional focus on the United States. The United States has been and will continue to be the largest consumer of Mexican hydrocarbons, a factor reinforcing the U.S. orientation of Mexico's foreign policy. But, in fact, oil may provide a real economic base to sustain the often-proclaimed goals of national independence, universalism, and diversification that had frequently seemed more rhetorical and unsubstantiated than real. Mexican foreign policy toward nations beyond Latin America has become important. Mexico's relations with oil-importing and oil-exporting nations will be analyzed, as well as Mexico's recent attempts to play a mediating role in the disputes that have characterized relations between these two blocs of nations.

Mexico and the Oil-Importing Nations

Some important tensions with the United States have arisen over Mexico's oil development program. The initial failure of the gas export deal discussed earlier and the 3-million-barrel oil spill in the Gulf of Mexico—the accident at the Ixtoc oil well in 1979 was the worst of its kind in history—are the clearest examples. Nonetheless, in general, the United States is pleased with its imports of Mexican oil and gas. We have said that some have gone as far as to propose the establishment of a *North American common market* that would include Canada, the United States, and Mexico.[26] Because the coordination of energy, monetary, and other policies among countries of unequal power, resources, and aims is perceived as a potential threat to the national sovereignty of the weaker parties involved, Canada and Mexico have so far rejected the proposal altogether.

Others have advocated developing a *special bilateral Mexico–United States relationship* on the grounds that stability in Mexico is essential to U.S. national security interests and that the United States should be prepared to pay the costs that such a situation entails.[27] Thus, for example, the United States could grant significant concessions in the immigration and trade areas in exchange for Mexico's commitment to increase oil exports to the United States. Henry Kissinger and David Rockefeller are among the most enthusiastic supporters of such a bilateral relationship.

In contrast with the central assumption implicit in the two proposals outlined above, a third view advises against allowing Mexican oil to be used as a pretext to further intensify bilateral relations. According to this view, a greater degree of interaction between the United States and Mexico might further complicate the relationship rather than increase cooperation. Instead, the United States should concentrate its efforts on bringing Mexico into *multilateral fora* (as it tried to do in 1979 by inviting Mexico to join GATT), where existing bilateral tensions could be more easily defused and hence become more manageable.[28] Any of these three options could become official U.S. policy in the future, but the United States has not yet developed an overall energy policy, let alone a particular energy policy toward Mexico. In any event, suffice it to say that oil remains one of many factors that together make up a complex but generally friendly relationship between Mexico and the United States. On the other hand, as President Ford learned from President Echeverría, and as President Carter learned from President López Portillo, Mexico has asserted its independence from the United States on oil and related energy issues. (Other factors influencing the Mexico–United States relationship have of course been discussed in Chapter 6.)

Oil has played an important role in the diversification of Mexico's economic and political relations with other industrial oil-importing nations—especially with West European nations and Japan. These countries depend heavily on oil imports to satisfy their energy needs; hence they seek secure supplies. Because Mexico has a long record of political stability and is more moderate than the Organization of Petroleum Exporting Countries (OPEC)—especially OPEC's radical Arab members— Mexico is generally perceived as a more secure source. Thus, some have even been willing to pay more for oil from Mexico than they would for oil coming from OPEC countries located nearer their borders! In addition, Mexico has been able to strike a series of bilateral deals including greater investments, loans, and technological assistance from these countries in exchange for long-term Mexican oil export contracts. For example, Spain has allowed PEMEX to take a majority interest in a refinery, Petronor, to process Mexican oil and compete in the European market. Japan is assisting Mexico with the most advanced technology available to expand port facilities and the national railroad network. Canada, France, and Sweden have been competing for a contract to sell Mexico the particular kind of nuclear energy production technology they know. Finally, all these industrial nations have agreed to encourage a greater flow of private capital to Mexico, and banks from these nations have underwritten many of Mexico's recent loan operations in the international financial market. Mexico has indeed awakened new interest and respect abroad. Following the controversy over Mexico's oil export prices in the summer of 1981, relations with these countries—especially with France—were temporarily strained. Contracts for oil purchases were terminated in some cases. Since then, PEMEX has reported that the conflict has been resolved, although it has not provided evidence that it has been able to restore its oil export contracts with these countries.

We argued in the preceding chapter that oil has also been instrumental in Mexico's policy toward Central America and the Caribbean. PEMEX has won several contracts to conduct oil exploration works in Cuba, Panama, and Nicaragua. More important, Mexico and Venezuela have signed the San José Agreement, whereby they will provide oil to some dozen nations in the area on preferential terms. The two major oil exporters in the Western Hemisphere have agreed to supply up to 80,000 barrels per day each of crude oil. The beneficiaries have to pay only 70 percent of the market price, and the rest becomes a credit to be paid according to either of two formulas. One is a credit for five years at an annual interest rate of 4 percent. However, if these financial resources are invested in priority economic development projects or in developing alternative energy sources, the terms of the credit change to twenty years at an annual interest rate of only 2 percent.[29] Mexico's and Venezuela's generosity can be attributed to the fact that both nations are concerned with the ongoing political turmoil in the region. Masters of political co-optation at home, the Mexicans agreed with the Venezuelans to try this formula in regional relations. It is hoped that lower oil prices will ease, if only to a certain degree, the economic and political tensions afflicting Central America and the Caribbean. As at home, political co-optation involves clear costs to the Mexican government, but, as at home, the costs seem well worth assuming.

Mexico and the Oil-Exporting Nations

The steady increase in Mexico's crude oil output has been concurrent with a declining world demand for oil due to the ongoing economic recession. Some recent reports are dramatic. While Mexico's crude oil output rose from 0.5 mbd in 1973 to 2.75 mbd in mid-1981, world crude oil production since the latter date has been held near the 1973 level, about 56 mbd.[30] This means that Mexico's share of total world crude oil production has risen from less than 1 percent to 5 percent during the period. Despite declining production due to the Iranian-Iraqi conflict, additional Mexican supplies combined with greater production from the North Sea and with an unusual output of more than 10 million mbd by Saudi Arabia to induce the supporters of higher oil prices within OPEC (e.g., Libya and Algeria) to cut down their production and freeze prices through the end of 1981. And in 1982, even though Saudi Arabia cut its own production to 6.5 mbd, there was a price-deflating glut in the world oil market.

To be sure, it is very difficult to assess the actual effect of greater Mexican oil production and exports on world oil prices. To date, Mexico has avoided direct confrontation with OPEC's price hawks by staying out of that organization. And it has been only in the early 1980s that higher Mexican oil production and exports have combined with surplus conditions in the world market. Nonetheless, as the relative weight of Mexico in the world oil market continues to increase, it would not be surprising if Mexico has to face new pressures from parties that may feel injured in the process. From this perspective, it is in Mexico's interest to evaluate thoroughly the advantages as well as the costs resulting from future decisions to increase its oil production and exports. Some would argue that Mexico should become a member of OPEC, or at least coordinate its production policies with OPEC in order to avoid affecting real oil prices negatively. This view takes on additional significance in the aftermath of the unilateral Mexican decision to cut oil export prices by more than US$4 per barrel in the summer of 1981, a decision reportedly intended to retain customers who felt Mexico's oil was overpriced.[31] Others would point out that as long as some industrial oil-importing nations continue to fight for a share of oil from "politically stable and reliable Mexico," offering special benefits, it is more likely that Mexico will not care so much about the fall in real oil prices over time.

These are difficult issues to which Mexico must give special consideration. Oil has inevitably introduced new variables into the foreign-policy-making process, but some have expressed the hope that Mexico will resist getting caught up in the intricacies of oil diplomacy. Domestically, for example, the Ministry of Foreign Relations will have to fight potential challengers (such as PEMEX) to its authority, who might want to make some decisions affecting relations with other nations independently, and the dreams of many who view oil as a means to increase Mexico's political influence abroad.[32] And beyond its borders, Mexico will be dealing with oil-importing and oil-exporting nations with different interests and objectives. Partly to avoid a clear-cut identification with the demands of one single bloc of these nations, Mexico has been seeking to play the role of broker or mediator. In pursuing this new role, Mexico tries to assert the current trend for the diversification of its foreign relations away from the United States.

Mexico as Mediator

Recent events have a flavor reminiscent of the Third World rhetoric of the Echeverría years, although because of the new Mexican place in the world oil market they may be much more firmly rooted. Material resources can now be used to back up the rhetoric. In particular, we are referring to President López Portillo's proposal before the United Nations General Assembly on September 27, 1979. He argued that energy resources should be managed in a way that helps to fulfill the needs of all nations, avoiding the chaos that has recently characterized world economic relations and that has the potential to spill over into politico-military conflicts. He proposed a *world energy plan*[33] with participation of all nations, although we must await the details of such a plan and the means to implement it. Mexico is not the first nation that has declared its intention to help resolve the disputes that result from the fact that only a few nations are well endowed with a resource that is of strategic importance for the economies of the world. Henry Kissinger led the first effort to bring all parties to the negotiating table. The United States convened a meeting of all major industrial nations in Washington in February 1974. In Kissinger's mind, the meeting should have been followed by another session with participation by all other oil-importing nations. After reaching a common position, a world conference including OPEC oil producers would be called. However, the project fell through at its first phase because the industrial nations themselves could reach no common position.[34]

In 1975, French president Giscard d'Estaing tried to use the prestige enjoyed by his country among some developing nations by convening the North-South Dialogue in Paris. The agenda linked oil to discussion of a complex set of issues such as aid, foreign debt, and trade and monetary relations. Once again, the effort fell apart after two years of frustrating negotiations.[35]

More recently, a new attempt has been made to revive the exchange of views between North and South. Former West German chancellor Willy Brandt was appointed to head a commission composed of world-renowned figures, which has produced a report calling for the reestablishment of the North-South Dialogue.[36] At that point, the heads of state of Austria and Mexico entered the picture. Austria is a neutral country par excellence, both in the European context and along the axis of East-West relations. And Mexico is a developing country that enjoys international prestige, is an important oil producer, and is *not* a member of OPEC. Following a preparatory meeting in Vienna in March 1981, it was agreed to invite several nations from all continents to a summit meeting in Cancún, Mexico. The Soviet Union declined to attend, but the heads of state or government of twenty-two other nations met at Cancún on October 22 and 23, 1981. The meeting was supposed to be chaired by the presidents of Mexico and Austria, but the latter fell ill, and Canada's prime minister, Pierre Trudeau, took his place. The meeting was very informal: There was no agenda and no actual negotiations took place. Its main objective was to strengthen support for the idea of a *global round of negotiations* dealing with various aspects of the world's deteriorating economic and energy situation. In this respect, the gathering could be termed a success, as all the participants agreed to conduct such negotiations in the near future within an institutional framework provided by the United Nations. Otherwise, as expected, the meeting did not produce any tangible outcome. Why, then, did Mexico spend so much time and effort to organize the summit?

Mexico's prestige was no doubt enhanced as a result of the Cancún Summit. In particular, Cancún highlighted Mexico's aspirations to universalism and national independence—two important goals of Mexico's foreign policy. And by being at the forefront of the efforts that made Cancún possible, Mexico reasserted the trend toward diversifying the focus of its foreign relations away from the United States. It was as if Mexico wanted "to jump away from the giant's shadow" and show the world that it had its own initiatives and could press its own views to help solve international problems. All this is, of course, highly symbolic—as was Cancún.

Another factor probably explaining Mexico's role in Cancún is that oil-exporting nations are feeling increasingly pressed to respond to the plight of oil-importing developing countries. The latter are experiencing phenomenal difficulties adjusting to the current international economic situation. In particular, some nations have been close to declaring themselves bankrupt because they cannot cope with the rising prices of strategic imports—especially oil imports. Conducting a *global round of negotiations* that would take into consideration the needs of all parties is perceived by many nations as the only means available to try to stabilize the world economy. There is a common view that a very strong and direct link exists between oil and the economic (and political) health of every single country.

CONCLUSIONS

In this chapter, we have analyzed some particular aspects of the role oil has played in Mexico's history, economy, and foreign policy.[37] For one thing, oil is a very important symbol of national independence. It is also a good example of the positive role the public sector has been playing in the economy. The government has provided oil abundantly and at low prices for industry and other consumers, contributing to economic growth. More recently, oil has become the central means of revitalizing the development model. During the 1970s, which we have termed a "decade of transition," several policies were implemented to revitalize that model. Revenues from oil exports are the primary source of funds for those projects that are supposed to propel Mexico into a new era of industrialization. These revenues are also instrumental for the government's programs to increase agricultural production. However, the economic reforms discussed in Chapter 5 must be implemented if oil is to play a very positive role in Mexico's future economy. Oil alone will not solve Mexico's economic problems, as had become painfully evident by 1982.

Oil has provided still another illustration of a common feature of Mexican politics: the centralization of power at the top. Decisions on this issue of national interest have been made by only a privileged few, without significant participation by the public. López Portillo's government has been relatively open insofar as it has encouraged public discussion of certain policies (e.g., the application for GATT membership). But oil policy has not been one of these. None of the societal actors analyzed in Chapters 3 and 4 is known to have influenced oil policy, although there has been freedom to express dissent. That is, political power in terms of being able to influence such an important policy has been lacking, while political liberty in terms of being able to oppose that policy has been maintained. Two important qualifications should be added, however. The first is that Mexico's new oil policy has generally pleased most of the business community. Perhaps business has participated privately more than publicly in the policymaking process. More important, we see that business interests are characteristically satisfied by the regime's basic development policies, whether or not the regime openly acknowledges and accepts business's points of view. The second qualification pertains to the political freedoms exercised. Very little group- or class-based dissent has found an *organizational* expression. Thus, the regime has not been seriously challenged by the individual expressions of dissent that have indeed been allowed.

We have tried to present as clearly as possible the little that is known about the ongoing debate among those who do affect oil policy. There are important differences concerning the role that oil should play in current attempts to revitalize the growth model. Some political forces, such as the business community, opposition parties, and intellectuals, have elaborated their own views about oil and, more generally, about other matters affecting the future course of Mexico's development. Analysis of their views on that future course is the focus of the concluding chapter of this book.

NOTES

1. Contrary to common practice in the international oil industry, PEMEX includes crude oil *and* gas in its proven reserve figures. In fact, only about 70 percent of total reserves are crude oil; gas, liquids, and condensates account for the rest.

2. For a comprehensive reading of various aspects of this history, see Lorenzo Meyer, *Mexico and the United States in the Oil Controversy, 1917–1942* (Austin: University of Texas Press, 1977); Secretaría de Relaciones Exteriores, *La expropriación petrolera* (Mexico City, 1974); Jorge Basurto, *El conflicto internacional en torno al petróleo de México* (Mexico City: Siglo XXI, 1976).

3. The 1884 law was actually passed during the administration of President Manuel González, but he was only a proxy acting, for all practical purposes, on behalf of the dictator from 1880 to 1884.

4. Cole Blasier, *The Hovering Giant: U.S. Responses to Revolutionary Change in Latin America* (Pittsburgh: University of Pittsburgh Press, 1976), p. 118.

5. Oil became the leading energy source in the United States only in 1950, and in Japan and Western Europe in the 1960s. Oil companies kept prices down for many years in order to gradually displace coal. OPEC was born in 1960, partly as a reaction of host governments who were interested in higher prices so that they could collect higher taxes and revenues from the companies operating in their territory. See Anthony Sampson, *The Seven Sisters* (New York: Viking Press, 1975); and Michael Tanzer, *The Political Economy of International Oil and the Underdeveloped Countries* (Boston: Beacon Press, 1969).

6. Universidad Nacional Autónoma de Mexico, *General Lázaro Cárdenas: Voz viva de México* (Mexico City, 1978), p. 7.

7. By contrast, British firms persuaded their government to break diplomatic relations with Mexico. These relations were reestablished following a compensation agreement in the early 1940s.

8. See Lorenzo Meyer, "La resistencia al capital privado extranjero: El caso del petróleo, 1938–1950," in Bernardo Sepúlveda et al., *Las empresas transnacionales en México* (Mexico City, El Colegio de México, 1974), pp. 107–156. President Miguel Alemán wrote a disclaimer following public release of copies of the contracts by the U.S. National Archives in 1974. See his *La verdad sobre el petróleo en México* (Mexico City: Editorial Grijalbo, 1977).

9. James C. Tanner, "Model Monopoly: National Oil Organization So Successful It Worries Industry," *The Wall Street Journal*, January 26, 1967.

10. The complete story regarding *when* PEMEX found out about the full extent of the oil and gas fields, and *why* such information was withheld from the public for some years, has yet to be written. It seems that an internal governmental debate developed around the very issue of disclosing the new reserve figures, although details are still largely unknown. It is also quite likely that the U.S. government learned of the information early and became very interested, although speculation on Washington's pressures on Mexico City to increase oil exports seems exaggerated. Some useful clues are provided in the following documents: PEMEX, *Informe del Director General, 1973* (Mexico City: PEMEX, 1973); Secretaría de la Presidencia, *El Gobierno Mexicano* ("Tercer Informe de Gobierno") (Mexico City, September 1973); *Platt's Oilgram News Service*, September 13, 1974; and articles in the *New York Times*, October 20–22, 1974.

11. *U.S. Department of State Bulletin*, November 18, 1974.

12. PEMEX, *Anuario Estadístico, 1978* (Mexico City: PEMEX, 1979), p. 30; and Gustavo Ortega, *La industria petrolera mexicana, sus antecedentes y su estado actual* (Mexico City: Secretaría de la Economía Nacional, 1936), p. 34.

13. "Aspectos del Presupuesto de 1981," *Comercio Exterior* 31, no. 1 (1981):14–19; and "The Largest Industrial Companies in the World," *Fortune*, August 10, 1981. Venezuela's PETROVEN and Brazil's PETROBRAS are the only two Latin American firms that are larger than PEMEX.

14. Castillo's arguments are similar to those made in the early 1960s by Juan Pablo Pérez Alfonso, Venezuela's minister of mines. Pérez Alfonso was a central figure in the efforts to establish OPEC in 1960. See Franklin Tugwell, *The Politics of Oil in Venezuela* (Stanford, Calif.: Stanford University Press, 1975).

15. For the PEMEX program and the gas project, see Instituto Mexicano del Petróleo, *Comparecencia del Sr. Ing. Jorge Díaz Serrano, Director General de PEMEX, ante el H. Congreso de la Unión* (Mexico City, 1977). See the data for gas flaring in annual speeches of the PEMEX director general (which he reads before the president); they are not consistent with much higher gas-flaring figures reported in PEMEX's own annual report, *Memoria de Labores*.

16. See Heberto Castillo's frequent articles in the weekly *Proceso* and his best presentation, *Necesario plan de energéticos* (Mexico City: Servicios y representaciones de ingeniería, 1978).

17. For a discussion of the reasons that the gas export deal did not materialize but instead became entangled in U.S. bureaucratic politics, see Richard Fagen and Henry R. Nau, "Mexican Gas: The Northern Connection," in *Capitalism and the State in U.S.–Latin American Relations*, ed. Richard Fagen (Stanford, Calif.: Stanford University Press, 1979), pp. 382–427.

18. Secretaría de Patrimonio y Fomento Industrial, *Plan nacional de desarrollo industrial, 1979–1982* (Mexico City, 1979); and *Programa de energía. Metas a 1990 y proyecciones al año 2000* (Mexico City, 1981).

19. "Programa de energía," *Energéticos* 4, no. 11 (1980):1–3.

20. PEMEX, *Memoria de Labores, 1980* (Mexico City: PEMEX, 1981); and U.S. Department of Energy, *Monthly Energy Review*, various issues in 1980 and 1981.

21. An interesting study of the initial social effects of the oil boom in the south is by Leopoldo Allub and M. A. Michael, "Petróleo y cambio social en el sureste de México," in *Foro Internacional* 18, no. 4 (1978):691–709. See also reports in the *Washington Post*, June 10, 1979, and January 20, 1981.

22. Guillermo Zetina, "Ningún extranjero perfora pozos: Díaz Serrano," *Excélsior*, September 21, 1979.

23. "Guessing Game Continues over Mexico's Oil Reserves," *Latin American Economic Report*, March 16, 1979.

24. Sources in both Mexico and the United States confirm the extent of this super-project. For technical details of the port development program, see Proyectos Especiales de Desarrollo, "Programa de Puertos Industriales," Mexico City, unpublished draft, November-December 1979. The estimate of total oil export capacity for 1985 is found in U.S. General Accounting Office, *Prospects for a Stronger U.S.-Mexico Energy Relationship* (Washington, D.C., May 1, 1980), p. 46.

25. Francisco Ortíz, "A cambio de contratos, el STPRM cede su exclusividad en la perforación de pozos," in *Proceso*, October 24, 1977; and Francisco Salinas, "Acepta el STPRM, como excepción," in *Excélsior*, November 30, 1977.

26. For the particular case of energy, see Kenneth E. Hill, *North American Energy: A Proposal for a Common Market Between Canada, Mexico and the US* (New York: Blyth Eastman Dillon and Co., 1979).

27. The best study about the various scenarios under which such a special relationship could materialize, although the author is not enthusiastic about the option, is Henry R. Nau, "U.S.–Mexican Oil and Gas Relations," in *United States Relations With Mexico: Context and Content*, ed. Richard D. Erb and Stanley R. Ross (Washington, D.C.: American Enterprise Institute, 1981), pp. 195–211.

28. Raymond Vernon has analyzed this position and its implications in "Trade and Investment in Mexican–US Relations," Cambridge, Mass., unpublished paper, December 15, 1980.

29. "Declaración conjunta de los presidentes de México y Venezuela," *Energéticos* 4, no. 10 (October 1980):27–28.

30. U.S. Department of Energy, *Monthly Energy Review*, various issues in 1981.

31. For the cut in Mexico's oil export prices and the temporary fall of its exports, the only available figures can be found in U.S. Department of Energy, *Weekly Petroleum Statistical Report*, various issues in 1981. We have no corresponding Mexican sources on this subject.

32. Samuel Berkstein has discussed this theme extensively, emphasizing the foreign policy challenges confronted by oil-exporting nations, in "Estrategia

petrolera y política exterior," *Foro Internacional* 21, no. 1 (1980):65–82. Other analyses have endorsed more enthusiastically the idea that oil has already turned Mexico into a well-established regional power. See for example Bruce Bagley, "Mexico in the 1980s: A New Regional Power," *Current History* 80, no. 469 (November 1981):353–357.

33. For the complete text of López Portillo's speech, see "Los energéticos constituyen la responsabilidad compartida de toda la humanidad," *Tiempo*, October 8, 1979.

34. Henry R. Nau, "US Foreign Policy in the Energy Crisis," *Atlantic Quarterly* 12, no. 4 (Winter 1974-1975):426–439.

35. Roger D. Hansen, *Beyond the North-South Stalemate* (New York: McGraw-Hill, 1979); Robert L. Rothstein, *The Third World and U.S. Foreign Policy: Cooperation and Conflict in the 1980s* (Boulder, Colo.: Westview Press, 1981).

36. Independent Commission on International Development Issues, *North-South: A Programme for Survival* (Cambridge, Mass.: M.I.T. Press, 1980).

37. For further readings on Mexico's oil policy, see George W. Grayson, *The Politics of Mexican Oil* (Pittsburgh: University of Pittsburgh Press, 1980); and Gabriel Székely, "The 1976 Oil Export Decision: Effects of the Oil Boom on Mexico's Political Economy," Ph.D. dissertation, George Washington University, 1983.

8

The Development Model
in the 1980s

The focus of this book has been on the central features of the Mexican political system, a system that has enjoyed a great degree of stability since 1929. One of our main purposes has been to understand, analyze, and explain this stability. But political stability does not preclude change. Therefore, our analysis has also stressed the flexibility and adaptability of the regime in the face of changing circumstances.

Since the mid-1930s, Mexico has transformed itself from a rural to a basically urban society. Of central importance to stability has been the fact that the regime has incorporated into the political system the groups that have emerged as a consequence of this transformation. It has also influenced the changing distribution of power in society. And even in those cases in which changes have not originated with it, the regime has proved capable of adapting to, and in due course attaining a degree of control over, many departures from the established order.

The most striking political (1968) and economic (1976) crises in Mexico during recent years, until the 1982 economic crisis, provide examples of regime responsiveness to challenges to the development model. In the aftermath of those two crises, the regime proposed and implemented policies geared to establishing the development model on new and firmer soil. Thus, the first section of this chapter analyzes the regime's recent planning efforts to deal with fundamental political and socioeconomic problems.

The regime has been remarkably successful in molding changes to its own ends, but this has not precluded other political actors from defining their own preferences regarding development policy for the coming years. Thus, we discuss here the alternative views of the business community, the nationalist left, and the Marxist left. These are by no means the only views that have been put forward, but they are certainly the most developed. Therefore, the book concludes by analyzing the major competing programs and perspectives on the future of Mexican development. This chapter is thus something of an epilogue rather than a summary presentation of our major arguments and conclusions; such summaries may be found at the end of each chapter.

THE REGIME'S VISION

One way of predicting what the major features of the regime's development policies will be in the 1980s is to look at the recent past—especially at the regime's development policies since the 1940s. This has been one of our primary concerns in previous chapters. Here, we merely reflect on how regime flexibility has translated itself into a constant search for new ways to adapt to emerging challenges and problems. In this respect, it could be argued that the regime has been involved in a trial-and-error process since 1970. On the political front, we have analyzed the regime's efforts to encourage greater political participation and even to permit greater media freedom. President Echeverría responded to the crisis of dissent and repression with certain measures to open up the political system (e.g., all eighteen-year-olds were granted the right to vote in 1973). Similarly, President López Portillo responded to the crisis of legitimacy with further political reforms (e.g., most political parties that had for many years sought legal status have finally reached their goal as a result of the 1977 political and electoral reforms).

There have been some important exceptions to this flexibility, however. We have discussed, for example, several cases in which the regime has forcibly limited its opening-up process (e.g., the *Excélsior* case). Moreover, it has remained clear that the regime is still prepared to offer much less in terms of organizational than purely personal freedoms. And, of course, we see the continued use of co-optation and repression, which are mechanisms aimed at maintaining political control.[1] In sum, the regime's political reforms show a commitment to flexibility; at the same time, the restrictions on freedom show that the regime is ready to go only so far in implementing changes. Perhaps it is somewhat undecided as to how far to go.

In the realm of socioeconomic policy, after discussing the dominant patterns prior to 1970, we suggested how the regime has tried since 1970 to respond to pressing problems, such as the neglect of the rural sector, insufficient health care and educational services, and income inequality. Reducing income inequality provides another illustration of an area in which the regime has been indecisive as to how far to go and in what ways.

However we ultimately assess recent policies concerning socioeconomic equality or political freedom, the regime has shown more confident resolve in how to pursue its three other historically and continuously glorified goals—national independence, economic growth, and political stability. It has, for at least half a century, made political stability paramount. The regime believes that with stability much is possible, including modifications and further improvements; without stability, much would be lost and little would be possible. It has stressed the strong relationship between political stability and economic growth. Partly for this reason, a discussion follows of the regime's development plans, initiated under López Portillo, which have been perhaps the most important official effort to date to define long-term policies to deal with current challenges to stability and growth. We give special attention to the Global Plan and the Industrial Plan, which are the most significant. These two plans include certain development aspects that are discussed at greater length in individual plans (e.g., the urban and the agricultural development plans).

Many of the assumptions and recommendations of the government's plans are inconsistent.[2] Such a situation partly reflects ongoing debate regarding which tools of economic policy are most likely to insure political stability, maintain high rates of economic growth, and achieve other objectives. This is not the place to discuss in detail the technical subtleties that set the Global Plan and the Industrial Plan apart.[3] Nevertheless, a summary is presented of the central objectives and some of the problems associated with each one.

President López Portillo entrusted the newly created Ministry of Programming and Budget with elaborating the Global Plan, hoping that the plan would provide policymakers with general guidelines for planning future development projects. The Global Plan includes a number of indicative quantitative and qualitative targets; it is designed to make the goals of the various government plans consistent; and it seeks to integrate federal budgeting into the planning process. The public sector's involvement in the economy, which we have seen to be very large, is thus reinforced. Furthermore, the management of many of the plan's policy incentives is expected to promote participation by regional political forces. The official political party (PRI) might also be strengthened, as it might play a mediatory role between the groups seeking the benefits included in the plan and the authorities who will provide them.

The Industrial Plan was elaborated by the Ministry of Natural Resources and Industrial Development to deal specifically with development problems in the industrial sector. Like the Global Plan, it was commissioned and subsequently endorsed by the president, and it included a number of indicative targets for the second half of López Portillo's administration.

246   THE DEVELOPMENT MODEL IN THE 1980s

A central objective of both plans is to attain annual rates of economic growth of around 8 percent. There is no split within the regime on the fundamental importance of economic growth. It is hoped that an extraordinary public and private investment effort (capital formation growing at unprecedented 13 percent annual rates) will help provide greater employment opportunities. The latter is an issue of special importance, partly because the migration of Mexicans to the United States has become a major issue of Mexico–United States relations, mostly because Mexico itself has not been able to provide sufficient employment for its citizens.

The Global Plan emphasizes a more balanced growth of the agricultural and industrial sectors than does the Industrial Plan. This is because only the Global Plan takes into consideration the recently elaborated program to increase agricultural production: the Mexican Food System. The Industrial Plan, for its part, stresses the desirability of expanding industry—especially some priority industries such as capital goods, steel, and petrochemicals. The business community is expected to participate importantly in all these projects. However, the Global Plan calls for a more moderate public participation in the economy in terms of investment and consumption. The proposed different degrees of public involvement in the economy reflect the traditional debate between those members of the ruling elite who favor the expansion of the public sector and those who prefer to strengthen the private sector's role. More important, business is not expected to share the high costs associated with the pursuit of high rates of economic growth. This theme has been extensively discussed (Chapter 5), and here we need only briefly refer to a few examples.

The regime plans contemplate no major fiscal reforms (e.g., increasing taxes on profits or reducing excessive subsidies to entrepreneurs), reforms that could be instrumental in keeping the public sector's finances in balance and in improving social services for the poor. Furthermore, there is no word about a more selective and qualified application of protectionist measures that favor domestic (often inefficient) producers. Finally, the government offers incentives to invest and produce more without due regard to how efficient and necessary the production of certain goods may be. For example, the Industrial Plan originally listed a number of firms eligible for special benefits because their products would help improve the standard of living of the poor (in regard to food, clothing, and other basic products); more recently, however, the list has been expanded to include products that the poor are very unlikely to purchase (e.g., automobiles and synthetic fibers).[4] These exceptions, favoring privileged groups, are consistent with the pattern of political and socioeconomic inequalities discussed throughout the book. But they are clearly inconsistent with the regime's ostensible objective of revitalizing the growth model on healthier and more equitable bases.

Regarding the external sector of the economy, two issues further illustrate some characteristics of and differences between the two plans. The Global Plan calls for a steady increase of exports (averaging 14 percent per year), including oil *and* gas exports. A corollary is that this plan seeks to maintain, at all times, a ratio of current account deficit to gross domestic product of only 1 percent. In comparison, the Industrial Plan expects that increases in domestic production of various goods will be geared toward satisfying domestic demand rather than toward export markets; it also calls for slowing down significantly the expansion of the oil industry, and it does not assume any exports of gas whatsoever. Thus, since a lower level of overall exports is expected, the ratio of current account to gross domestic product is set at 2 percent, double the ratio in the Global Plan.[5] It could be argued that the goals of the Global Plan in this area imply a somewhat greater effort to open the economy than does the Industrial Plan, while the latter's stress on fewer exports (including less oil exports) would make Mexico more dependent on foreign credit.

Oil is supposed to provide an important share of the financial resources necessary to fund various projects discussed in both these plans. Regrettably, however, the specific links between oil policy and other economic policy objectives are not always specified. And when they are, there are contradictions associated with the actual implementation of policies. For example, the National Energy Plan proposes to hold down domestic energy prices to about 70 percent of the level of prices prevailing internationally in order to promote greater investments and exports and to avoid the greater inflation that could result from the hike in domestic energy prices.[6] Surely, promotion of exports and control of inflation are two important goals of both the Global Plan and the Industrial Plan. In fact, however, energy prices at home have been held to much lower levels than the 70 percent prescription, while inflation is high and exports (other than oil) are lagging. More important, little has been done in other areas that could more effectively help to achieve stated government objectives in these areas. Gerardo Bueno, a respected economist from El Colegio de México, has been particularly critical of this situation. Bueno has argued that reducing protectionism would make more goods available at lower prices (assuming imported products were more competitive than domestic products), thus helping to curb inflation somewhat. And adjusting the exchange rate of the peso closer to its true value would help promote exports by making Mexican goods cheaper. Bueno asked the poignant question: "Why formulate plans, why approve and sanction them, if in the final analysis the decision-making process concerning these crucial questions continues as if such plans never existed or never were approved?"[7]

Bueno is not the only one to express skepticism regarding some aspects of the regime's plans to revitalize the growth model. René Villarreal, another prominent economist, at the Ministry of Finance in the López Portillo administration, has contended that even though oil may be instrumental in dealing with some of the traditional constraints on economic growth (e.g., availability of foreign exchange resources), the government has not designed ways to deal with other issues, such as inflation and the public deficit. He argued that public savings should be increased to finance investments from the government's own resources and that the economy should be open to greater competition in order to force domestic producers to be more efficient and to increase their exports.[8] Thus, Bueno and Villarreal are among those who have strongly criticized the continued and unqualified pursuit of an import substitution industrialization strategy. It should be recalled that emphasis on producing certain goods for export is an alternative strategy to import substitution and that opening the economy to greater competition does not necessarily mean that Mexico must become a member of GATT. The point is that government plans do not deal explicitly and at the same level of analysis with all issues—issues that are critical for revitalizing the growth model.

Employment is a problem that receives a good deal of attention in the regime's plans but that nonetheless is not dealt with effectively. It is true that one of the central goals of both plans is to provide jobs at a faster pace than the growth of the population. The Industrial Plan goes as far as to spell out several incentives (e.g., tax rebates) that would be awarded to firms that create new jobs, especially outside Mexico City and other big cities. It is also true that the ongoing expansion of oil plants and the construction of new plants, as well as public works, have reduced the level of unemployment in 1980 and 1981. However, the jobs created thereby are temporary. Once the construction of new facilities comes to an end, many workers will find themselves without employment. More important, there is a contradiction between the pursuit of greater levels of employment and the concentration of investments in projects that are clearly capital-intensive: Production of capital goods, steel, and petrochemicals, for example, is accomplished primarily by machines and not by workers. Again, little is said in either plan about these issues.

Finally, the government plans are indicative, rather than compulsory. Much is said about rewards for those willing to cooperate, but means for enforcement are lacking. In this respect, the Global Plan and the Industrial Plan are similar to many other planning efforts conducted in the past, all of which were shelved after some time without having achieved significant results.[9] These critical comments are intended to

The PRI's candidate, Miguel de la Madrid, on the campaign trail, Mexico City, November 1981. What future for Mexico? (Photo courtesy of Rodolfo Romo de Vivar)

caution those who hope that oil surpluses and very elaborate plans are adequate means to solve the complex issues faced by Mexico's development model. The events of 1981–1982 seem to confirm the more cautious view.

Nonetheless, the prospects for the continued application of these new plans may have been improved somewhat by the election of Miguel de la Madrid as president (1982–1988). After all, he was head of the Ministry of Programming and Budget that worked out the Global Plan, the master plan designed by the López Portillo administration. Never elected to a political position (his links with the PRI are not very impressive), de la Madrid worked his way up through the complex bureaucratic system. As mentioned in Chapter 4, he has a solid background in economics and capped his educational studies with a Harvard master's degree. His most frequently cited qualities include honesty, earnestness, organizational abilities, and strong discipline. We have argued that the good qualities of a man—even in a strong presidential system such as Mexico's—are not enough to secure the successful implementation of government goals. The point is that, because de la Madrid played a prominent role in the elaboration of crucial regime plans, he is more likely (than other candidates might have been) to support the main thrust of those plans—plans that are of course subject to any changes the new administration may consider appropriate.

Given the fact that the success of any official development plans depends largely on the behavior of the business community, it is essential to consider the latter's perspective on the development model in general and its attitudes toward the regime's plans in particular.

THE BUSINESS COMMUNITY'S VISION

It is feasible to talk of a common position within the business sector insofar as it has established an organization that tries to represent its views. That organization is the Coordinating Business Council (CCE), established in 1975. A central point is that, through the CCE, members of the business sector express positions that conflict with those of the regime. This is obviously not the first time that business has dissented from the regime. For example, many entrepreneurs opposed the 1938 oil nationalization, while others unsuccessfully pressured the government to withdraw its support of the Cuban regime in the early 1960s.[10] However, this is the first time that most organizations of the business community have formulated their own perspective of Mexican development in a clear and coherent manner. Many of their views, were they to become actual policies, would imply a significant departure from Mexico's current system of political and socioeconomic relations. In the words of Carlos Arriola, an expert on regime-business relations: "Businessmen have elaborated their own development project by seeking to put the state's political and economic resources at the service of private enterprise."[11]

It could be argued that the business sector has advocated a different development model from that of the regime ever since the revolution. For this sector, an ideal development model would be one with less public involvement in the economy, in which private interests would assume control of many firms currently owned by the state. In such an ideal model, credit would be more readily available, without having to deal with the government in the process. Mexican businessmen would engage in joint investment ventures with their counterparts in the United States and other nations, without having to face stiff government regulations or critical public opinion. In this respect, great efforts would be made to change public perceptions, fed by the regime's rhetoric, of the business community as evil. And, some would argue, tougher social and political control of popular dissent would be included in such a business-oriented model. In short, this model would be antithetical in many ways to the revolutionary and nationalistic rhetoric expounded by the regime.

To date, however, the business sector has gotten enough of what it wants and has therefore usually supported the regime. On occasion, such as when Cárdenas and Echeverría were in office, the degree of overlap between the regime's and the business sector's development models diminished, and business spelled out its ideals more forthrightly. Then, when the regime returned to more probusiness policies, under an Alemán or a López Portillo, business preferred to reestablish a modus vivendi with the regime.

Events during the 1970s lend support to this interpretation of regime-business relations and their implications for the development model. In 1975, the CCE published a "Declaration of Principles" and a "Declaration about National Problems." Both documents include a number of highly controversial demands, varied in character. One such demand is that the state sell public enterprises to entrepreneurs as a means of reversing the ongoing expansion of the public sector. The business community also calls for an end to state-sponsored shops that sell basic products to the poor at low prices, a change that would clearly run counter to the regime's social goals. A further proposal is that Mexico grant foreign firms permission to hold majority interests in certain economic sectors, practically doing away with the 1973 Law to Regulate Foreign Investment. The business documents also express the hope that the government's use of commercial banks' legal reserve requirement to finance the public deficit, a practice that has limited the amount of credit available to private entrepreneurs, would come to an end. Furthermore, the business sector opposes any type of centralized and compulsory planning system.[12] In sum, *these measures would lead to a process of "reprivatization" of the economy*, at least somewhat similar to those that have occurred in recent years in some major South American countries. Such hopes were obviously dealt a serious jolt by the government's 1982 takeover of all private banks.

Is the business community actually seeking dramatic changes in the current development model? We believe that although that is a possibility, its declarations are more likely to be part of a short-term strategy with more limited objectives. It should be remembered that the radical expression of these views took place in the midst of the mid-1970s confrontation with the Echeverría administration. The key aspect of the business sector's position is that it put forward an alternative to the frame of reference and analysis expounded by Echeverría. This is not to say that the business sector does not actually hold the conservative views included in those documents. In fact, most industrialists, pre-expropriation bankers, and landlords hold these or somewhat similar views. Nonetheless, once the López Portillo administration took power, abandoning the use of hostile rhetoric and implementing more favorable policies, the business sector toned down its own political pronouncements. The CCE's documents are nonetheless a reminder that there are actors other than the regime whose strength is formidable and who now have formally elaborated their own perspectives regarding the orientation that national development should follow. They are also a reminder that the business sector supports the regime because it usually gets most of what it wants. That is, business does not want either to confront the regime too directly or to alienate or weaken it, because the regime basically does well for business interests.

An important caveat is in order, one that further minimizes business-regime differences. It would be an oversimplification to say that Mexican business is always against government involvement in the economy. In fact, business relies on several subsidies and incentives and a wide range of government investment and infrastructural projects. One thinks of the government's development banks, of its role in irrigation projects, of roads and communications networks without which many businesses could not flourish. More generally, business relies on a strong government role in insuring inexpensive labor and political-economic tranquility. Thus critics of the business sector can argue that business is selective indeed in applying its free-market doctrines.

Generally speaking, entrepreneurs have been enthusiastic about the new government plans.[13] This is understandable largely because of the generous incentives for investment included in the plans and because there are no penalties for those unwilling to cooperate. More important, as we have seen, the regime's projects to put the development model on a sounder footing do not include measures that would make the business sector share the high costs associated with the pursuit of high rates of economic growth. Partly reacting to this situation, several voices have been raised that advocate tougher policies toward the private sector and a greater public role to help fulfill the goals of the Mexican Revolution. We turn our attention to analyzing the position of the "nationalist left."

THE NATIONALIST LEFT'S VISION

A third perspective on the future of Mexican development has been advocated by what we call the "nationalist left." This includes some members of the political elite as well as many intellectuals. It has been referred to in the past as "the left wing of the PRI," or "the left of the regime coalition." We believe the term "nationalist left" is more appropriate, because many of its members are in no way related to the PRI or the regime.

The most recent, and perhaps the most sophisticated, presentation of the nationalist left position can be attributed to former minister of programming and budget Carlos Tello and to the National University's economics professor Rolando Cordera.[14] Note that author Tello was appointed head of the Banco de México immediately following the government takeover of private banks. Briefly, the thrust of the Tello-Cordera argument is that only the fulfillment of the goals of the Mexican Revolution—as embodied in the 1917 Constitution—could lead to the significant improvement of the dismal socioeconomic situation of the poor and thus to continued stability. Moreover, they have demanded that the government exercise full control over the general conditions in which production takes place. That is, a major priority should be to guarantee the nation's economic independence, and the government should resist ongoing trends leading toward the further internationalization of the economy. Similarly, it should resist business-oriented proposals geared to a reprivatization of the economy. Using as a historical reference point the experience under the Cárdenas administration, they advocate the strengthening of the old alliance between the regime and organized labor (CTM and other organizations in the Congress of Labor). Only then will the government be able to effect substantial economic and social reforms, despite resistance from domestic and foreign entrepreneurs.

This position is more than what many would label a "reformist" position. It reflects a well-founded concern that the regime has been unable (if not unwilling) to fulfill its *own* self-imposed revolutionary objectives: The regime has allegedly become less and less responsive over time to the aspirations of the working classes, thus undermining its own legitimacy. Instead, it has been responsive to the demands of a small economic elite that has not shared many of the costs of economic growth. The nationalist left fears that the continuation of this trend will lead either to instability or, should stability be maintained, to a far more authoritarian system. Indeed, the nationalist left sees many of the challenges discussed in Chapter 1 as true threats to regime stability.

It is easier to find sympathizers with the positions of the nationalist left when seemingly radical acts of foreign policy, rather than domestic policy, are involved. There are many who might support the government's anti-U.S. rhetoric and its close ties with Cuba but who would be much more reserved in regard to the character of necessary domestic reforms. This parallels the juxtaposition of foreign policy leftism and domestic policy conservatism that characterizes the regime (see Chapter 6).

Perhaps the most telling criticism that can be made of the nationalist left is its excessive reliance on "either-or" propositions to support its position. For example, it views a "neoliberal model" as the only alternative to its nationalistic development model. In the words of Tello and Cordera: "The neo-liberal project is a metropolitan project. It seeks a fundamental re-structuring of the international capitalist system according to the analysis and the perspectives of key financial and transnational centers. In the Mexican case, the neo-liberal vision would lead to an economy increasingly integrated to the United States economy . . . to a political congruence between the Mexican state and the United States."[15]

It is not surprising that the nationalist left opposed Mexico's application for GATT membership. As we have noted, however, no concrete proposals have been forthcoming to solve, for example, such a severe problem as excessive protectionism, which has contributed to undermining the financial health of the very actor the nationalist left wants to strengthen: the state. Rather, we could argue for the nationalist left's goals by arguing against its policy: The regime should force domestic producers to be more efficient and competitive, making Mexico become less dependent on foreign creditors to compensate for insufficient exports. Of course, a comprehensive fiscal reform—which the nationalist left supports—might be another very important means of improving the public sector's finances, hence reducing the need for foreign credit to balance the national accounts. The point is that a more consistent attitude on the part of the nationalist left is necessary if it wants to help shape national policy.

The nationalist left's program shows some interesting similarities and differences with the regime's two major development plans. It seems that some of its goals are closer to those of the Industrial Plan than to those of the Global Plan. For example, it favors a very slow opening of the economy to foreign competition. But in its support of a strong public sector, the nationalist left is largely in accord with both major regime plans. In contrast to the regime's plans, however, the nationalist left model views the strengthening of political alliances with less privileged groups (e.g., labor), rather than automatic "trickle-down effects," as the only means to improve the lot of the poor. The nationalist left advocates a substantial tax reform, the intensive use of labor rather than capital to help solve unemployment, and increased state regulation of domestic and foreign private interests. For its part, the regime would not be unsympathetic to many statements of the nationalist left, but it would regard several as too naive, as not appreciating the subtle but all-important bases of stability or the great importance of stability.

The nationalist left model, particularly the reforms it advocates, are at odds (in most respects) with the business community's model. In fact, the nationalist left regards domestic and foreign (U.S.) private entrepreneurs—not the Mexican regime—as Mexico's principal enemy. In this way, the nationalist left buttresses the regime's political legitimacy: The nationalist left's views even perpetuate the image that the regime truly has revolutionary (that is, opposed to domestic and foreign business) instincts and interests. Thus, it should not be surprising that the nationalist left still falls short of calling for a fundamental transformation of Mexico's socioeconomic and political systems. By contrast, the Marxist left calls for fundamental changes. It is worried by problems that also concern the nationalist left. However, the Marxist left does not hope to handle these problems within the basic framework of preserving the regime and its successes in stability and growth. The Marxist left feels that stability and growth, as pursued by the regime, are incompatible with improved socioeconomic equality and true democratization. In the final analysis, the Marxist left may see the regime itself as the most important obstacle to building a new political and economic system. So the Marxist left may acknowledge that the regime has been right in its policies, although frightfully wrong in its goals and priorities. It does not like what the regime does, but it "gives the devil his due" and says that it does it well. The nationalist left, on the other hand, is much more supportive of the regime regarding goals, but harsher regarding means and policies. It tries to work with the regime by promoting its "revolutionary left," by encouraging the positive and progressive tendencies within the regime. Given these different perceptions of the regime held by the nationalist left and the Marxist left, it should not be surprising that these political forces often find themselves in conflict with one another. What are, in more specific terms, the perspectives and goals of the Marxist left?

THE MARXIST LEFT'S VISION

Mexico's Unified Socialist party (the former Mexican Communist party), occupies a prominent position within the Marxist left. However, the Marxist left also encompasses several small parties (such as Heberto Castillo's Mexican Workers party). It has the allegiance as well of several prestigious intellectuals (such as the former head of the National University, Pablo González Casanova).

The Marxist left seeks fundamental changes in Mexico's development model: the socialization of the economic means of production, and a political regime that would not include the PRI. According to this view,

> Socialism is the solution, particularly a socialism that would solve (as has been shown by the socialist countries themselves) not only the problems of insufficient employment, housing, health, and educational services; but a socialism that would also solve the problems of bureaucraticism and authoritarianism, objectives that are increasingly shared—with Cuba at the forefront—by all socialist and communist forces in the world.[16]

In order to build such a model of political and socioeconomic relations, emphasis is put upon the decisive and leading role of the working class.[17] Here we can identify a very important difference between the nationalist left and the Marxist left. The former argues for an alliance between labor and the regime to implement certain reforms, whereas the latter advocates that the working class should pursue its interests independently. This does not mean that the Marxist left opposes the fiscal, social, and political reforms advocated by the nationalist left. What it means is that the Marxist left views such reforms with suspicion, as it views historical experiences such as the close alliance between the regime and labor during the Cárdenas years. It feels that these experiences did not result in a more just and democratic society. The main reason for predominant failure amid sporadic and limited success, the Marxist left argues, is that the regime is in fact generally responsive to domestic and foreign private interests, rather than to the demands of the poor.

The Marxist left favors a revolutionary transformation of society, but most of its followers do not expect to realize its goals immediately or violently. In fact, the Marxist left shares many objectives with the nationalist left in this respect. It favors nationalizations, comprehensive fiscal reform, more limited foreign investment, extension of medical care and educational services to all, expropriation of large landholdings, unemployment benefits for the people who do not find jobs, and so forth.[18]

Politically, the Marxist left claims to support the democratization and independence of labor unions, the independent organization of peasants, and freedom of dissent. It tends to view the recent political and electoral reforms positively, although it would like to carry them much further. For example, because some members of the Marxist left now participate in Congress, they would like to strengthen the powers of the Chamber of Deputies and limit those of the president. The Marxists have proposed that the political parties, and not the Federal Electoral Commission dominated by the PRI regime, organize and supervise all aspects of the electoral process. Thus, the Marxist left's support for the recent reforms by the regime is very qualified.

It goes without saying that the Marxist left's perspective on the development model is totally antagonistic to the perspective of the business community. While business wants to reprivatize the economy, for example, the Marxists strive for the socialization of the means of production. While business wants significantly reduced restrictions on foreign investment, the Marxists want more nationalizations. And while business generally benefits from the status quo, the Marxists want a revolution!

Critics of the Marxist left, including some who endorse its major goals, argue that revolutions usually involve very high political, economic, and human costs. Furthermore, there are many who would view skeptically the Marxist left's professed commitment to political democracy and freedoms, even though they may not question the sincerity of some Marxist leaders. Other critics add that a social revolution in Mexico is unrealistic because the Marxist left lacks a broad popular base of support.

Finally and obviously, aside from all questions of cost, sincerity, and feasibility, many critics simply do not endorse the principles of the Marxist left.

CONCLUSIONS

Both the business and the Marxist models represent radical alternatives to the regime's model. However, to date the regime retains substantial resources with which to pursue, and even to effect, important modifications in its own development model. Mexican development is still largely shaped by decisions emanating from Mexico's ruling political elite. This does not mean that the regime will succeed in its efforts to revitalize the model or that its policies will not take into consideration the interests of other political actors—especially the privileged actors. In this respect, the regime has on balance been closer to business than to the left. But, significantly, the regime has been flexible enough to avoid complete identification with either, to grant concessions to both sides, and to allow for, indeed insist on, varying its own approach across administrations. Thus, for example, after Echeverría drew close to the nationalist left, López Portillo went much closer toward business. Yet at no time does the regime fully surrender its autonomy by subsuming itself to any actor or side.

The Mexican regime remains a politically strong and autonomous actor. It is also flexible, carrying out reforms in response to pressures from societal actors (such as business and organized labor) and adapting to the desires of traditional institutions (such as the military and the university). Indeed, reform has continually been a tool to achieve stability. But the capacity of the regime to effect reforms—which are so central to sustaining its autonomous role in society and therefore to stability— may be severely limited. Among the several challenges that we have identified throughout this book, three stand out most prominently. First, there is the continuing economic problem associated with generating sufficient public revenue even for the very basic social and political needs the regime itself is pledged to meet. Thus far, the regime has been unable to extract sufficient resources (e.g., higher taxes on private capital) from society in order to improve the public sector's economic posture, fund social programs, and strengthen national independence. Second, there is the potential alienation of organized labor as a result of persistent, difficult economic conditions and, beyond that, the potential response of unorganized workers who might increasingly find themselves without jobs if efforts to re-establish sustained economic growth do not succeed. Finally, there is the ongoing political challenge involved in maintaining political legitimacy and support while not extending freedom and participation so far as to risk a significant loss of regime control or regime ability to maintain stability.

Mexico's development model in the 1980s, both in political and in economic terms, will be shaped to a very important degree by the regime's policies to deal with these and other problems, and by the demands and responses of an increasingly complex Mexican society.[19] We hope that our analysis has contributed to a better understanding of contemporary Mexico, of its problems and aspirations. The extent to which such problems will be solved, and such aspirations will be fulfilled, only time will tell.

NOTES

1. José Luis Reyna has defined the objective of political control as "keeping the number of political demands limited and turning them into bureaucratic-administrative issues." See Reyna's *Control político, estabilidad y desarrollo en México,* Cuadernos del Centro de Estudios Sociológicos 3 (Mexico City: El Colegio de México, 1974), p. 25.

2. México, Secretaría de Programación y Presupuesto, *Plan global de desarrollo, 1980–1982* (Mexico City, 1980); and México, Secretaría de Patrimonio y Fomento Industrial, *Plan nacional de desarrollo industrial, 1979–1982* (Mexico City, 1979).

3. Interested readers might refer to Calvin P. Blair, "Economic Development Policy in Mexico," in *United States Relations with Mexico. Context and Content,* ed. Richard D. Erb and Stanley R. Ross (Washington, D.C.: American Enterprise Institute, 1981), pp. 233–257; and Gabriel Székely, "Mexican Oil and Economic Policies, 1976–1980," Ph.D. dissertation, George Washington University, 1982, especially Chapter 2.

4. "Decreto que reforma y adiciona el que establece los estímulos para el fomento del empleo y la inversión en las actividades industriales," in *Diario Oficial* (Mexico City, June 8, 1981).

5. The Global Plan's current-account-to-GDP ratio has been subsequently adjusted to 2 percent, largely because (despite high exports of oil and gas) the deficit in current account has continued growing dramatically, as is shown in Chapter 5. México, Secretaría de Programación y Presupuesto, *Plan global de desarrollo. Primer informe de avance, 1980–1982* (Mexico City, 1981), p. 24.

6. México, Secretaría de Patrimonio y Fomento Industrial, *Programa de energía. Metas a 1990 y proyecciones al año 2000* (Mexico City, 1981).

7. Gerardo M. Bueno, "Petróleo y planes de desarrollo en México," *Comercio Exterior* 31, no. 8 (1981):839.

8. René Villarreal, "Petroleum and Mexican Economic Growth and Development in the 1980s," in Jerry R. Ladman et al., *U.S.-Mexican Energy Relationships: Realities and Prospects* (Lexington, Mass.: Lexington Books, 1981), pp. 69–86.

9. For a discussion of past development plans, see Leopoldo Solís, *Planes de desarrollo económico y social en México* (Mexico City: Secretaría de Educación

Pública, 1975). See also the PRI's *Plan básico de gobierno, 1976–1982* (Mexico City, 1976).

10. Well-documented case studies include Lorenzo Meyer, *Mexico and the United States in the Oil Controversy, 1917–1942* (Austin: University of Texas Press, 1977); and Olga Pellicer de Brody, *México y la revolución cubana* (Mexico City: El Colegio de México, 1972).

11. Carlos Arriola, *Las organizaciones empresariales y el estado* (Mexico City: Fondo de Cultural Económica, 1981), p. 126.

12. Consejo Coordinador Empresarial, "Declaración de Principios," and "Declaración sobre problemas nacionales," in Arriola, *Las organizaciones*, appendix, pp. 168–204.

13. Félix Arciniega, "Businessmen Make 180° Turnabout," *The News* (Mexico City), April 26, 1979, quoted in Blair, "Economic Development Policy," p. 241.

14. Carlos Tello and Rolando Cordera, *México: La disputa por la nación. Perspectivas y opciones del desarrollo* (Mexico City: Siglo XXI, 1981).

15. Ibid., p. 81.

16. See the introduction by editors Pablo González Casanova and Enrique Florescano to their recent volume *México, Hoy* (Mexico City: Siglo XXI, 1979), p. 14.

17. Arnaldo Córdova, *La política de masas y el futuro de la izquierda en México* (Mexico City: Serie Popular Era, 1979).

18. See the following document: "Llamamiento del Partido Socialista Unificado de México," *Excélsior*, December 3, 1981.

19. For further reference, see Leopoldo Solís, *Alternativas para el desarrollo* (Mexico City: Cuadernos de Joaquín Mortiz, 1980); Joseph Hodara, *Los futuros de México* (Mexico City: Fondo de Cultura BANAMEX, 1978); and Miguel Basáñez, *La lucha por la hegemonía en México, 1968–1980* (Mexico City: Siglo XXI, 1981).

Selected Bibliography

BOOKS AND ARTICLES

Alba, Francisco, *The Population of Mexico: Trends, Issues and Policies.* Trans. by Marjory Mattingly Urquidi. New Brunswick, N.J.: Transaction Press, 1982.

Alcázar, Mario. *Las organizaciones patronales en México.* Mexico City: El Colegio de México, 1970.

Alisky, Marvin. *Latin American Media: Guidance and Censorship.* Ames: Iowa State University Press, 1981.

Almeida, Vania, and Appendini, Kristen de. *Agricultura capitalista y agricultura campesina en México.* 2d ed. Mexico City: El Colegio de México, 1977.

Arriola, Carlos. *Las organizaciones empresariales y el estado.* Mexico City: Fondo de Cultura Económica, 1981.

Aspra, L. Antonio. "Import Substitution in Mexico." *World Development* 5, no. 1/2 (1977):111–124.

Anguiano, Roberto. *Las finanzas del sector público en México.* Mexico City: Universidad Nacional Autónoma de México, 1968.

Bailey, David C. *¡Viva Cristo Rey!* Austin: University of Texas Press, 1973.

Balassa, Bela. *The Newly Industrializing Countries in the World Economy.* New York: Pergamon Press, 1981.

Banco de México. *Informe anual.* Various issues.

———. *The Mexican Economy in 1977.* Mexico City, 1978.

———. *Producto interno bruto y gasto, 1970–1978.* Mexico City, 1979.

Banco Nacional de Comercio Exterior. *Mexico: La política económica del nuevo gobierno.* Mexico City, 1971.

Basáñez, Miguel. *La lucha por la hegemonía en México, 1968–1980.* Mexico City: Siglo XXI, 1981.

Bermúdez, Antonio J. *La política petrolera mexicana.* Mexico City: Cuadernos de Joaquín Mortiz, 1976.

Brandenburg, Frank. *The Making of Modern Mexico.* Englewood Cliffs, N.J.: Prentice-Hall, 1964.

261

Bueno, Gerardo., *Opciones de política económica en México: Después de la devaluación.* Mexico City: Técnos, 1977.

Bustamente, Jorge A. "El estudio de la zona fronteriza México–Estados Unidos," *Foro Internacional* 19, no. 3 (1979):471–516.

———. "Migración indocumentada." *Foro Internacional* 19, no. 2 (1978):317–325.

Calvert, Peter. "The Mexican Revolution: Theory or Fact." *Journal of Latin American Studies* 1, no. 1 (1969):51–68.

Camp, Roderic. "Intellectuals and the State in Mexico" (book manuscript in progress).

———. *Mexico's Leaders: Their Education and Recruitment.* Tucson: University of Arizona Press, 1980.

———. "The Middle-Level Technocrat in Mexico." *Journal of Developing Areas* 6, no. 4 (July 1972):571–582.

Cardoso, Fernando Henrique. "On the Characterization of Authoritarian Regimes in Latin America." In *The New Authoritarianism in Latin America,* edited by David Collier, pp. 33–57. Princeton, N.J.: Princeton University Press, 1979.

Castañeda, Jorge. *México y el orden internacional.* Mexico City: El Colegio de México, 1981.

Castillo, Heberto. *Necesario plan nacional de energéticos.* Mexico City: Servicios y Representaciones de Ingeniería, 1979.

Cline, Howard. *Mexico: Revolution to Evolution, 1940–60.* London: Oxford University Press, 1962.

Collier, David, ed. *The New Authoritarianism in Latin America.* Princeton, N.J.: Princeton University Press, 1979.

Comisión Federal Electoral. *Ley federal de organizaciones políticas y procesos electorales.* Mexico City, 1977.

Conklin, John. "Elite Studies: The Case of the Mexican Presidency." *Journal of Latin American Studies* 5, no. 2 (1973):247–269.

Connor, John M., and Mueller, Willard. *Market Power and Profitability of Multinational Corporations in Brazil and Mexico.* Report to the Subcommittee on Foreign Economic Policy of the Committee of Foreign Relations, U.S. Senate. Washington, D.C.: Government Printing Office, April 1977.

Consejo Nacional de Ciencia y Tecnología, editor. *El Petróleo en México y en el Mundo.* Mexico City, 1979.

Cordero, Salvador, and Santín, Rafael. *Los grupos industriales: Una nueva organización económica en México.* Cuadernos del Centro de Estudios Sociológicos 23. Mexico City: El Colegio de México, 1977.

Córdova, Arnaldo. *La ideología de la revolución mexicana: La formación del nuevo régimen.* Mexico City: Era, 1973.

Cornelius, Wayne. "La migración ilegal mexicana a los Estados Unidos: Conclusiones de investigaciones recientes, implicaciones políticas y prioridades de investigación." *Foro Internacional* 18, no. 3 (1978):399–429.

———. "Nation-Building, Participation, and Distribution: The Politics of Social Reform Under Cárdenas." In *Crisis, Choice and Change: Historical Studies of Political Development,* edited by Gabriel A. Almond, Scott C. Flanagan, and Robert J. Mundt, pp. 392–498. Boston: Little, Brown and Co., 1973.

———. "Urbanization as an Agent of Latin American Political Stability: The Case of Mexico." *American Political Science Review* 63, no. 3 (1969):833–857.

Corredor, Jaime. "Oil in Mexico." Mexico City: Office of Advisers to the President, November 1980.

Cosío Villegas, Daniel. *American Extremes*. Trans. by Américo Paredes. Austin: University of Texas Press, 1964.

———. *El sistema político mexicano: Las posibilidades de cambio*. Mexico City: Cuadernos de Joaquín Mortiz, 1974.

———. *La sucesión presidencial: Desenlace y perspectivas*. Mexico City: Cuadernos de Joaquín Mortiz, 1975.

Craig, Richard. "La Campaña Permanente: Mexico's Antidrug Campaign." *Journal of Interamerican Studies and World Affairs* 20, no. 2 (1978):107–132.

———. "Operation Condor." *Journal of Interamerican Studies and World Affairs* 22, no. 3 (1980):345–364.

Domínguez, Jorge, ed. *Mexico's Political Economy: Challenges at Home and Abroad*. Beverly Hills, Calif.: Sage Publications, 1982.

Eckstein, Shlomo, et al. *Land Reform in Latin America: Bolivia, Chile, Mexico, Peru and Venezuela*, Staff Working Paper 275 (Washington, D.C.: World Bank, April 1978).

Erb, Richard D., and Ross, Stanley R., eds. *United States Relations with Mexico: Context and Content*. Washington, D.C.: American Enterprise Institute, 1981.

Fagen, Richard R., and Nau, Henry. "Mexican Gas: The Northern Connection." In *Capitalism and the State in U.S.–Latin American Relations*, edited by Richard Fagen, pp. 382–424. Stanford, Calif.: Stanford University Press, 1979.

Fagen, Richard R., and Tuohy, William S. *Politics and Privilege in a Mexican City*. Stanford, Calif.: Stanford University Press, 1972.

Feinberg, Richard E. "Bureaucratic Organization and U.S. Policy Toward Mexico," in *Mexico–United States Relations*, edited by Susan Kaufman Purcell, pp. 32–42. Proceedings of the Academy of Political Science 34, no. 1. New York: Academy of Political Science, 1981.

Fernández Kelly, María Patricia. "The U.S.-Mexico Border: Recent Publications and the State of Current Research." *Latin American Research Review* 16, no. 3 (1981):250–267.

Fitzgerald, E.V.K. *Patterns of Public Sector Income and Expenditures in Mexico*. Austin: University of Texas, Institute of Latin American Studies, 1978.

———. "The State and Capital Accumulation in Mexico." *Journal of Latin American Studies* 10, no. 2 (1978):263–282.

Fuentes, Carlos. *The Death of Artemio Cruz*. Trans. by Sam Hileman. New York: Farrar, Straus, 1964.

Furtak, Robert K. *El partido de la revolución y la estabilidad política en México*. Mexico City: UNAM, 1978.

Garza, Rodolfo O. de la. "Demythologizing Chicano-Mexican Relations," in *Mexico-United States Relations*, edited by Susan Kaufman Purcell, pp. 88–96. Proceedings of the Academy of Political Science 34, no. 1. New York: Academy of Political Science, 1981.

González Casanova, Pablo. *Democracy in Mexico*. Trans. by Danielle Salti. London: Oxford University Press, 1970.

González Casanova, Pablo, and Florescano, Enrique, eds. *México, Hoy*. Mexico City: Siglo XXI, 1979.

Grabendorff, Wolf. "Mexico's Foreign Policy—Indeed a Foreign Policy?" *Journal of Interamerican Studies and World Affairs* 20, no. 1 (1978):87–88.

Grayson, George W. *The Politics of Mexican Oil*. Pittsburgh: University of Pittsburgh Press, 1980.

Green, Rosario. *El endeudamiento público de México, 1940–1973*. Mexico City: El Colegio de México, 1976.

––––––. "México: La política exterior del nuevo regimen." *Foro Internacional* 18, no. 1 (1977):1–9.

Grindle, Merilee. *Bureaucrats, Politicians, and the Peasantry in Mexico*. Berkeley: University of California Press, 1977.

––––––. "Power, Expertise and the 'Técnico': Suggestions from a Mexican Case Study," *Journal of Politics* 39, no. 2 (1977):399–426.

Hamilton, Nora. "Mexico: The Limits of State Autonomy." *Latin American Perspectives* 2, no. 2 (1975):81–108.

Hansen, Roger D. "The Evolution of U.S.-Mexican Relations. A Socio-Political Perspective," in *United States Relations with Mexico: Context and Content*, edited by Richard D. Erb and Stanley R. Ross, pp. 39–48. Washington, D.C.: American Enterprise Institute, 1981.

––––––. *The Politics of Mexican Development*. Baltimore: Johns Hopkins University Press, 1971.

Hellman, Judith Adler. *Mexico in Crisis*. London: Holmes and Meier, 1978.

––––––. "Social Control in Mexico." *Comparative Politics* 12, no. 2 (1980):225–242.

Hewitt de Alcántara, Cynthia. *La modernización de la agricultura mexicana 1940–1970*. Mexico City: Siglo XXI, 1978.

Hill, Kim Quaile, and Hurley, Patricia A. "Freedom of the Press in Latin America: A Thirty-Year Survey." *Latin American Research Review* 15, no. 2 (1980): 212–218.

Huntington, Samuel P. *Political Order in Changing Societies*. New Haven, Conn.: Yale University Press, 1968.

Independent Commission on International Development Issues. *North-South: A Programme for Survival*. Cambridge, Mass.: M.I.T. Press, 1980.

Inter-American Development Bank. *Economic and Social Progress in Latin America*. Washington, D.C., 1981–1982.

Johnson, Kenneth F. *Mexican Democracy: A Critical View*. Rev. ed. New York: Praeger Publishers, 1978.

Kaufman, Clifford. "Urbanization, Material Satisfaction and Mass Political Involvement: The Poor in Mexico City." *Comparative Political Studies* 4, no. 3 (1971):295–320.

Koslow, Lawrence E., and Murnane, Stephen P. "The Evolution of the Mexican Political System: A Paradigmatic Analysis." In *The Future of Mexico*, edited by Lawrence Koslow, pp. 47–98. Tempe: Arizona State University Press, 1979.

Ladman, Jerry R., et al. *U.S.-Mexican Energy Relationships: Realities and Prospects.* Lexington, Mass.: Lexington Books, 1981.

Laichas, Thomas Michael. "Mexico in the U.S. Press: A Quantitative Study, 1972–1978." In *Statistical Abstract of Latin America,* edited by James W. Wilkie, Vol. 20, pp. 581–594. Los Angeles: UCLA Latin American Center Publications, 1980.

Lajous, V. Adrián. *Mexico: Energy Sector.* Mexico City: Secretaría de Patrimonio y Fomento Industrial, 1981.

Larin, Nicholás. *La rebelión de los cristeros (1926–1929).* Trans. by Angel C. Tomás. Mexico City: Ediciones Era, 1968.

Leñero, Vicente. *Los periodistas.* Mexico City: Editorial Joaquín Mortiz, 1978.

León-Portilla, Miguel, ed. *Visión de los vencidos: Relaciones indígenas de la conquista.* 8th ed. Mexico City: UNAM, 1980.

Levy, Daniel. "Comparing Authoritarian Regimes in Latin America: Insights from Higher Education Policy." *Comparative Politics* 14, no. 1 (1981):31–52.

————. "The State and Higher Education in Latin America: Private-Public Patterns" (book manuscript in progress).

————. *University and Government in Mexico: Autonomy in an Authoritarian System.* New York: Praeger Publishers, 1980.

Lewis, Oscar. *Five Families.* New York: Basic Books, 1959.

Lieuwen, Edwin. *Mexican Militarism: The Political Rise and Fall of the Revolutionary Army, 1910–1940.* Albuquerque: University of New Mexico Press, 1968.

Lindblom, Charles E. *Politics and Markets.* New York: Basic Books, 1977.

Loaeza, Soledad. "La política del rumor: México, noviembre–diciembre 1976." *Foro Internacional* 17, no. 4 (1977):557–586.

Lomnitz, Larissa. *Networks and Marginality: Life in a Mexican Shantytown.* New York: Academic Press, 1977.

Looney, Robert E. *Mexico's Economy: A Policy Analysis with Forecasts to 1990.* Boulder, Colo.: Westview Press, 1978.

Loyoza, Jorge Alberto. *El ejército mexicano (1911–1965).* Mexico City: El Colegio de México, 1970.

Lustig, Nora, ed. *Panorama y perspectivas de la economía mexicana.* Mexico City: El Colegio de México, 1980.

Mancke, Richard. *Mexican Oil and Natural Gas: Political, Economic and Strategic Implications.* New York: Praeger Publishers, 1979.

Marshall, F. Ray. "Economic Factors Influencing the International Migration of Workers." In *Views Across the Border: The United States and Mexico,* edited by Richard W. Weatherhead and Stanley R. Ross, pp. 163–182. Albuquerque: University of New Mexico Press, 1978.

Martínez Verdugo, Arnoldo. *Crisis política y alternativa comunista.* Mexico City: Ediciones de Cultura Popular, 1979.

México, Oficina de Asesores del C. Presidente de la República. "Sistema alimentario mexicano." Mexico City, unpublished draft, 1980.

México, Proyectos Especiales de Desarrollo. "Programa de puertos industriales." Mexico City, unpublished draft, November/December 1979.

México, Secretaría de Gobernación. *Ley electoral mexicana, 1812–1973.* Mexico City, 1974.

————. "Ley de fomento agropecuario." In *Diario Oficial*. Mexico City, January 2, 1981.

México, Secretaría de Patrimonio y Fomento Industrial. *Plan nacional de desarrollo industrial, 1979–1982*. Mexico City, 1979.

————. *Programa de energía, Metas a 1990 y projecciones al año 2000*. Mexico City, 1981.

México, Secretaría de Programación y Presupuesto. *La industria petrolera en México*. Mexico City, 1979.

————. *Plan global de desarrollo, 1980–1982*. Mexico City, 1980.

México, Secretaría de Patrimonio Nacional. *Law to Promote Mexican Investment and to Regulate Foreign Investment*. Mexico City, 1973.

México, Secretaría del Trabajo y Previsión Social. *Projecto. Plan nacional de empleo, 1980–1982*. Mexico City, November 1979.

Meyer, Lorenzo. *Las empresas transnacionales en México*. Mexico City: El Colegio de México, 1974.

————. "Historical Roots of the Authoritarian State in Mexico." In *Authoritarianism in Mexico*, edited by José Luis Reyna and Richard Weinert, pp. 3–22. Philadelphia: Institute for the Study of Human Issues, 1977.

————. *Mexico and the United States in the Oil Controversy, 1917–1942*. Austin: University of Texas Press, 1977.

Meyer, Lorenzo, et al. *Lecturas de política exterior mexicana*. Mexico City: El Colegio de México, 1979.

Meyer, Michael C., and Sherman, William L. *The Course of Mexican History*. New York: Oxford University Press, 1979.

Middlebrook, Kevin J. "Energy Security in U.S.-Mexican Relations." In *Energy and Security*, edited by David A. Deese and Joseph Nye, pp. 152–180. Cambridge, Mass.: Ballinger Publishing Co., 1980.

————. "Political Change in Mexico." In *Mexico-United States Relations*, edited by Susan Kaufman Purcell, pp. 55–66. Proceedings of the Academy of Political Science 34, no.1. New York: Academy of Political Science, 1981.

Mosk, Stanford. *Industrial Revolution in Mexico*. Berkeley: University of California Press, 1954.

National Financiera. *50 años de la revolucion mexicana en cifras*. Mexico City, 1963.

————. *Statistics on the Mexican Economy*. Mexico City, 1977.

Nau, Henry R. "U.S.-Mexican Oil and Gas Relations: A Special Relationship?" In *United States Relations with Mexico: Context and Content*, edited by Richard D. Erb and Stanley R. Ross, pp. 195–211. Washington, D.C.: American Enterprise Institute, 1981.

Needler, Martin. *Politics and Society in Mexico*. Albuquerque: University of New Mexico Press, 1971.

Ojeda, Mario. *Alcances y límites de la política exterior de México*. Mexico City: El Colegio de México, 1976.

————. "México ante los Estados Unidos en la coyuntura actual." *Foro Internacional* 18, no. 1 (1977):32–53.

Organization of American States. *México: Informes económicos de corto plazo*

México, 1980. Washington, D.C., August 18, 1980.

Oteyza, José Andrés. "México y el mercado internacional del petróleo." *Energéticos* 5, no. 6 (1981):27–28.

Padgett, L. Vincent. *The Mexican Political System.* 2d ed. Boston: Houghton Mifflin Co., 1976.

Paz, Octavio. *The Labyrinth of Solitude: Life and Thought in Mexico.* New York: Grove Press, 1961.

———. *The Other Mexico: Critique of the Pyramid.* Trans. by Lysander Kemp. New York: Grove Press, 1972.

———. "Reflections: Mexico and the United States." Trans. by Rachel Phillips. *New Yorker,* September 17, 1979, pp. 136–153.

Pellicer de Brody, Olga. "Cambios recientes en la política exterior mexicana." *Foro Internacional* 13, no. 2 (1972):139–154.

———. *México y la revolución cubana.* Mexico City: El Colegio de México, 1972.

———. "Veinte años de política exterior mexicana: 1960–1980." *Foro Internacional* 21, no. 2 (1980):152–159.

Peñaloza, Tomás. "La formulación de la política exterior en los Estados Unidos de América y su impacto sobre México." *Foro Internacional* 18, no. 1 (1977):26.

Portillo, José López. *Informe de Gobierno.* Mexico City: Ministry of Planning and Budget, various issues.

Poulson, Barry W. "The Brain Drain from Mexico to the United States." In *U.S.-Mexico Economic Relations,* edited by Barry W. Poulson and Noel Osborn, pp. 245–260. Boulder, Colo.: Westview Press, 1979.

Purcell, John F. H., and Purcell, Susan Kaufman. "El estado y la empresa privada." *Nueva Política* 1, no. 2 (1976):229–250.

Purcell, Susan, and Purcell, John F. H. "State and Society in Mexico: Must a Stable Polity be Institutionalized?" *World Politics* 32, no. 2 (1980):194–227.

Purcell, Susan Kaufman. "Business-Government Relations in Mexico: The Case of the Sugar Industry." *Comparative Politics* 13, no. 2 (1981):211–232.

———. *The Mexican Profit-Sharing Decision: Politics in an Authoritarian Regime.* Berkeley: University of California Press, 1975.

Purcell, Susan Kaufman, ed. *Mexico-United States Relations.* Proceedings of the Academy of Political Science 34, no. 1. New York: Academy of Political Science, 1981.

Reyna, José Luis. *Control político, estabilidad y desarrollo en México.* Cuadernos del Centro de Estudios Sociológicos 3. Mexico City: El Colegio de México, 1974.

Reyna, José Luis, and Weinert, Richard. *Authoritarianism in Mexico.* Philadelphia: Institute for the Study of Human Issues, 1977.

Reyna, José Luis, et al. *Tres estudios sobre el movimiento obrero en México.* Mexico City: El Colegio de México, 1976.

Reynolds, Clark. *The Mexican Economy: Twentieth Century Structure and Growth.* New Haven, Conn.: Yale University Press, 1970.

———. "Why Mexico's 'Stabilizing Development' Was Actually Destabilizing (with Some Implications for the Future)." *World Development* 6, no. 7-8 (July-August 1979):1005–1018.

Ríos-Bustamente, Antonio, ed. *Mexican Immigrant Workers in the U.S.* Los Angeles: UCLA, 1981.

Ronfeldt, David, Nehring, Richard, and Gandara, A. *Mexico's Petroleum and U.S. Policy: Implications for the 1980s.* Santa Monica, Calif.: Rand Corporation, June 1980.

Ross, Stanley, ed. *Is the Mexican Revolution Dead?* New York: Knopf, 1966.

Safford, Frank. "Bases of Political Alignment in Early Republican Spanish America." In *New Approaches to Latin American History,* edited by Richard Graham and Peter H. Smith, pp. 71–111. Austin: University of Texas Press, 1974.

Sanderson, Steven E. *Agrarian Populism and the Mexican State: The Struggle for Land in Sonora.* Berkeley: University of California Press, 1981.

Sante, Angela M. Delli. "The Private Sector, Business Organizations, and International Influence: A Case Study of Mexico." In *Capitalism and the State in U.S.–Latin American Relations,* edited by Richard R. Fagen. Stanford, Calif.: Stanford University Press, 1979.

Schmitt, Karl M. *Mexico and the United States 1821–1973: Conflict and Coexistence.* New York: John Wiley, 1974.

Scott, Robert. *Mexican Government in Transition.* Urbana: University of Illinois Press, 1964.

――――. "Mexico." In *Comparative Politics Today,* edited by Gabriel Almond, pp. 366–402. Boston: Little, Brown and Co., 1974.

Segovia, Rafael. *La politización del niño mexicano.* Mexico City: El Colegio de México, 1975.

Sepúlveda, Bernardo, and Chumacero, Antonio. *La inversión extranjera en México.* Mexico City: Fondo de Cultura Económica, 1973.

Shafer, Robert. *Mexican Business Organizations.* Syracuse, N.Y.: Syracuse University Press, 1973.

Siglo XXI, editors. *El perfil de México en 1980.* 3 vols. Mexico City: Siglo XXI, 1970.

Silva Herzog, Jesús. *Trayectoria ideológica de la revolución mexicana.* Mexico City: S.E.P., 1973.

Smith, Peter. *Labyrinths of Power: Political Recruitment in Twentieth Century Mexico.* Princeton, N.J.: Princeton University Press, 1979.

Solís, Leopoldo. *Alternativas para el desarrollo.* Mexico City: Cuadernos de Joaquín Mortiz, 1980.

――――. *A Monetary Will-o-the-Wisp: Pursuit of Equity Through Deficit Spending.* Princeton, N.J.: Princeton University Discussion Papers, no. 77, 1977.

――――. *La realidad económica mexicana: Retrovisión y perspectivas.* 10th ed. Mexico City: Siglo XXI, 1980.

Spalding, Rose J. "State Power and Its Limits: Corporatism in Mexico." *Comparative Political Studies* 14, no. 2 (1981):139–161.

――――. "Welfare Policymaking: Theoretical Implications of a Mexican Case Study." *Comparative Politics* 12, no. 4 (1980):419–438.

Stevens, Evelyn. *Protest and Response in Mexico.* Cambridge, Mass.: M.I.T. Press, 1974.

Story, Dale. "Entrepreneurs and the State in Mexico: Examining the Authoritarian Thesis." Technical Papers Series No. 30, Institute of Latin American Studies, University of Texas, Austin, Tex., 1980.

Székely, Gabriel. "The 1976 Oil Export Decision: Effects of the Oil Boom on Mexico's Political Economy," Ph.D. dissertation, George Washington University, 1983.

Tannenbaum, Frank. The Struggle for Peace and Bread. New York: Columbia University Press, 1950.

Tello, Carlos, and Cordera, Rolando. México: La disputa por la nación: Perspectives y opciones del desarrollo. Mexico City: Siglo XXI, 1981.

Tenenbaum, Barbara H. "Straightening Out Some of the Lumpen in the Development." Latin American Perspectives 2, no. 2 (1975):3–16.

Thorp, Rosemary, and Whitehead, Lawrence. Inflation and Stabilization in Latin America. New York: Holmes and Meier, 1979.

Turner, Frederick C. The Dynamic of Mexican Nationalism. Chapel Hill: University of North Carolina Press, 1968.

United Nations Economic Commission for Latin America. México: Notas para el estudio económico de América Latina. Washington, D.C., 1979.

United Nations Educational, Scientific and Cultural Organization. Statistical Yearbook 1977. Paris: UNESCO, 1978.

U.S. Central Intelligence Agency. The International Energy Situation: Outlook to 1985. Washington, D.C., April 1977.

_____. The World Oil Market in the Years Ahead. Washington, D.C., August 1979.

U.S. Congress, Joint Economic Committee. Recent Developments in Mexico and Their Economic Implications for the United States. Hearings before the Subcommittee on Inter-American Economic Relationships of the Joint Economic Committee, January 17 and 24, 1977. Washington, D.C., 1977.

U.S. Congressional Budget Office. The World Oil Market in the 1980s: Implications for the United States. Washington, D.C., May 1980.

U.S. Congressional Research Service. Mexico's Oil and Gas Policy: An Analysis. Washington, D.C., December 1978.

U.S. Council of Economic Advisors. Economic Report of the President. Washington, D.C.: Government Printing Office, January 1981.

U.S. General Accounting Office. Prospects for a Stronger U.S.-Mexico Energy Relationship. Washington, D.C., May 1, 1980.

U.S. House of Representatives. Intelligence on the World Energy Outlook and Its Policy Implications. Hearings before the Subcommittee on Oversight of the Permanent Select Committee on Intelligence. Washington, D.C., 1980.

_____. U.S.-Mexican Relations: An Update. Hearings before the Subcommittee of Inter-American Affairs of the Committee of Foreign Affairs. Washington, D.C., June 1981.

_____. U.S.-Mexican Relations and the Energy Crisis. Washington, D.C.: Committee on Foreign Affairs, June 1980.

U.S. House of Representatives, Committee on Science and Technology. U.S.-Mexico Relations and Potentials Regarding Energy, Immigration, Scientific

Cooperation and Technology Transfer. Washington, D.C.: Government Printing Office, 1979.

U.S. Senate. *Mexico: The Promise and Problems of Petroleum.* Washington, D.C.: Committee on Energy and Natural Resources, March 1979.

———. *The Western Hemisphere Energy System.* Hearings before the Committee of Energy and Natural Resources. Washington, D.C., November 1979.

Vargas, Armando. "Coup at Excélsior." *Columbia Journalism Review* 15, no. 3 (1967):45–48.

Vásquez, Carlos, and García y Griego, Manuel, eds. *Mexican-U.S. Relations: Conflict and Convergence?* Los Angeles: UCLA, 1981.

Vaughan, Mary Kay. *The State, Education, and Social Class in Mexico, 1880–1928.* DeKalb, Illinois: Northern Illinois University Press, 1982.

Vernon, Raymond F. *The Dilemma of Mexico's Development: The Roles of the Private and Public Sectors.* Cambridge, Mass.: Harvard University Press, 1963.

Villarreal, René. "El petróleo como instrumento de desarrollo y de negociación internacional: México en los ochentas." *El Trimestre Económico* 48, no. 1 (1981):3–44.

———. "The Policy of Import-Substituting Industrialization." In *Authoritarianism in Mexico,* edited by José Luis Reyna and Richard Weinert, pp. 67–107. Philadelphia: Institute for the Study of Human Issues, 1977.

Weil, Thomas E., et al. *Area Handbook for Mexico.* Washington, D.C.: Government Printing Office, 1975.

Weintraub, Sidney. "Case Study of Economic Stabilization: Mexico." In *Economic Stabilization in Developing Countries,* edited by William R. Cline and Sidney Weintraub, pp. 271–296. Washington, D.C.: Brookings Institution, 1981.

Whitehead, Lawrence. *Mexico: From Bust to Boom: A Political Evaluation of the 1976–1979 Stabilization Program.* Latin American Program Working Paper no. 44. Washington, D.C.: Woodrow Wilson International Center for Scholars, June 1979.

Wilkie, James. *The Mexican Revolution: Federal Expenditures and Social Change Since 1910.* Berkeley: University of California Press, 1967.

Wionczek, Miguel. "On the Viability of a Policy for Science and Technology in Mexico." *Latin American Research Review* 16, no. 1 (1981):57–78.

———. *La sociedad mexicana: Presente y futuro.* Mexico City: Fondo de Cultura Económica, 1973.

Womack, John. *Zapata and the Mexican Revolution.* New York: Knopf, 1969.

Workshop on Alternative Energy Strategies (WAES). *Energy: Global Prospects, 1985–2000.* New York: McGraw-Hill, 1977.

World Bank. *Annual Report.* Various issues.

———. *Energy in the Developing Countries.* Washington, D.C., August 1980.

———. *Mexico, Manufacturing Sector: Situation, Prospects and Policies.* Washington, D.C.: World Bank, 1979.

———. *A Program to Accelerate Petroleum Production in the Developing Countries.* Washington, D.C., 1979.

———. *World Development Report.* Washington, D.C., 1980, 1981.

PRINCIPAL NEWSPAPERS AND MAGAZINES CONSULTED

Comercio Exterior
Energéticos
Excélsior
El Heraldo
Latin American Political Report
Latin American Weekly Report
New York Times
Novedades
Proceso
Razones
El Trimestre Económico
Uno Más Uno

Abbreviations

CANACINTRA	National Chamber of Manufacturing Industry
CCE	Coordinating Business Council
CCI	Independent Peasant Confederation
CONASUPO	National Staple Products Company
CONCAMIN	Confederation of Industrial Chambers
CONCANACO	Confederation of Chambers of Commerce of Mexico
COPARMEX	Confederation of Employers of the Mexican Republic
CROM	Mexican Regional Labor Confederation
CTM	Confederation of Mexican Workers
FSTSE	Federation of Unions of State Workers
GATT	General Agreement of Tariffs and Trade
GDP	gross domestic product
IEPES	Institute of Political, Economic and Social Studies
ISI	import substitution industrialization
NAFINSA	National Development Bank
OAS	Organization of American States
PAN	National Action party
PARM	Authentic Party of the Mexican Revolution
PCM	Mexican Communist party

273

PDM	Democratic Mexican party
PEMEX	Petróleos Mexicanos (Mexico's state oil company)
PIPSA	Producer and Importer of Paper
PMT	Mexican Workers party
PPS	Popular Socialist party
PRI	Institutional Revolutionary party
PST	Socialist Workers party
PSUM	Mexico's Unified Socialist party
SAM	Mexican Food System
UNCTAD	United Nations Conference on Trade and Development
VAT	value added tax

Index

275

42
Bolivia, 1, 217
Book publishing, 90
Border transactions, 134(table), 136, 194
Bracero program, 176
Brandt, Willy, 236
Brazil, 1, 9, 13, 42, 138, 139, 150, 187
Brown and Root (U.S. company), 229
Bucareli Agreements (1923), 175, 215, 216
Bueno, Gerardo, 247–248
Bureaucracy, 28, 102, 109–110, 149
Bush, George, 228
Business community. *See* Coordinating Business Council; Economic development, capital investment, private; Politics, and business community

Cabañas, Lucío, 7
Caciques, 30, 33, 39, 40, 140
Calles, Plutarco Elías, 31–32, 33, 38–39, 41–42, 43, 59, 107, 175–176, 215, 216
Camarilla, 113
CANACINTRA. *See* National Chamber of Manufacturing Industry
Canada, 232, 233. *See also* Mexico, and Canada; United States, and Canada
Cancún, 197, 236
Capital goods, 135(table), 137–138, 140, 141, 149, 159, 230
Capital-intensive
  goods, 193, 248
  societies, 200
  technologies, 143
Caracas Conference (1954), 187
Cárdenas, Lázaro, 32–33, 34, 35, 39, 42, 43, 46, 59, 61, 71, 107, 139, 176, 216–217, 256
Cardenistas, 36, 46, 47
Caribbean, 114, 185. *See also* Mexico, and Caribbean; United States, and Caribbean
Caribbean Basin Initiative, 186
Carranza, Venustiano, 29, 30, 31, 38, 58, 175
Carter, Jimmy, 13, 16, 177, 183, 232
Casa del Obrero Mundial (1912), 58
Castañeda, Jorge, 182
Castillo, Heberto, 75, 76, 221–222, 255

Castro, Fidel, 179
Catholic Church, 12, 26, 41–42, 65, 71, 83, 176
CCE. *See* Coordinating Business Council
CCI. *See* Independent Peasant Confederation
Central America, 42. *See also* Mexico, and Central America; United States, and Central America
Central Bank (1925), 53, 127, 143, 225
Centralists, 25
Cervantes del Río, Hugo, 106
Chapopote, 214
Chapultepec Castle, 173
Charter of Economic Rights and Duties of States, 181
Chávez, Carlos, 34
Chiapas (state), 225
Chicago (Ill.), 16
Chicanos. *See* Mexican-Americans
Chihuahua (state), 10
Chile, 1, 42, 64, 114, 150. *See also* Mexico, and Chile
Cinema, 88
CNC. *See* National Peasant Confederation
Coahuila (state), 10
Cocaine, 195
Colby, William, 199
Colegio de México, El, 90
Colombia, 11, 114
Comic books, 89
Commerce, Ministry of, 53, 157, 158
Common energy market, 194, 232
Communes. *See* Marxist communes
Communications, 10, 36, 127, 128, 129(table)
Compadrazgo, 12
CONASUPO. *See* National Staple Products Company
CONCAMIN. *See* Confederation of Industrial Chambers
CONCANACO. *See* Confederation of Chambers of Commerce of Mexico
Confederation of Chambers of Commerce of Mexico (CONCANACO) (1917), 62–63
Confederation of Employees of the Mexican Republic (COPARMEX), 63
Confederation of Industrial Chambers (CONCAMIN) (1918), 63

178, 179, 187
Organization of Petroleum Exporting
  Countries (OPEC), 178, 220, 227,
  233, 234, 235
Orozco, José Clemente, 34
Osorio, Reyes, 139
Otezya, José Andrés de, 224

Pakistan. *See* Mexico, and Pakistan
PAN. *See* National Action party
Panama. *See* Mexico, and Panama
Panama Canal Treaty (1977), 179
Paramilitary groups, 152
PARM. *See* Authentic Party of the
  Mexican Revolution
Party of the Mexican Revolution, 39, 59
Paz, Octavio, 14, 22, 34, 97
PCM. *See* Mexican Communist party
PDM. *See* Democratic Mexican party
Peasants, 27, 28, 33, 34, 39, 68, 84,
  140–141, 156, 169(illus.)
  and politics, 57, 58, 60–62, 96,
  100–101
  See also Social development, and
  urban migration
PEMEX. *See* Petróleos Mexicanos
Pendulum theory, 111–112
Peninsulares, 23, 24
Perfil de México en 1980, El, 147
Pershing, John, 175
Persian Gulf, 216
Peru, 1, 23
Peso
  devaluation (1954), 230
  devaluation (1976), 36, 65, 110, 111,
  152
  devaluation (1982), 37, 112, 198, 201
  exchange rate, 132, 138, 149
  overvaluation, 138
Petróleos Mexicanos (PEMEX), 53, 141,
  153, 218, 219–220, 221, 222,
  223–224, 225, 226, 227, 233, 235
  union, 228–229
Petroleum Law (1925), 215–216
Petronor (Spanish refinery), 233
Piedad para el Indio (Lamicq), 34
PIPSA. *See* Producer and Importer of
  Paper
Pluralism, 101, 114, 115, 116, 118
PMT. *See* Mexican Workers party
Political parties, 7, 17, 26, 38–39, 51,

65–77, 82–83, 244, 256. *See also*
  individual parties
Political power, 99–104, 116–117
Politics, 2, 9
  as authoritarian, 114–118
  and business community, 62–65, 102,
  103–104, 237–238
  and Catholic Church, 41–42
  centralization, 13, 25, 27, 38, 237
  and change, 81, 105–113, 117–118,
  156–157, 243
  conservatives, 25, 26, 144
  corporatism in, 57
  crisis (1968), 7
  democratic, 114, 115
  elite, 26, 29, 34, 40, 44, 108–110,
  127, 252, 257
  equality, 26, 29, 46, 81, 99–104, 114,
  116
  and guerrilla activity, 6–7
  leftist, 33, 36, 42, 73–76, 95, 196,
  198, 243, 252–255, 256. *See also*
  Marxist left
  legitimacy, 7, 56, 71, 185, 244, 253,
  254
  liberals, 25, 26, 28, 41, 45, 46, 47
  liberty, 21, 26, 27, 28, 29, 30, 33, 36,
  42, 45, 46–47, 81–99, 114,
  115–116, 237–238, 245, 257
  and military, 40, 114
  paradoxes of, 81
  participation, 51, 66, 114, 257
  reform, 26, 29, 30, 32–33, 36, 76–77,
  114, 244, 257
  rural and urban, 73
  stability, 1–3, 6–8, 17, 21, 23, 25, 26,
  27, 28, 32, 33, 35, 36, 39, 45–46,
  47, 57, 77, 81, 104–105, 113,
  117–118, 125, 141–142, 144, 155,
  199, 243, 245
  and universities, 43–44, 102
  See also Mexico, cabinet; Mexico,
  presidents; Political parties
Polk, James, 172, 173
Popular sector, 39, 57, 62–65, 68
Popular Socialist party (PPS) (1948),
  70(table), 72(table), 74–75, 76, 77
Porfiriato (1876–1910), 26, 27, 28, 29,
  32, 41, 45, 46, 174, 206
¿Por Que?, 93, 95
Port facilities. *See* Economic

About the Book and Authors

MEXICO
Paradoxes of Stability and Change
Daniel Levy and Gabriel Székely

Mexico's political stability is unique in twentieth-century Latin America and, indeed, unusual in the Third World as a whole. How the country appears after a half-century of rule by a single regime is significant as a case study—or even a model—of political stability. Certainly from the U.S. viewpoint, Mexico is the most important nation in the Spanish-speaking world.

Professors Levy and Székely briefly discuss Mexico's geography, population, culture, and especially its history, before analyzing both the stated and the real functions of institutions, groups, and political parties in a paradoxical system that simultaneously permits and circumscribes political participation. One of their central concerns is the phenomenon of the country's extraordinary political stability coexisting with the possibilities of—and restrictions on—political freedom, equality, and change. They go on to explore how that political stability has been accompanied by economic growth and by a cruel social structure. While examining the relationship between domestic and foreign policy, the authors give particular emphasis to Mexican-U.S. relations and oil policy. They conclude by considering the balance between stability and change in Mexican politics and speculating on how that balance might relate to the most prominently proposed alternatives for Mexico's future.

Daniel Levy, who is on the staff of the State University of New York at Albany, received his Ph.D. in political science from the University of North Carolina. He was formerly a research associate at Yale University's Institution for Social and Policy Studies and is now a visiting research associate there. Dr. Levy is author of *University and Government in Mexico: Autonomy in an Authoritarian System.* **Gabriel Székely,** who received his Ph.D. in political science from the George Washington University, is on the staff of El Colegio de México. Dr. Székely was a visiting fellow at the Overseas Development Council in Washington, D.C.